MW01172473

Astrology and the Zodiac Signs

Unlocking Astrological Secrets and Mysteries of Sun, Moon, and Rising Signs

© Copyright 2023

The content contained within this book may not be reproduced, duplicated or transmitted without direct written permission from the author or the publisher.

Under no circumstances will any blame or legal responsibility be held against the publisher, or author, for any damages, reparation, or monetary loss due to the information contained within this book, either directly or indirectly.

Legal Notice:

This book is copyright protected. It is only for personal use. You cannot amend, distribute, sell, use, quote, or paraphrase any part, or the content within this book, without the consent of the author or publisher.

Disclaimer Notice:

Please note the information contained within this document is for educational and entertainment purposes only. All effort has been executed to present accurate, up-to-date, reliable, complete information. No warranties of any kind are declared or implied. Readers acknowledge that the author is not engaging in the rendering of legal, financial, medical, or professional advice. The content within this book has been derived from various sources. Please consult a licensed professional before attempting any techniques outlined in this book.

By reading this document, the reader agrees that under no circumstances is the author responsible for any losses, direct or indirect, that are incurred due to the use of the information contained within this document, including, but not limited to, errors, omissions, or inaccuracies.

Free Bonus from Silvia Hill available for limited time

Hi Spirituality Lovers!

My name is Silvia Hill, and first off, I want to THANK YOU for reading my book.

Now you have a chance to join my exclusive spirituality email list so you can get the ebooks below for free as well as the potential to get more spirituality ebooks for free! Simply click the link below to join.

P.S. Remember that it's 100% free to join the list.

~~$27~~ FREE BONUSES

- 9 Types of Spirit Guides and How to Connect to Them
- How to Develop Your Intuition: 7 Secrets for Psychic Development and Tarot Reading
- Tarot Reading Secrets for Love, Career, and General Messages

Access your free bonuses here

https://livetolearn.lpages.co/astrology-and-the-zodiac-signs-paperback/

Table of Contents

Part 1: Astrology

Unlocking the Secrets of the Zodiac, Tarot, and Numerology along with Moon, Sun, and Rising Signs

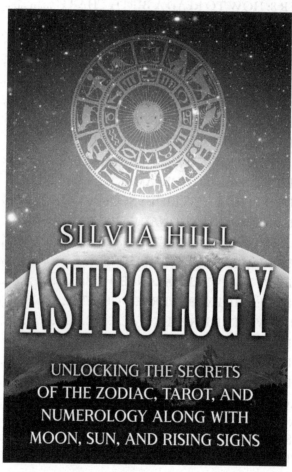

Introduction

Astrology and the concept of horoscopes thrive in a symbiotic relationship and alter each other's course at every step. The study of astrology and its related elements has been in existence for centuries. In fact, it can be dated back to the point when time was first measured and studied. The word "astrology" is divided into two parts - Astra, meaning "star," and Logos, meaning "reason" or "logic." The movement, position, and alignment pattern of the stars and celestial bodies are studied to interpret the vibrations and energies around us. These energies can then be utilized to manifest your dreams and understand the essence of life.

Astrology and astrological energies exist without forcing anyone to believe in them. Whether or not you believe in astrology and the energies surrounding you, their existence is not affected. However, if you take an interest and try to analyze these energies, you can benefit from them. You can learn more about your true personality and inner traits and use this knowledge to discover your inner calling and life's purpose. With time, you can also study effective ways to use your internal power and turn the tides of change in your favor.

Fundamentally, astrology combines the study of different celestial bodies, their positions, people's intuition, and a bit of science and mathematics. The study is conducted through symbols, patterns, and cycles that systematically present the findings. Since the movements of the planets are measurable, the results can be recorded, allowing us to understand the fundamental aspects of our physical realm. These movements and events trigger the cosmic waves and frequencies of the universe, which can be altered and aligned with our internal vibrations. In turn, this will cause an expected and successful outcome. It is not as easy as it sounds, though!

You must learn the right way to interpret these cosmic waves using your intuition and spiritual voice. With these things, you can discover the secrets of the world around you and use the language of astrology to interpret the singularities of the universe. One effective way to do that is to draft your horoscope or astrology chart based on the position of the celestial bodies at the time of your birth. Every person has a dedicated horoscope or a personal map and ruling planets indicated by their time and date of birth. Simply put, your astrological chart is a snapshot of the universe's position during the exact moment of your birth. This is your personal blueprint that acts as a toolkit throughout your life. You can use this toolkit to know yourself better, listen to your inner or true voice, and make desirable changes to your life.

Interestingly, every astrologer has their own way of interpreting astrological charts. While some refer to the cosmic influence and its related theories, others use the concept of space and time to perceive the Earth and heaven as one. Other domains include the study of numbers known as numerology and reading a set of illustrated cards related to one's intuition known as the Tarot. A set of root numbers is extracted in the former, based on the person's date of birth. This unique number can be used to study a person's traits, motivations, and life direction.

The essence and motto of astrology are that each person is unique and possesses an unprecedented calling. Furthermore, every person falls under one of twelve zodiac signs based on their birth month. These groups represent unique archetypes, each with its own emotional, mental, and spiritual traits. Each zodiac sign is represented by a symbol, a set of numbers, colors, and natural elements. When studying your zodiac sign and linking it to your horoscope, you can relate to your past and present, as well as foretelling your future. While the zodiac signs are stationary, you can measure your progress and future based on the position and movement of the planets. Using accurate data on the place, date, and time of your birth, you can correlate your existence to the Astral charts and one of the houses you fall under.

With the right information and practice, you can dramatically improve the quality of your life and gain emotional independence. Astrology abides by the notions of living with free will and having a strong sense of purpose, unlike those who are demotivated and fail to understand the meaning of life. It does not ask you to believe in fatalism or superstition but rather persuades you to recognize your unique skills and talents. This study helps unveil the "real" you and encourages spiritual maturation.

Since most people are unaware of the actual reasoning and fail to comprehend astronomical phenomena, they have false notions and refuse to believe the authenticity of this discipline. Now, if you are one of them, it is time to unravel the truth and legitimacy of this study, so you may become more self-aware and understand your true self. This is where this book will help you. It will enable you to examine the contrasting nature of horoscopes and astrology. Since astrology is intricately linked to our sense of being and reality, it is necessary to dispel the myths surrounding it to better understand and appreciate it. With time and practice, you can study the signs and alignment of the stars on your own and alter your perspective to achieve favorable effects.

This book contains valuable information related to astrology, numerology, the positioning of planets, sun signs, moon signs, and Tarot. It will walk you through the distinct facets of astrology and various domains in the simplest manner. Whether you are a novice or an avid practitioner, you will gain useful insights to help you on your life journey. Each chapter is broken down into fragments that can be easily absorbed. Take this opportunity as a guiding thread that will allow you to lead a more content life. Finally, this book will provide insights and tips to apply these postulates and shift your perspective to better life outcomes.

Read on to grasp the concept and philosophy behind astrology and its related entities in detail and experience its positive effects to turn your life around. Without further ado, let our exploration journey begin!

Section One: Astrology Basics

Chapter 1: The Planets and the Signs

Astrology has been a subject of fascination for centuries. Each civilization had its own notions about the stars and the planets in the sky. Many ancient civilizations developed their own unique systems of astrology. It is believed that the Mesopotamians pioneered the science and practice of astrology around 2000 BCE. The system they created greatly influenced those devised by other civilizations in the future.

The Romans, Greeks, Persians, Hindus, and Chinese all possessed knowledge in reading the planets and stars. The ancient civilizations used these readings to predict events like wars, droughts, floods, or deaths. This shows just how important and influential astrology has been throughout history and across the globe.

The classic phrase "As above, so below" is the essence of astrology. It is believed that the set of instructions written in the sky will affect worldly matters to a great extent. Since the position of the stars and the planets is ever-changing, the precise arrangement of celestial bodies at the time of a person's birth supposedly influences their destined course in life. This means that planets and zodiac signs obey the natural laws of the universe. It is these laws that all civilizations have attempted to study and codify to determine their fate.

The most common features in most astrological systems comprise planets and signs. Planets have always been considered significant in influencing a person's life events, personality, and more. Zodiac signs have existed in most cultures, with most cultures having 12 signs.

In this opening chapter, we'll set out to explore the different meanings and interpretations of terms like planets, zodiac signs, natal charts, etc. These concepts all play major roles in our lives, and understanding them helps us uncover many mysteries surrounding our destiny and desires.

Natal Charts

First things first, it's essential to understand the role and significance of the individual components we're about to discuss. Then, later in this chapter, numerous things will be covered, such as houses, planets, and zodiac signs.

Natal Charts, also known as Birth Charts, are the exact positioning of the different planets in different houses on the day you were born. These are prepared using your name, date of birth, and sometimes your place of birth. You'll find free tools available online to get your Natal Chart mapped out.

A Natal Chart will reveal a great deal about your tendencies, personality, hidden desires, and even the decisions you will take in life. This chart will be more detailed and accurate than any horoscope you may read since a Natal Chart is unique to everyone. Now, let's find out which components make up a Natal Chart.

Planets

Ten planets in astrology influence us, thanks to their unique characteristics. While planets help express various aspects of our personality, the zodiac works differently. Everyone has a different zone of comfort depending on the planets. A domicile planet is the one that rules your zodiac sign and harbors where you are most efficient.

It is important to understand that we also refer to the sun and moon as planets in astrology. This might go against the notions of human-defined modern science, but our perspective here is different. Any celestial body visible from the earth is considered a planet in the realm of astrology. What follows is a brief overview of the qualities that the different planets have. The influence that each planet has on your life will be defined by the qualities it possesses.

- **Sun:** The sun symbolizes vitality, vigor, ego, stamina, and radiant energy.
- **Moon:** The moon is a symbol of emotions and governs our moods and instincts.
- **Mercury:** The symbol of intellect and reasoning. Mercury controls how you learn.
- **Venus:** The symbol of love, attraction, and beauty. Venus determines how you attract your desires.
- **Mars:** The planet of aggression, desire, ambition, and passion. This planet determines how you act.
- **Jupiter:** This planet represents luck, optimism, and growth in life.
- **Saturn:** A symbol of discipline and hard work. This planet influences structure in life.
- **Uranus:** Freedom, sudden change, eccentricity, and rebellion are the features of this planet.
- **Neptune:** This planet represents a mystic and intuitive mind. It influences a person's artistic creativity.
- **Pluto:** This small yet powerful planet is responsible for the transformation and evolution of life.

Zodiac Signs & Planets

Think of a zodiac as an imaginary belt of the heavens through which planets move across the sky. The different stars are divided and grouped according to their shape and size into larger groups, known as constellations. Since the Sun moves through this belt once a year, we obtain a 360-degree eclipse. This eclipse, when divided into 12 equal parts, forms the components of a zodiac sign.

The zodiac signs are further grouped into four categories based on the basic constituent elements of the universe:

Elements	Zodiac Signs
Earth	Taurus, Virgo & Capricorn
Fire	Aries, Leo & Sagittarius
Water	Cancer, Scorpio & Pisces
Air	Gemini, Libra & Aquarius

The planets play a much larger role in the zodiac as each is responsible for influencing people's lives. Each planet is thought to influence the human mind in a particular manner. However, this influence varies from one individual to the next as it changes according to the different positions of the planets at different given times.

Each zodiac sign has its own domicile planet with which it is associated. A domicile planet plays an important role in determining the qualities attributed to a zodiac sign. In this section, we will explore some of how the ruling planet influences a zodiac sign.

1. Aries: Mars

As the Roman god of war, Mars perfectly matches the temperament of the first sign of the zodiac. Mars stands for ambition, passion, instinct, and aggression, and with the fiery personality of an Aries, Mars can actually bring forth its aggressive nature. Those born under the sign of Aries are adept at leadership and are known for having high energy levels. The true nature of an Aries influenced by Mars comes out when challenged or confronted in any situation.

2. Taurus: Venus

Taurus is an earth sign, meaning it has a natural affinity for earthly pleasures and materialism. While Venus is the goddess of love and beauty, the planet also symbolizes luxury and pleasure. The sensual and pleasure-seeking Taurus exemplifies the nature of Venus.

3. Gemini: Mercury

The fast-footed and sharp-tongued messenger of the gods, Mercury, is at its best when expressed in Geminis. Gemini is an air sign known for being quick-witted, chatty, and inquisitive. Geminis are usually gifted with high intellect and love to socialize. Mercury allows Geminis to think and analyze, which is something they naturally like doing.

4. Cancer: The Moon

Those born under the sign of Cancer are the most emotional of all the zodiac signs due to their being very sensitive and caring. The Moon's intuitiveness perfectly complements the nurturing nature of Cancers. They are empathetic and in touch with what everyone around them is feeling. The Moon influences our emotions, feelings, and a general sense of comfort, which is why being coupled with a gentle sign like Cancer allows these qualities to shine through.

5. Leo: The Sun

Leos like to be the center of attention at any place or event. This is why the center of our solar system is the ideal planet for this sign. A Leo's loyal, dramatic, confident, and generous nature is the perfect channel for the Sun's radiant positivity, warmth, and generous, life-giving sunlight. So, thank the Sun for your high confidence levels and positive outlook, Leos!

6. Virgo: Mercury

We know that the Roman god Mercury had multiple tasks to handle. Likewise, the planet Mercury has also been assigned to two zodiac signs. The witty and quick side of Mercury is channeled by Geminis, while Virgos channel the other side. Mercury is also a translator and interpreter, which is reflected by Virgo's keen intellect and analytical skills. As a Virgo, you love organizing your belongings, and all your plans are well prepared and executed. Be grateful to Mercury for making you so meticulous.

7. Libra: Venus

Venus is the second planet on our list to govern more than one zodiac sign. The goddess of love has a lot of love to share, after all! As the zodiac symbol of balance and harmony, the Libra seeks balance in everything in their life. The romantic and loving nature of Venus manifests itself when Libras try to maintain a happy, fulfilling love life. Libras are also artistic and have an eye for beauty, which matches Venus perfectly since the planet also represents beauty.

8. Scorpio: Pluto

A dark and mysterious sign like Scorpio was bound to be associated with the strangest of all planets. Pluto, the god of the underworld, represents the eccentricity and extreme nature of Scorpios to perfection. The little planet has a significant impact when it comes to life-changing transformations, birth, death, creation, and destruction. Scorpio energies evolve and transform when influenced by Pluto, which makes them the perfect partners.

9. Sagittarius: Jupiter

Jupiter is the planet that symbolizes expansion, free spirit, carelessness, and optimism. Those born under the sign of Sagittarius are often happy-go-lucky people who exude positive vibes around them. The joyful planet Jupiter perfectly complements the optimism of a Sagittarius. In addition, Sagittarians have a thirst for knowledge due to the effects of Jupiter. They are also keen on trying out new things and rarely turn down new experiences.

10. Capricorn: Saturn

Saturn is the planet that deals tough love to its zodiac signs and adds some structure. As such, only a Capricorn can properly align with Saturn. Capricorns are disciplined and hardworking, which is necessary to satisfy Saturn's demand for structure. The impact of Saturn can be restrictive at times, but it also teaches Capricorns not to take shortcuts in life and always to work hard.

11. Aquarius: Uranus

Uranus is the planet that inspires rebellion, brilliant ideas, and innovation. The air sign Aquarius is the perfect match, thanks to the revolutionary energy resting inside of it. An Aquarius is naturally innovative and easily comes up with solutions that exhibit "out of the box" thinking. With the presence of Uranus, an Aquarius can have brilliant new ideas, but it is also responsible for the rebellious nature of the zodiac sign. Sudden changes, which are the signature feature of an Aquarius, shine through when Uranus interacts with the sign.

12. Pisces: Neptune

The god of the oceans is naturally suited to the mutable water sign that is Pisces. Neptune brings with it an aura of illusions and poetic beauty. The Pisceans are particularly receptive to this influence - thanks to their emotional and spiritual nature. Neptune can inspire a Piscean to be more artistic and to dream bigger. This helps turn the dreams and ambitions of a Piscean into reality.

The Houses

The houses are yet another important aspect of the science of astrology. Each house has a different set of traits that will influence your life. This depends on the location of the planets in each house at the time you were born. Astrologers often use this knowledge to predict the areas of your life in which you will experience trouble or find opportunities.

Whenever a planet visits a house, that part of your chart is influenced, and you acquire that house's traits. The first six houses are called "Personal Houses," and the last six are called "Interpersonal Houses." These houses move from self to society as we move counterclockwise.

So, let's have a look at all the different houses and discover which areas of life they have the most influence on:

- **1st House:** Also known as the house of Aries, this house is all about the beginning of things. It covers first impressions, new beginnings, your self-image, and any new initiatives you undertake.

- **2nd House:** This house governs your perception and immediate surroundings. All the things like the smells, sights, sounds, and even tastes in your life fall under this house. Led by Taurus, this house also deals with how you handle material possessions.

- **3rd House:** This house is presided by Gemini and tells us all about communication in our lives. It reveals how we interact with our siblings, parents, and society in general.

- **4th House:** This house lies at the bottom of the zodiac wheel, controlling all the foundations of life. It is home to cancer, the most sentimental sign, and it has to do with our roots and origins, which is why it determines the type of relationship a person has with their father. The parental home, childhood circumstances, and even the relationships with our family members can all be determined by this house.

- **5th House:** Leo is the ruler of this house and has imbued it with the dramatic attributes they are known for having. This house concerns all matters related to creativity in our lives and pleasure in the form of love affairs.

- **6th House:** The house ruled by Virgo commands all the aspects of one's life regarding health, wellness, organization, and discipline. Healthy and natural living and being of service to others are the fundamental traits that govern this house.

- **7th House:** Ruled by Libra, this house is all about relationships, both personal and professional. For instance, how we select our romantic partners and business partners is all determined by this house.

- **8th House:** This dark house, which the mysterious Scorpio governs, deals with all the metaphysical aspects of life and loss. Loss, which can be material loss or loss through death, falls under the purview of this house. It tells us how a person deals with the various losses they face and can even reveal how people deal with other's property.

- **9th House:** Sagittarius rules this house, and it is concerned with how we learn about spirituality in our lives. It governs philosophy and existentialism. This house is also the house of journeys to foreign lands, enriching our spiritual development as well.

- **10th House:** This house rests at the top of the zodiac wheel and is responsible for the choice of profession or career a person makes. It also governs the relationship that one will have with their mother throughout their life. This is why the 10th house, ruled by Capricorn, is the one that affects our general development in life.

- **11th House:** Aquarius rules this house, determining how we interact with our friends, teachers, and other well-wishers. This house shows us how we fit in with society and is often the determining factor in our friendships.

- **12th House:** Last, this is a house that paints the larger picture. Not surprisingly, Pisces governs this house since it deals with self-sacrifice and escapism. This final house covers all the loose ends left by the other houses, such as old age, seclusion, isolation, and much more. This house is also responsible for creativity and an interest in arts in light of its isolated nature.

These are all the basics you need to know about astrology. The basic terminologies and variables have been clarified by now. Using this information, you can easily determine what a Natal Chart represents. These are the first steps in understanding astrology, and the subject will be developed in detail in the next few chapters. So, once you have made your way to the end of this book, you will be able to appreciate the beauty and logic of astrology like never before!

Chapter 2: The Sun Sign: Your Identity

Finding yourself and understanding who you are can be quite a difficult thing to do. Essentially, you are a complex combination of emotions, ideas, values, and traits that sometimes seem contradictory. This is where your sun sign comes in. It can tell you things about yourself that you may not have recognized or even realized were a part of your personality. By interpreting your sun sign, you can get a concrete idea of who you are and learn more about your identity. If you don't know the first thing about sun signs, that's okay! Just read on to discover everything you need to understand better what they are and how they can help you figure out what kind of a person you truly are.

What Is Sun Sign Astrology?

Sun sign astrology is an iteration of Western astrology that only considers the sun's position when determining your sign. No matter which of the twelve zodiac signs, where the sun is at the time of your birth is considered your sun sign. This sun sign can determine your personality, character traits and predict events throughout your life. There are also planets, elements, modalities, and polarities associated with each sign, all working together to make up a personality map you can follow. As such, you can use your sun sign to help light your path and guide you throughout your life's journey.

History of Sun Signs

While the science of astrology dates to the 1600s, sun sign astrology as a system wasn't codified until 1930. A newspaper astrologer named R. H. Naylor coined the term for his column in the Sunday Express. When he wrote a horoscope for the recently born Princess Margaret, Queen Elizabeth II's younger sister, his popularity soared, and people began clamoring for horoscopes about themselves. This led to Naylor producing them regularly.

Shortly after this famous horoscope, Naylor predicted the crash of the R101 airship. He foretold that a British airship would be in danger in October, and on the 5th of October 1930, the R101 went down in flames over Beauvais, France. Other newspapers thus began including horoscopes and predictions of their own, and Naylor was pressed to reveal how the event was predicted. Over the next seven years, he outlined his system for others to follow.

In 1937, Naylor unveiled his completed astrology system, which he dubbed sun signs or star signs. It made predictions based on a person's date of birth, dividing the year into twelve distinct signs based on the zodiac. This allowed for twelve different horoscopes to appear in each column, giving readers a somewhat personalized overview of what their future held. The system of sun sign astrology used today has been refined over time and combined with other astrological concepts for a complete forecast of a person's personality, character traits, and likes and dislikes.

Sun Signs and Their Meanings

There are twelve sun signs within the zodiac. Each has its own associated characteristics and personalities ascribed to those born under it. While the sun's alignment upon your birth isn't the only factor in astrology, it is the most important when determining who you will be as a person. Every sun sign has a specific celestial body connected to them and a fixed, mutable, or cardinal modality (explained further below). Sun signs are grouped into four categories that correspond with the four base elements: fire, water, earth, and air. They also have either a positive or negative polarity assigned to them. The twelve zodiac sun signs are:

Aquarius

Aquarians are born between January 20 and February 18. You are associated with the element of air and the planet Uranus. Your modality is fixed, and your polarity is positive. The name Aquarius means the "Water-Bearer."

If you were born under the sign of Aquarius, you are independent by nature and refuse to conform to societal norms. You prefer to march to the beat of your own drum, and you will often seek tough challenges rather than take the safer and easier options. You don't mind being alone, but you enjoy the company of others. Aquarians are intelligent but can easily become bored when they lack stimulation. You may also have trouble expressing yourself emotionally.

Pisces

Pisceans are born between February 19 and March 20. You are associated with the element of water and the planet Neptune. Your modality is mutable, and your polarity is negative. The name Pisces means the "Fish."

If you were born under the sign of Pisces, you are a compassionate person and are selfless with others. You are a creative and intuitive individual, having wisdom far beyond your years. Because of your great capacity for empathy and emotional expression, you can be a bit too trusting. Pisceans are romantic and dislike cruelty of any kind. Music is very important to you, and you will most likely have developed a strong connection to it from an early age.

Aries

Ariens are born between March 21 and April 19. You are associated with the element of fire and the planet Mars. Your modality is cardinal, and your polarity is positive. The name Aries means the "Ram."

If you were born under the sign of Aries, you are a strong and direct person with plenty of energy. You tend to be optimistic in most situations and hold honesty as an important trait in people. Ariens are highly organized individuals, although they can also be temperamental. You work well with others, often taking on a leadership position when in a team or group. Your impulsiveness means you may find yourself in dangerous situations, but your willingness to fight for your goals will help you get through the challenges life throws at you.

Taurus

Taureans are born between April 20 and May 20. You are associated with the element of earth and the planet Venus. Your modality is fixed, and your polarity is negative. The name Taurus means the "Bull."

If you were born under the sign of Taurus, you are dependable and hardworking. You take a practical approach to life and are a loyal friend. Although you don't do well with change and can be stubborn, you are also patient and willing to remain committed to your goals. Taureans make excellent advisors and have a knack for making money. You like doing things with your hands, such as gardening and cooking, and are fond of fashion and trends.

Gemini

Geminin's are born between May 21 and June 20. You are associated with the element of air and the planet Mercury. Your modality is mutable, and your polarity is positive. The name Gemini means the "Twins."

If you were born under the sign of Gemini, you are the curious kind, often seeking answers and willing to learn new things. You are a gentle person who feels the need to express yourself emotionally. You can easily adapt to new situations, which is why you are constantly looking for interesting new hobbies and ideas. Geminians often have trouble making up their minds because they are interested in a variety of things. You like to show others affection and aren't afraid to engage with new people.

Cancer

Cancerians are born between June 21 and July 23. You are associated with the element of water and the Moon. Your modality is cardinal, and your polarity is negative. The name Cancer means the "Crab."

If you were born under the sign of Cancer, you are a very imaginative, sympathetic, and artistically inclined individual. You have no problem showing your emotions but are also prone to mood swings. You can be quite persuasive, which can be construed as manipulative, especially with those close to you. However, you enjoy being surrounded by loved ones and don't take kindly to those who try to harm or mess with them. Cancerians understand the difficulties of dealing with the outside world, so they will do their best to help others overcome their challenges and navigate through life.

Leo

Leos are born between July 24 and August 22. You are associated with the element of fire and the Sun. Your modality is fixed, and your polarity is positive. The name Leo means the "Lion."

If you were born under the sign of Leo, you are a passionate person with a generous spirit. You are creative and confident, tackling life's challenges with enthusiasm. Sometimes, your self-assuredness can come across as arrogance, yet your cheerfulness, warmth, and humor will often win people over. Leos thrive on attention, seeking validation from others through material possessions and status. You enjoy spending time with friends, having fun, and taking a break from your responsibilities every now and then.

Virgo

Virgins are born between August 23 and September 22. You are associated with the element of earth and the planet Mercury. Your modality is mutable, and your polarity is negative. The name Virgo means the "Maiden."

If you were born under the sign of Virgo, you are a practical and analytical person. You are well-organized and have defined goals in life. You may tend to get stuck on details due to your perfectionism, but this attention to detail also means you always put your best into everything you do. Virgins often close themselves off emotionally due to their shyness and fear of being hurt. You like to keep your environment clean and orderly, just like your mind.

Libra

Librans are born between September 23 and October 22. You are associated with the element of air and the planet Venus. Your modality is cardinal, and your polarity is positive. The name Libra means the "Scales."

If you were born under the sign of Libra, you are peaceful and diplomatic. You would rather solve conflicts with words than fists and are very easy to get along with. Equality and justice are important to you, so when you feel you've been wronged, you can hold grudges for a long time. Librans are sharp-minded and find inspiration all around them. You enjoy spending time with others and are good at working cooperatively. You like things in your life to be balanced, from your work and relationships to the leisure activities you engage in.

Scorpio

Scorpios are born between October 23 and November 22. You are associated with the element of water and the former planet Pluto. Your modality is fixed, and your polarity is negative. The name Scorpio means the "Scorpion."

If you were born under the sign of Scorpio, you are a brave and passionate person. You are very assertive, resourceful, and emotionally expressive. Scorpios are dedicated to the truth and facts, making it difficult for them to admit when they are wrong. You, despite dishonesty and tend to be suspicious of others that haven't proven themselves loyal and forthright. Due to your passion, you can be quick to anger, sometimes resulting in violence. Your natural leadership abilities mean others often look to you for guidance. You must keep your temper in check so they don't learn the wrong lessons from your actions.

Sagittarius

Sagittarians are born between November 23 and December 21. You are associated with the element of fire and the planet Jupiter. Your modality is mutable, and your polarity is positive. The name Sagittarius means the "Archer."

If you were born under the sign of Sagittarius, you are an idealist with a great sense of humor. You can be very generous and enjoy having the freedom to do the things you want. Sagittarians often love to travel. You are open-minded and allow yourself to learn about new cultures and philosophies without judgment. You tend to be enthusiastic and an extrovert who always speaks your mind, which can sometimes come off as disrespectful. However, your optimism means you will always try to find the best in any given situation and do what's necessary to achieve your goals.

Capricorn

Lastly, Capricorns are born between December 22 and January 19. You are associated with the element of earth and the planet Saturn. Your modality is cardinal, and your polarity is negative. The name Capricorn means the "Mountain Sea-Goat."

If you were born under the sign of Capricorn, you are a responsible and disciplined individual. You are well-mannered and treat others with respect. You are a serious person who doesn't like to waste time fooling around, meaning you can come off as strict and condescending at times. Capricorns make plans with realistic goals and don't indulge in fantasies. Because you hold yourself to such a high standard, you expect the same out of everyone else. You may seem like an unforgiving person when you hold others accountable for their mistakes, but you also greatly appreciate it when they work hard and do well. You are family-centered and traditional in many regards, which can sometimes lead to conflict with those who don't share similar values.

Modalities

In sun astrology, modalities refer to the part of a season that your sun sign falls under, each having defining characteristics shared by those born under the same modality, even if it comes during a different part of the year. There are three modalities: cardinal, fixed, and mutable. Here are the main characteristics for each one:

Cardinal

This modality comes at the start of a season. People with a cardinal modality are active, dynamic, entrepreneurial, and are a powerful force.

Fixed

This modality comes in the middle of a season. People with a fixed modality have great willpower, are inflexible, and resist change.

Mutable

This modality comes at the end of a season. People with a mutable modality are flexible, resourceful, and can adapt to almost any situation.

Elements and Polarities

The elements of air, fire, earth, and water are based on the four personality types proposed by Hippocrates, namely being sanguine, choleric, melancholic, and phlegmatic. These instill in you specific traits and characteristics depending on which element your sun sign is associated with. For example, the polarities determine whether you are more active or passive. These are the four elements and their personality types:

Air: Sanguine

This has a positive polarity. Associated traits include good communication, the ability to socialize, and developing goals and turning them into reality.

Fire: Choleric

This has a positive polarity. Associated traits include being strong-willed, assertive, and driven.

Earth: Melancholic

This has a negative polarity. Associated traits include cautiousness, practicality, and a focus on material things.

Water: Phlegmatic

This has a negative polarity. Associated traits include being empathetic, sensitive, and having strong emotions.

Ultimately, your sun sign can tell you a lot about your own self. You can use this information to help you grow as a person, learn your strengths and what weaknesses on which you must work. It can also help you figure out what will make you happy and what kind of people you will get along with best. The purpose behind understanding your sun sign is that you will be able to understand yourself better.

Chapter 3: The Rising Sign: Your Mask

Once you know your sun sign, the next important facet of your birth chart is your rising sign. It will set the tone for the rest of your chart. There may be aspects of yourself that you've only been presenting unconsciously, and your rising sign can help explain the reasons behind those parts of your personality. However, your rising sign isn't always the same as your sun sign. It can be any of the twelve zodiac signs, including your sun sign. Knowing what your rising sign is can go a long way towards helping foster a better understanding of who you are as a person.

What Is the Rising Sign?

Also known as an ascendant sign, a rising sign is an astrological sign rising on the eastern horizon when and where a specific event occurs. For you, this means which one was rising at the exact moment of your birth. It's one of the three pillars of your birth chart, along with your sun sign and your moon sign. Astrologists believe that combined, these create the foundation for your upbringing and personality. In addition, your rising sign dictates your "external" characteristics, that is, those aspects of yourself you show to other people. It's the mask you wear in public or the facade you put up to keep others from seeing what's underneath.

History of Rising Signs

Rising signs go all the way back to ancient Babylonians, who observed and recorded the specific times of the celestial phenomena of signs ascending in the sky. Then, in the 3rd century BC, Egyptians used the rising time of different clusters of stars to estimate the current time of night. The ancient Greeks later adopted this system called the rising sign, the "hour marker," or horoskopos. This is where the modern term for "horoscopes" originated.

Calculating Your Rising Sign

To calculate your rising sign, you must first know your sun sign and the precise time of your birth. You can find which rising sign is yours by referring to the chart below:

Your Sun Sign	12 AM to 2 AM	2 AM to 4 AM	4 AM to 6 AM	6 AM to 8 AM	8 AM to 10 AM	10 AM to 12 PM	12 PM to 2 PM	2 PM to 4 PM	4 PM to 6 PM	6 PM to 8 PM	8 PM to 10 PM	10 PM to 12 AM
♒	♐	♑	♒	♓	♈	♉	♊	♋	♌	♍	♎	♏
♓	♑	♒	♓	♈	♉	♊	♋	♌	♍	♎	♏	♐
♈	♒	♓	♈	♉	♊	♋	♌	♍	♎	♏	♐	♑
♉	♓	♈	♉	♊	♋	♌	♍	♎	♏	♐	♑	♒
♊	♈	♉	♊	♋	♌	♍	♎	♏	♐	♑	♒	♓
♋	♉	♊	♋	♌	♍	♎	♏	♐	♑	♒	♓	♈
♌	♊	♋	♌	♍	♎	♏	♐	♑	♒	♓	♈	♉
♍	♋	♌	♍	♎	♏	♐	♑	♒	♓	♈	♉	♊

♎	♌	♍	♎	♏	♐	♑	♒	♓	♈	♉	♊	♋
♏	♍	♎	♏	♐	♑	♒	♓	♈	♉	♊	♋	♌
♐	♎	♏	♐	♑	♒	♓	♈	♉	♊	♋	♌	♍
♑	♏	♐	♑	♒	♓	♈	♉	♊	♋	♌	♍	♎

Symbol Key

Aquarius = ♒

Pisces = ♓

Aries = ♈

Taurus = ♉

Gemini = ♊

Cancer = ♋

Leo = ♌

Virgo = ♍

Libra = ♎

Scorpio = ♏

Sagittarius = ♐

Capricorn = ♑

Rising Sign Personalities

Each rising sign has certain traits and characteristics that can determine your overall personality. They also have specific strengths and weaknesses assigned to them.

Aquarius

Strengths: You are an independent and unique person. You remain calm and collected in most situations and are tolerant of other people's views. In addition, you are sociable, using your intelligence and charitable nature to make friends.

Weaknesses: You tend to rebel against norms, even when it isn't advantageous. You often act before you think, which can get you into trouble. Due to your strong spirit, you dislike authority and taking orders.

Pisces

Strengths: You are kind and friendly to others, usually taking their feelings into account during interactions. You have an even temper, which helps you make good decisions instead of acting on emotions. You are a creative dreamer, always striving to reach the goals you set for yourself.

Weaknesses: You don't like confrontation, leading to you avoiding or running away from problems. You tend to be overly sentimental, clinging to the past. You sometimes struggle with making decisions, and your nature as a dreamer means you may have unrealistic goals and standards for yourself.

Aries

Strengths: You are adventurous, showing passion and bravery in everything you do. You can easily adapt to new situations and usually keep a cheerful and hopeful attitude in your endeavors. You are dynamic, have plenty of energy, and value honesty. You are a warm and generous person, giving to others without reservations.

Weaknesses: You can be slightly impatient and impulsive, which can cause trouble. You may be naive about the realities of certain people and situations. You are also prone to bickering, especially with those who you perceive as dishonest. Your willpower can cause issues with others, as you don't shy from getting your way with things.

Taurus

Strengths: You are a hard-working and passionate person. You can be decisive and patient, persevering against all odds. You are logical and practical and prefer to be realistic in any situation. You also have a romantic side and can be kind to others. In addition, you are very artistic, pouring your energy into creative endeavors.

Weaknesses: You can be stubborn and needy at times. You hold your values in such high esteem you may be prejudiced against those who don't share them. Your pursuit of hedonistic activities can also take you down a very selfish path. Because of your logical mind, you don't get along well with those who are fantastical dreamers.

Gemini

Strengths: You are smart and quick-witted, a warm, charming person who can get others to like you with ease. You can be very insightful have a cheerful disposition. You get along with different types of people, understand their points of view, and connect with them on many levels.

Weaknesses: You can be capricious, especially when it comes to friends. You tend to gossip, especially since you often see deeper into a person's mind than others. Your ability to charm people can also evolve into manipulation, which may cause others to perceive you in a negative light.

Cancer

Strengths: You are a kind and caring person with a gentle heart. You are dedicated and persevering, never letting obstacles stop you from achieving your goals. You have a great imagination that serves you well in creative undertakings. You also have an acute sixth sense and can perceive things about people and the world by instinct.

Weaknesses: You can be greedy at times, wanting more of the things you desire than you deserve. You are very possessive about people and material things and rarely want to share them with others. You may be a touch too sensitive, often getting your feelings hurt over the slightest offenses. You are also somewhat prudish, and you see people who are comfortable expressing themselves with a skeptical eye.

Leo

Strengths: Like the lion of your sign, you are a proud individual. You show unwavering loyalty to those you consider friends or family, having their back through thick and thin. You are charitable, giving to others without a second thought, and are enthusiastic in all your endeavors. You also can reflect on things, garnering a better understanding of any situation.

Weaknesses: Your pride can quickly turn into arrogance if you're not careful. You may behave conceitedly, believing you are above others. You tend to be somewhat wasteful, especially when you've got what you needed from something. Your willfulness can also land you in trouble since you refuse to back down.

Virgo

Strengths: You are highly intelligent and use your powerful mind to your advantage. You strive for perfection in everything you do, holding yourself to very high standards. You are precise in your actions and prefer to be practical. Your sense of style is elegant, and you enjoy the finer things in life. You are also very perceptive, picking up on subtle hints and social cues that others often miss.

Weaknesses: Your perceptiveness can sometimes lead to you becoming nosey, getting involved in other people's affairs when they may not want you to do so. Your preciseness and elegance may come across as fussiness. Also, your perfectionist nature can become overbearing, making excessive demands of others.

Libra

Strengths: You are an idealist, always seeing the best in people and situations. You are very reasonable and show a willingness to compromise. You are charming, have excellent social skills, and can deal with many personalities without trouble. You are kind and fair-minded and always want to see justice done. As an artistic being, you enjoy things like music, painting, and various crafts.

Weaknesses: You have a penchant for laziness and procrastination. Because of how easy socializing comes to you, you may be careless, especially when it comes to other people's feelings. You are prone to egotistically behaving since you are often the center of attention. You don't like to commit to things and prefer to live a free-spirited life.

Scorpio

Strengths: You are an intelligent and rational person. You have great intuition and are insightful, discovering things about others that people often overlook. You are independent and don't rely on others for your own happiness. You are devoted to those you care about and are very reasonable, acting in a manner that benefits everyone in difficult situations.

Weaknesses: You tend to obsess over things until it becomes unhealthy. You are often suspicious of other people's motives, partly because you can perceive aspects of them they may be trying to hide. You can be arrogant and complicated at times. As a possessive person, you don't want to let anyone else have what you hold close to your heart.

Sagittarius

Strengths: You are outspoken about your views and aren't afraid to stand up for yourself. You have an upbeat personality, lifting the spirits of others when they're down. You are brave and adventurous, never afraid to take on a new challenge. You always look on the bright side and manage to stay optimistic even in the face of uncertainty. You are also rational, using your mind to solve problems as efficiently as possible.

Weaknesses: You can be forgetful, constantly losing things like your keys or failing to remember important dates and events. This can seem like being thoughtless, as when you forget someone's birthday or overlook their contributions, it may come across as malicious. You are also somewhat rash, letting your outspokenness take over, which doesn't always lead to positive results.

Capricorn

Strengths: You are a very dependable and reliable person. You are intelligent, and there is something endearing about you, helping you make many friends. You can be persistent, pushing forward even when you face setbacks, and are determined to persevere no matter what. You are generous to others and have an unfailing optimism. You prefer practicality in things, such as buying a plain vehicle that gets great gas mileage over a flashy sports car that burns through fuel.

Weaknesses: You are a solitary person who would rather do things on your own. While this isn't always a bad thing, you avoid asking others for help, even though you're the first to offer it. You can be stubborn, refusing to admit you're in the wrong, or do things someone else's way. You may be suspicious of others, and you question their honesty during everyday interactions.

Houses of the Birth Chart

Birth charts are divided into individual "houses" that correspond to the twelve signs of the zodiac. It involves a complex system that charts the zodiac signs based on the movement of the Earth as it rotates on its axis. The first six houses are considered to be below the horizon, whereas the other six are above the horizon. They possess specific traits assigned to them, and all have a name that expresses their overarching meaning. These houses are:

1. Aries: Life: House of Self

2. Taurus: Gain: House of Value

3. Gemini: Sisters: House of Sharing

4. Cancer: Parent: House of Home and Family

5. Leo: Children: House of Pleasure

6. Virgo: Health: House of Health

7. Libra: Spouse: House of Balance

8. Scorpio: Death: House of Transformation

9. Sagittarius: Passage: House of Purpose

10. Capricorn: Kingdom: House of Enterprise

11. Aquarius: Good Deeds: House of Blessings

12. Pisces: Rehabilitation: House of Sacrifice

Effects of Your Rising Sign

Various factors can determine the potency of a force in your birth chart. Most astrologers believe that the closer to the start of a given sign a person's birth falls under, the more strength it will possess. This is because most of the first house will be within that sign. When their birth comes later in the sign, the majority of the first house falls into the next sign, causing it to be weaker. When the sun is in a weaker position, like at the bottom of your birth chart, the rising sign is believed to have more influence, this is because the sun would have been on the other side of the Earth at the time you were born.

The influence of your rising sign may weaken at the age of 29, at which point you will become more like your sun sign. This is due to people becoming more confident as they get older, meaning there's less reason to wear a mask in public. However, this isn't true for everyone, as there are still plenty of people who put on a facade their entire lives. With more self-esteem and a better-developed ego, you can express your true inner self without fear. Ultimately, you can use your understanding of your rising sign to help you grow and become a stronger individual.

Understanding Your Rising Sign

Once you understand your rising sign, you gain deeper insights into how you behave around other people. You'll know the strengths you can take advantage of and offset your weaknesses. Knowledge of your rising sign can help you adjust your attitudes and tendencies, allowing you to connect with others on a deeper and more genuine level.

It's worth remembering that your rising sign is only but a part of your identity. Your actions and decisions are still up to you, but knowing and understanding your rising sign can inform these actions and decisions to help you make better ones. The sun, moon, and stars aren't responsible for how you interact with other people; they merely provide guidance to assist you in your development and growth as a person.

Chapter 4: The Moon Sign: Your Emotions

When it comes to exploring behavioral tendencies and character traits in astrology, most people only refer to the star or sun sign. Many people fail to realize that the sun, the moon, Mercury, Venus, Mars, Jupiter, Saturn, Uranus, Pluto, and their rising sign are all significant celestial bodies in the realm of astrology. Each planet, along with the sun and the moon, symbolizes a different set of characteristics and qualities in us humans. Each rules over a certain aspect of our lives, contributing its energy and direction. Every celestial body is a character of its own. They all have their unique interests, goals, and functions. Based on the zodiac sign they are positioned in, they express themselves and act independently.

We constantly feed off the energy of the sun, the moon, and the planets. However, how they affect us typically depends on their position in the zodiac at any given moment. As we've seen, who you are is a collection of your natal planets at the time of your birth. You may consult an astrologer or look for an online birth chart calculator to know your natal planets. Once you discover where the celestial bodies lie in your natal chart, you can tell how they impact different parts of your life and affect your energy. You can also explore the relationships between the planets.

Now, to better understand how your natal chart determines who you are as a person, you must first understand the role and functions of each celestial body. As explained previously, the sun sign reflects yourself and your conscious mind. It determines your life's purpose and fosters your creative energy. In simple terms, it is the most solid and genuine version of who you are.

The sun naturally rules over Leo. Mercury is the planet of expression, communication, intellect, and reason. It represents your ability to carry out coherent and reasonable conversations.

Mercury naturally rules over Virgo and Gemini. Venus rules over Taurus and Libra and is the planet of love, romance, pleasure, and beauty. It symbolizes how you construe value, love, and experience luxury and pleasure. Mars represents your desire and sexual drive. It determines raw energy and aggression, namely your fundamental physical instinct.

Mars rules over Aries. Jupiter is the planet that pushes you to chase your loftiest dreams. It's associated with good luck, optimism, and abundance and naturally rules over Sagittarius. Saturn is renowned as the rigid celestial body. While its energy can be harsh, it is intended to help you learn and grow.

Saturn is associated with discipline and life lessons and naturally rules over Capricorn. Uranus is perhaps the most unpredictable planet. Its energy is innovative and original, and it represents awakenings, inspiration, and insights. Uranus naturally rules over Aquarius.

Neptune is the planet of sensitivity and spirituality. It is the most ethereal planet, representing intuition, artistic expression, and dreams. It rules over Pisces. Although it is no longer considered a planet in science, Pluto is still as much of a powerful planet as any other planet in astrology. Pluto represents transformations, death, darkness, and rebirth. It has an intense energy that symbolizes extremities, from the newest beginnings to all endings. Pluto was even named after the god of the underworld and rules over Scorpio.

Finally, the moon. Throughout this chapter, we will explore how the moon plays a central role in the zodiac world. The moon, which naturally rules over Cancer, can be thought of as your internal emotional compass. It is a gentle and emotionally driven celestial body.

The Moon

In astrology, the moon symbolizes those aspects of yourself that you can't express. It represents your innermost emotions and rules over your most vulnerable and hidden parts. The moon holds the key to what makes us feel comfortable, safe, and emotionally secure. It regulates all the aspects of yourself that you don't show to others unless your emotional and safety needs are met. The moon is often called the cosmic mother. Just like it represents our emotions, it symbolizes our motherly, feminine, and maternal side. It also represents our memories and even the simplest things we find joy in. It is also a representation of our inner child. In other words, the moon reflects our basic, natural reactions, profound personal needs, and our unconscious.

Our moon signs are a reaction to our suns' activities. It has a reflective power, receptive energy, and responsive reactions. The moon is spontaneous and ultimately instinctual. The role of the moon in the solar system mirrors its purpose in the zodiac. The moon's circular motion around the sun can be viewed as a symbol of protectiveness, just like how it teaches us, or rather, wants us to protect ourselves.

The moon grants us our liveliness and spirit. It controls the rhythmic rise and fall of our energy and activity. It is the arbitrator between the exterior world and the inner world. It is irrational, unlike the sun. Everything, including our habits, prejudices, spontaneous thoughts, reactions, and feelings, is ruled by the moon. The sun censors most of it, which is why these feelings may not be acted out.

The Moon and the Sun

For some people, the moon drives and affects their personality much more than the sun does. This holds true, especially if your moon falls in a water sign, namely Scorpio, Cancer, or Pisces. Your moon can also be predominant in your personality if your moon is at a conjunct angle in your natal chart. This means it can be near a 4th or 10th house cusp, a Descendant, or an Ascendant. To attain happiness in your life, it's best to give your moon neither too little nor too much attention. Remember it without obsessively analyzing your actions or emotions accordingly. Grant Lewi, an Astrologist, offered the most accurate description of the moon. He explained that when you feel something that you can't quite explain, it's because your moon is aware of it, but your sun refuses to say it. He claimed that the things you feel too deeply (things you can't even cry out) are the thoughts that emerge from the nature of your moon.

Silent sorrows, clandestine dreams, indescribable ecstasy, and the cryptic version of yourself that no one seems to know, value, or understand all originate in your zodiac's moon. When you feel misunderstood, it indicates that the nature of your moon is not in line with the sun's energy. Sometimes, most of us experience the frustration of knowing what needs to be done but not knowing the right way to do it. This typically happens when your moon and your sun fall out of tune. It's the moon that's aware, but it's the sun that refuses to cooperate. When you question your actions or words, it is because either your sun or your moon acted despite the other. Most of the time, if you find yourself satisfied with your unexpected speech or action, it's the moon that acted against the sun's will. By contrast, if you find yourself bothered or critical of yourself, it's the other way around.

Seeking Balance

Once you've analyzed your natal chart and understood the energies of your sun and moon, you can figure out a way to maintain a balance in your life. If, as it happens, your sign and moon fall under the same sign, this suggests that the things you want and the things you need are in alignment. When you think of your path in life and your ability to express yourself cohesively and freely, it's because you may feel less resistance in doing so typically.

If your sun and moon are downright incompatible, you may be prone to internal stress and tension. This is because the two celestial bodies are constantly trying to find a way to satisfy each other's needs along with their own. Our emotional needs differ from our conscious ones. For instance, if your sun is in Virgo and your moon is in Gemini, you may find yourself constantly fighting a battle between seeking practicality and wanting variety. You may have to overcome several obstacles before finally finding true happiness and balance. You can set yourself out on the path to self-discovery once you understand and accept the differences between your sun and your moon. This is needed so you can unite and please both aspects of who you are.

The sun and moon always work together, whether to maintain life in the universe or within your inner self. However, just like they've found harmony in existence, it is your role to help them achieve harmony within you. This doesn't necessarily mean that you should attempt to make your moon and sun seek the same things, which is impossible. It simply means you should look for the good in what each offers. Besides, their inherent polarity is what allows you to grow and progress. As they work together, despite their differences, they allow you to move on and let go of the things that hold you back and hinder your progress. At the end of the day, your sun and your moon want you to thrive in their unique ways.

How Moon Signs Manifest

Like sun signs, moon signs manifest themselves differently. Moon signs have different emotional needs, express themselves differently, and have different reactions. Unlike the sun, the moon moves quickly around the zodiac. The moon stays in the same sign for a two-day period. This is why you need the date, time, and place of birth to calculate your moon sign accurately.

Emotional Aries

If your moon is in Aries, you may be very short-tempered. You probably like competition and challenges and feed off any form of excitement. You find satisfaction in releasing built-up energy, and while this is good, it may severely hurt the other person even when it no longer affects you. However, one of the best things about emotional Aries is that they don't hold grudges. Once you talk about your emotions, you are quick to move on, forgive and forget.

Emotional Taurus

You feel safe only when you are provided with stability. It's almost impossible to satisfy this need with the constant unpredictability of life. As a result, you tend to be practical, relying on the material aspects of the world. You will easily get hurt if you don't accept that change is inevitable.

Emotional Gemini

Gemini moons tend to run away from their emotions by unintentionally playing vicious mind games. Once their emotions are challenged, they find a way to view things exactly as they want, rather than how they ought to be. However, Gemini moons are intelligent and curious. They have a fun nature, and when they allow their feelings to surface, they can be open and sentimental.

Emotional Cancer

If you are an emotional Cancer, you feed off your feelings. Even when things seem logically solid, you rarely contradict your emotions. Most of your decisions are made based on instinct. You may get hurt easily, though you still have a protective layer that will instinctively come into play to safeguard itself. You are somewhat tactical and resilient and are emotionally strong. You can easily walk out on people and never look back once they run out of warnings or second chances. When treated well, though, you are a very nurturing, loyal, and warm individual.

Emotional Leo

You find security in your ability to impress others. Receiving admiration and praise is your drive and makes you feel safe. However, when you find yourself the center of attention, you can feel confused. You naturally desire success, money, and eminence and can attain it all.

Emotional Virgo

Your security rests on clarity and structure, even when it comes to your emotions. You may feel a strong urge to get everything in order. This can cause you severe damage and hinder your mind, which is why you must accept that things are typically imperfect. It's simply the nature of life.

Emotional Libra

If your moon is Libra, you probably seek safety in your relationships. In addition, you wish to be a source of happiness to others and favor an abundant and rewarding social life. In the end, though, focus on yourself more and figure out the things that satisfy you. As an emotional libra, you have a strong desire for a harmonious and balanced life.

Emotional Scorpio

With your moon in Scorpio, you may feel the need to go as deep in your emotions as possible. Normally, delving this far into your feelings can cause you to feel vulnerable. While exploring and understanding your emotions is a good thing, it also means you can never let go of anything that hurt you. This also makes it difficult for you to do anything that you aren't willing to do.

Emotional Sagittarius

As someone with a moon in Sagittarius, you are always searching for something. This is your ultimate desire. You find safety in adventure and exploration. You like intriguing beliefs and philosophies. You are always searching for things, missions or goals, to give your life meaning. You choose to experience the higher vibrations of life, allowing you to let go of negative emotions rather quickly.

Emotional Capricorn

You get your safety from feeling useful. You want to benefit those surrounding you. You want to help society and seek explanations from the external world. Unfortunately, your need for validation can cause you to feel unloved and useless, leading you to overlook your own needs. You must trust your potential instead of worrying about others ignoring you.

Emotional Aquarius

If you're an emotional Aquarius, chances are you have a complex relationship with your emotions. You feel the need to liberate yourself from negative emotions. You want to free yourself from anger, jealousy, fear, and other unwanted feelings. While this may temporarily grant you peace of mind, this will build a lot of pressure and bottle up your emotions in time. Besides, when others show negative emotions, they will expect you always to tolerate them.

Emotional Pisces

Those with Pisces moon are characterized by their discernment and sensitivity, which may leave them feeling insecure at times. Motional Pisces are usually passive when it comes to their future and life in general. They will simply sit back and watch things as they unfold. However, if you are into spirituality and creativity, you can unlock boundless chambers of imagination.

When it comes to the world of zodiacs, people mostly direct their attention to their sun or star signs. However, what they don't know is that the positioning of their moon matters just as much. Your moon is everything that your sun represses. It's the unconscious and your hidden, unspoken emotions. Exploring your moon can be your key to unleashing your creativity and your path to self-discovery.

Section Two: The Secret Power of Numerology

Chapter 5: What Is Numerology?

Whether we're talking about our everyday life or in spiritual terms, not surprisingly, numbers hold significant value. Throughout this chapter, we explore the significance of numbers in the spiritual world. Numerology, simply put, is the correspondence between a number and its spiritual nature on individuals and the concept of existence as a whole. Keep in mind that numerology can also refer solely to the study of the alphabet's numerical value.

For centuries, people have experimented with different ideas and concepts in numerology. However, it wasn't until 1907 that the word numerology itself was scripted in the English language. Babylon, ancient Egypt, China, Japan, Rome, and Greece were among the earliest civilizations where the first records of numerology emerged. Pythagoras, the Greek Philosopher, is historically known as "the father of numerology." He was highly celebrated for being an incredible mathematician and scholar. Although much of Pythagoras' life is a mystery, his interest in numbers is well-recognized in history. Driven by his passion, he traveled to Egypt, where he spent 22 years studying Chaldean numerology. He believed that the power of numbers is the essence of all existence and that the entire world was built upon it. According to Pythagoras, everything in life can be translated into a numerical form. This led to developing the Pythagorean number system, which is still applied in modern technology. This system is based on the idea that letters can be assigned numerical values.

Numbers also have a major significance in religion. For instance, some say that the number 888 represents Jesus, the Holy Trinity's infinite nature, and Hanukkah, which lasts for eight nights. The number 666, on the other hand, is linked to the beast. In Tarot, every card has a number with a unique and distinct meaning, and in the Chinese tradition, bad luck is highly associated with the number 4. Thus, numerology is important in every aspect of our lives. We subconsciously use it to find meaning in different things. Some people even unintentionally master the art of numerology to employ it in the stock market! But most combine numerology and astrology to set themselves on the path to clairvoyance and self-discovery.

Let's point out that numerology is not to be confused with astrology. While they are very different studies, they both aim to discover individuals' unique qualities, characteristics, and traits. Astrology and numerology rest upon distinct concepts and ideas. However, they can be and typically are, used together in various ways. For example, people combine the two fields to make predictions and attempt to understand themselves and others. Numerology and astrology both use mathematics, science, and spirituality to decipher readings for the future. In fact, Prem Jyotish, a numerology and astrology expert, offers one of the clearest explanations as to how numerology can be used to that end. He explains that numerology employs significant numbers in your life (numbers that revolve around it) as signs that can allow you to find different things that can help you without being tied to a specific timeline or schedule.

On the day you are born, the planets, the sun, and the moon align to create your energy. Their positions in your zodiac continue to affect you as they move. Understanding their position in relation to your zodiac can help you get a better sense of your behavior, emotions, reactions, and ultimately, who you are as a person. Meanwhile, by combining the letters of your birth name with their respective numbers, numerology can help you gather insight into your future. This will reflect your personality traits, motives, challenges, talents, and karma energy. Astrology and numerology are both needed to leverage the readings you gather from both studies. Your astrological inferences can be faulty if not based on divisional charts and an accurate interpretation of them. This applies to numerology as well. How freely you express your emotions and blend with the environment that surrounds you can both affect your numerology readings.

How It Works

The science of numerology can be very esoteric. If you are looking for accurate and highly detailed readings, you may need to resort to a certified numerologist. However, simple calculations such as those for your personality, expression, life path, and soul's urge numbers can be easily obtained. Connecting the dots and figuring out how all of these numbers come into play together is why you need an expert. Invariably, numerology predictions can provide profound insights into different aspects of life. They can also help you learn more about other people. The most basic readings and calculations can reveal incredible revelations. Like the infinite nature of numbers, a numerology chart can be read and interpreted in endless ways.

What It Can Do for You

Besides providing the keys for predictions and self-discovery, numerology, when used correctly, can help you discover the hidden meanings of existence. Think of numerology as your own personal guide to life. It dictates your possibilities, potential, strengths, and weaknesses. The three numbers derived from your name (the personality, power, and soul's urge numbers), along with the other three derived from your birthdate (life path, attitude, and birth numbers), each have their own meaning and purpose. Some say that the most prominent of them all is your life path number. Specific energies are tied to designated numbers. For example, the number "1" is associated with innovation, leadership, and independence, while the number "3" is linked to self-expression, allure, and optimism. Number 6 reflects harmony and responsibility and 9 of healing, compassion, and perfection.

While it can be confusing at first glance, understanding the concept behind the calculation is quite simple. For starters, the cosmos of your life is affected by your birth date. It determines your life's path and provides an interpretation of the relationships you cultivate. You can think of it as a beneficial insight into the unknown, a way to prepare for what's ahead. Numerology can help you tap into your potential and abilities and teach you how to make your character shine through. This is intended to help you change your own life by choosing the path you want to walk down. Many people refer to numerology when looking to make difficult or life-altering decisions. It gives them a clear insight into whether it's a suitable time to embark on new life journeys. When you set out to explore the unknown, numerology typically sends you signs to warn you about both positive and negative incomings.

Numerology can help you find your spirit's purpose and guide you towards the paths along which you can form meaningful professional and personal relationships. It gives you a clear insight into the person who will walk you through life. Numerology can also help drive you towards opportunities by letting you know the avenues that promise auspicious results. Not only that, but it also enables you to understand the mindsets, ambitions, drives, desires, and inhibitions of important people in your life. For instance, it can help you understand why some people succeed and others fail even though they work towards the same goal (wealth, status, happiness, enlightenment).

You can use numerology to discover more about your traits, set goals, and establish plans to help you attain them. It helps you make the right choices regarding education, work, finances, love, and marriage. It also allows you to find surefire ways to overcome your challenges. By using numerology to assess the energies of your environment, you will always be in the right place at the right time.

The Traits of Numbers

Have you ever wondered why numbers are divided into odd and even? This is because they share similar traits. However, odd numbers and even numbers have their own strengths and weaknesses.

Odd Numbers

Odd numbers epitomize the spirit of adventure, creativity, and inspiration. They are symbols of intangible things linked to the brain's right hemisphere. Odd numbers like to do things differently.

They go against the grain, which is perhaps why they are called "odd" numbers. Let's further dig into these symbolisms:

The number 1 symbolizes the urge to drive forward and initiate. The sun and intellection are both associated with it. The number 1 is considered masculine. As visionaries and leaders, the number 1s are pioneering, direct, and groundbreaking. Their weakness, though, is that they may be too dominant and bossy. They can be overly aggressive and poor listeners.

The number 3 symbolizes the urge for artistry, self-expression, and creativity. Number 3s are thought to be gifted and naturally talented. They are lucky and optimistic, have a heightened sense of imagination and a great sense of humor. That said, number 3s are not all blessings. They tend to gossip and be unorganized. They are lost and don't have a strong sense of direction. They talk a lot, but they never act on their words.

The number 5 represents the yearning to experience every aspect of life. This longing manifests itself in mundane emotions such as the love of adventure, curiosity, and change. Naturally, the number 5 tends to be peculiar. It is also the number of boundlessness. Number 5s choose to explore and expand in all directions at all times. However, as "odd" as it may sound, number 5 may be deemed fearful. They are also usually moody, unhappy, and can even be thought of as escape artists.

The numbers 1 through 6, in both odd and even groups, represent mundane, everyday concerns. By contrast, the numbers 7 and beyond deal with higher transcendental matters.

The number 7 symbolizes the need for knowledge and wisdom and seeks to understand the realm of technicalities. The number 7s are skeptics and hermits. They like to research, observe, and investigate. On the other hand, number 7s can seem sarcastic and cynical. They are quite analytical, which is why they may sometimes appear withdrawn and depressed.

The number 9 is representative of the desire to find acceptance and amicable love. It is also associated with appreciation and compassion. The number 9 tends to be forgiving and tolerant, although they may seem bitter and moody. Number 9s are also possessive and prone to depression. Because it's the greatest odd number, 9 embodies the idea of completion. As we'll see, it is similar to the number 6 but a much wiser and grown version of it.

Even Numbers

Even numbers are tied to the brain's left hemisphere. They symbolize structured and laid-out things. As opposed to odd numbers, even numbers represent tangible things and like to conform to the norms. They don't like the unexpected and prefer that their lives go very smoothly. Generally, even numbers are associated with the "right" things in society.

The number 2 embodies tranquility, harmony, and unity. Number 2s are typically gentle and soothing. Their patience and sensitivity also characterize them. The number 2 is thought to be feminine and representative of the moon. It expresses abstract energies, feelings, intuitions, and vibrations that are hard to put into words. But number 2s can be perceived as timid. They are self-critical, overly consumed by details, and are usually reluctant to advocate for what they believe in.

The number 4 symbolizes the need for orderliness. It is structured, systematic, and seeks practicality and efficiency. Number 4s are considered down-to-Earth. The downside of the number 4 is that they can be closed off, stringent, and very opinionated. They may also lack imagination.

The number 6 feels the need to provide service. It is also symbolic of tenderness, care, and romantic love. It represents the benevolence of individuals who are very loving toward other people. This makes them patriotic, family-oriented, and devoted to others and their welfare. Unfortunately, this also makes them self-sacrificing and somehow over-protective. They can be nagging and resentful, often to unhealthy extremes.

The number 8 embodies the spirit of the law. It is majorly associated with the law of retribution. Number 8 goes by the statement, "for every action, there is an equal and opposite reaction." Number 8s are concerned with causes and effects and the concept of karma. They are structured, authoritative, and driven by the need for balance and the commandments of Jesus and Moses. Number 8s are potent and directed, although they can be obsessive and overly driven. The number 8 is typically compulsive and miserly. However, the number 8 mysteriously stands out from the rest. It holds high energies and power.

The number zero, or the cipher, is symbolic of the fulfillment of possibilities. Zero can elevate and draw out whichever number it accompanies. It doesn't change the number's value, however. It only makes it more mature and grown. It is a way to show that the other numbers have experienced an entire cycle and are now ready to operate from higher perspectives. The cipher is an emblem of the whole world.

The Master Numbers

As the master numbers, 11, 22, 33, 44 are phenomenally special. They convey a strong sense of dedication to help with the substantial awakening of consciousness. When a master number shows up in a numerology chart, this suggests that maturity and wisdom are needed to deal with various responsibilities and life choices successfully. Master numbers comprise two single digits, and these digits can result in greater things than single digits can achieve on their own. You can know the single digit that any master number can be reduced to. For instance, the number 11 can be reduced to 2 (1+1=2), and 22 can be reduced to 4 (2+2=4). Similarly, 33 is 6, and 44 is 8.

The master number 11 encompasses the qualities of numbers 1 and 2. Eleven can also be written as 11/2. It symbolizes the force that lights up the path towards a higher sense of consciousness. Great inner flexibility and strength are required to go down that path. On the downside, 11 can be perceived as high-strung and anxious. It is easily disenchanted and contradictory. Some go as far as to say that it holds "schizophrenic" traits. It constantly swings back and forth between personalities. The need for balance drives 11/2.

The master number 22 displays the qualities of numbers 2 and 4 and can be written as 22/4. It symbolizes the need to reconstruct the world in accordance with the laws of human dignity and equal participation. However, 22/4s may indulge in self-destructive behaviors. They may be considered very negative, lazy, and even cruel.

The master number 33, written as 33/6, includes all the qualities of numbers 3 and 6. It is driven by the desire to lighten up and vitalize the world by offering humor and laughter. However, this

---

47

number may feel burdened and aimless. It is viewed as a people-pleaser.

Last, the master number 44 (or 44/8) embodies the qualities of the numbers 4 and 8. It symbolizes the need for reconciliation and bridging the gap between god and goddess by employing inner spirituality and aligning the mind and body. On a mundane, social, and personal level, it is concerned with healing children. It is easily overwhelmed which challenges and the burdens of life. Ironically, 44 may seem oppressive and heartless.

Ultimately, the study and practice of numerology can help us understand the essence of existence, ourselves, and others. It offers great insights into the future, aiding us in making major life decisions. By using numerology, you can guide yourself down positive paths and find ways to overcome challenges.

Chapter 6: Discover Your Destiny Number

Numerology uses a person's Destiny Number to determine their goals in life and how those goals are to be pursued. This number, also known as the Expression Number, is easy to calculate and can help you garner meaningful insights into your true nature. However, remember that this number does not tell who you are right now but rather indicates the kind of person you could be if you fulfill your duties and follow your instincts.

The most commonly suggested way to calculate your Destiny Number is by adding up the individual digits corresponding to the letters of your birth name. While many people suggest using your nickname, others think that the only proper way to calculate it is by using the name given to you by your parents on your birth certificate. However, you can try it with variations of your name to obtain interesting results that might give you hidden insights. Of course, you should also avoid including any prefixes or suffixes like Jr, Sr, or 1st, and even the changes made to your name later in life should be avoided.

The chart used to discover the Destiny Number is rather simple and can easily be found online. It goes as follows:

1	2	3	4	5	6	7	8	9
A	B	C	D	E	F	G	H	I
J	K	L	M	N	O	P	Q	R
S	T	U	V	W	X	Y	Z	

Let's take a random name and discover the Destiny Number for it by utilizing the table. For example, if a person is named Jack Black, then the steps to discover their Destiny Number by using the values in the table will be:

1. JACK = 1+1+3+2 = 7
2. BLACK = 2+3+1+3+2 = 11 (add both individual numbers, so 1+1) = 2
3. **Destiny Number** = 7+2 = 9

After discovering the Destiny Number, you have only to match the resulting number with the given description for each number. We will later discuss how Destiny Numbers affect every individual's path in life in detail to help you better understand what your life's goals should be aligned with. These are basic guidelines to give you an overview and might include more points as applicable.

So, let's take a look at the number you calculated for your name:

Number 1

As a number 1 Destiny Number holder, you strive to be the best, and your path lies in leading others. You have a strong drive for leadership and attaining power which makes you a naturally adept leader. The unyielding determination, perseverance, and courage you exhibit inspire others to follow you. You have a strong sense of initiative and don't wait for anyone else to take the first step.

You are free of self-doubt, which is a characteristic that should not be exhibited by you when following your destiny. Your self-confidence and boldness against insurmountable odds make you a born leader. You crave independence and don't want to be stuck in a rat race like the others. This is why you'll often dive into decisions headfirst without thinking about the consequences.

With such a strong drive for success and the ability to innovate, you would excel at starting a business of your own. Your determination and the creative solutions you come up with are likely to bring great financial gains in your life. But sometimes, you might need to be gentle and more considerate towards others. Your Destiny Number will inherently drive you towards self-centeredness and egotism since your leadership approach is ruthless and aggressive. However, understand that things can be accomplished even without resorting to such extremes.

Number 2

Being a number 2, your job is to be a harbinger of peace, harmony, love, and cooperation. For you, the purpose of everything in life is to maintain love and harmony. As a result, you thrive in environments free of conflicts, and you'll always strive to appease any situation where tensions run deep.

You can excel at diplomacy and people skills if you devote the time to groom yourself properly. For you, a larger cause can be the motivation that pushes you to greatness. Even though you might not get credit for what you did, you will still be content with your contribution since your ideas matter more to you than money or wealth. However, you might be more of a dreamer than a doer, and you'll often have a hard time being practical and realizing that some things are out of reach.

You can be shy, but socializing is an essential activity for you since a lack of it would make you depressed and pessimistic. Working on your shyness, indecisiveness, and oversensitivity will enable you to cultivate great interpersonal skills. You will be admired and liked by everyone around you, thanks to your capacity to understand and empathize.

Number 3

As a holder of the number 3 destiny, you will be the life of every party or conversation around you. Being optimistic, inspiring, enthusiastic, and friendly is in your nature and will help you attract others towards you. You will easily impress people with your charms, and people will love to make conversation with thanks to your remarkable social skills.

You can develop yourself along creative lines like writing, speaking, singing, or any other performance arts. Even your destiny will align with proper devotion, so you get maximum opportunities to be on stage. For you, life is a journey that's meant to be enjoyed, and your optimism will increase as you mature. However, you must follow your passions and don't let go of what your heart truly desires, or else you may fall into a cycle of anger, depression, and self-destructive behavior.

With your ability to inspire and influence others, you'll be able to do well in a career like sales. Your only weaknesses might be superficiality and attempting to please everyone. Suppose you can overcome these obstacles and develop your personality to be positive, uplifting the spirits of others. In that case, you will fulfill your destiny of being an inspiration to those around you.

Number 4

As a wielder of the number 4 destiny, you will be naturally bestowed with the tenets of hard work and responsibility. You thrive in order and stability and will often go as far as sacrificing your own comforts to establishing and maintaining a well-functioning system. Number 4 makes for an excellent partner, whether in business or marriage, due to their unyielding devotion to a cause.

You will be happy in planning, organizing, and executing a strategy, which makes you an ideal candidate for managerial positions. You serve as a bedrock to many institutions around you, be it your family or your community. People trust you because of your demonstrated dedication and pragmatism.

You must learn to take risks if you wish to maximize your potential. You might think that if you fail, then people will think less of you, but this is only an irrational fear you must overcome sooner or later. If you pursue qualities like impeccable morals, honesty, loyalty, and seriousness, you will be the happiest since it will bring you a step closer to your destiny.

Number 5

If there's one word that can be associated with a number 5 destiny, it's freedom. You are a free soul who doesn't like to be bound by anything. You get frustrated whenever your life gets mundane or stagnates. While many others might want stability, you enjoy the sense of adventure and change. You want to explore the world and live life to the fullest.

A sedentary life is your worst nightmare, and you don't want to be stuck in a rut. For you, traveling is as much about the journey as it is about the destination. You might border into the self-centered category, and your relationships might not last a long time either. This is because you get bored of repetition and routine, even in relationships.

However, you are also a versatile person with multiple talents. You have a curious mind that allows you to be more spiritually aware and conscious than others. If you can overcome your weaknesses like fearfulness, selfishness, and myopia, then you can endorse the role that your destiny will drive you to.

Number 6

Anyone with a destiny number 6 is blessed with the ability to love, support, and nurture those in their life. You will not distinguish between friends, family, or society while sending out your love. The only thing you will care about is treating everyone with kindness and compassion.

A number 6 will find happiness in lifting the mood and raise the spirit of other people who might feel depressed. As long as you are dependable, friendly, and open to others, you will have no issues when it comes to meeting your destined goals. Those with this destiny number are often prone to overly empathizing with everyone, and they go out of their way to help out the ones in need. Unfortunately, this can sometimes work against them as they get too invested in others and overlook their own needs.

A number 6 might have many other talents, but they will most likely devote themselves to helping the poor, hungry, old, and needy. Work involving charity of any kind will be the most appealing to you due to your inherent compassion and love for others. The family life of a number 6 will be prosperous and full of love, but the negative traits you might exhibit are dominance and self-righteousness. If a number 6 can eliminate any vestiges of these negative behaviors and accept others with an open heart, then they can fulfill the role chosen for them by their destiny.

Number 7

If your destiny number is 7, you are a lifelong learner and a teacher. The purpose of your existence is to obtain knowledge and share it with others. Due to your desire for knowledge, you will most likely have a contemplative nature and find yourself poring over religion, spirituality, philosophy, and yourself.

You are a gentle soul at heart, but since your wisdom extends beyond what others might comprehend, your words may hurt others who are not aware of your intentions. You might feel the need to spend most of your time alone, but this will harm you. If you don't share your knowledge with others by interacting with them, this will lead to unforeseen frustration and depression.

Your destiny will most likely lead you towards a career of similar nature with your thirst for knowledge. You will do well as a scientist, teacher, or spiritual guru since you naturally want to share your knowledge and enlighten others.

Your only downsides are skepticism, cynicism, and superficiality. However, if you can overcome these vices, then you will fulfill your true potential and destiny.

Number 8

People blessed with the number 8 have a naturally high drive for success in the material world, and they seek to command respect and power from others. A number 8 is not an easy destiny to live up to, but if you master what is demanded of you, this number becomes one of the most rewarding ones.

A number 8 has immense potential for financial success. You will make a great businessman, and your administrative prowess will be unparalleled if you exercise proper judgment. The number 8 will have authority issues at times, making them feel like they exercise authority wherever they go. This is one of those problems that come with great power and skill. Once you overcome these basic personality issues, you will achieve a lot in the material world.

You might also face issues like stubbornness and over-ambition, but these can easily be turned to your advantage by acknowledging and addressing them. For example, stubbornness can be turned into strong self-belief and confidence in whatever you pursue, whereas your ambition can help you be more driven to achieve the true path laid down by your destiny.

Number 9

Last, a number 9 likes to be around people and interact with them with compassion and care. If this is your destiny number, you will be happiest when collaborating with others and helping them reach their full potential. You will most likely be a romantic at heart and see everything through your prism of romanticism, but when people don't measure up to your expectations, you can get disappointed.

People often see you as a mentor and expect you to guide them on their own journey since your life seems well sorted out. Friendships and other relationships are vital for your journey, as you cannot function without meaningful connections with others. You can heal and repair broken-spirited people with your charismatic and unconditional support, which helps you grow as a person.

If you don't cultivate your personality in line with your destiny, you will end up the exact opposite of what you were meant to be. For example, you can turn out to be emotionless, cold, and arrogant if you don't invest time in others since this is the only way for you to accomplish your destiny fully.

Now, after you discover your destiny number and the path laid out for you, it is your duty to follow through. There is no guarantee that you'll turn out exactly as described in the above points if you don't invest in yourself. You must work actively to sideline the negative aspects of your personality, or else they might become dominant over time. If this happens, then you can never unleash the potential of your destiny.

You can also try to find the destiny number for your nicknames to see if they paint a similar picture. Often, when you get the different destiny numbers, you can identify a mix of different qualities from both the numbers into your personality. This will help you better understand the different facets of your personality, and in turn, you will be able to follow the course of your destiny in a much more comprehensive way.

Chapter 7: Find Your Life Path Number

Numerology is the study of the relationship between numbers and the physical world. As we've seen, it is based on the teachings of the Ancient Greek philosopher Pythagoras, also known as the father of mathematics. According to Pythagoras, all things in the physical world contain the energetic vibrations of numbers. Apart from providing quantitative, real-world solutions, he believed that numbers are interconnected. Repeating numbers and numerical synchronicity have been observed for thousands of years. Numerology is a great tool for identifying patterns and making sense of recurring numbers in your life. The study and practice of numerology can help you better understand the world around you and your character traits by observing numerical patterns in your daily life.

Pythagoras and his contemporaries believed that since mathematical concepts are easy to regulate and classify, they could easily be connected with reality. Today, numerology practitioners believe that everything in this world has a numerical representation, and it is up to humans to understand the divine relationship between numbers and the events that occur throughout their lifetime. Modern numerology provides a comprehensive system to identify the main number influences found through people's names and dates of birth. Pythagoras devised a method that attributes a numerical value to alphabets. Based on his theories, the practice of numerology can help you better understand yourself.

Life Path Number

Your life path number can help you gain insight into your skills, habits, tendencies, and possible obstructions you might have to face in life. With the mystical power of numerology, and more importantly, through your life path number, you can focus on your strengths, understand and accept your weaknesses, realize your ambitions, hone your natural talents, and accomplish your life's purpose. With the help of your life path number, you can identify why certain events occurred in your past, why you are going through a certain phase in your life, or why you feel like you are running around in circles. The life path number is a meaningful tool to appreciate what you have, push your boundaries, and create a better future with the understanding of your life's greater purpose.

How to Find Your Life Path Number

To discover your life path number, you have only to solve a simple equation. According to numerology, by reducing your date of birth to a single digit, you will find your life path number. To do so, you must take the individual digits in the date, month, and year of your birth date and add them separately. You will get three different numbers. Now, add those three numbers. If it is a double-digit number, add the individual digits of that double-digit number again until you reach a single-digit number. If you got a single-digit number, that is your life path number!

Still confused? Let us take an example to find your magical life path number. How about we take some help from the renowned wizard, Harry Potter? Harry was born on the 31st of July 1980. We'll consider the day, month, and year separately to find Harry's life path number. Let's start with the day. Since he was born on the 31st, we'll add 3 and 1, giving us 4. Since July is the 7th month of the year, we get 7 as our second number. Suppose he was born in December, which is the 12th month. We would add 1 with 2 and get 3 as our second number. Now, consider the year 1980. We add 1, 9, and 8 and get 18 as a result (a double-digit number). So, we add 1 with 8 from the number 18 and get 9 as our third number. To sum it up, we have the numbers 4, 7, and 9 corresponding to the day, month, and year of Harry's birth date. Last, we'll add the three numbers until we reach a single-digit number. So, adding 4, 7, and 9 together gives us 20. Adding 2 with 0 means that 2 is the final number and Harry's life path number.

Equation

Step 1:

$31/07/1980 = (3+1) + (7) + (1+9+8+0)$

Step 2:

$31/07/1980 = (4)+(7)+(20) = (4)+(7)+(2+0)$

Step 3:

$31/07/1980 = (4)+(7)+(2) = 20 = (2+0) = 2$

Life Path Number = 2

By reducing Harry's date of birth to a single digit, we've found his life path number to be 2. However, there's a catch. If, during the calculations, you end up with a number like 11 or 22, you can't reduce them further. The reason behind it is that 11 and 22 are known to be "Master Numbers," according to numerology. People who have any of these two numbers as their root number are considered special. Maybe Albus Dumbledore was one of them. Who knows?

Numerology experts believe that the formula mentioned above for calculating life path numbers is important to follow. However, they also believe that the science behind numerology has an integrated nature and a brilliant architecture of its own. Therefore, blindly adding numbers will not do you any good. Instead, you might get confused with the outcome.

Now, what are you supposed to do with your life path number? What's the meaning of all this? The explanation is simple. Each number is believed to have a specific vibration associated with different traits, skills, and challenges. Using our previous example, Harry Potter's life path number reveals that he is caring, deeply kind, and empathetic. You certainly can't deny that! To discover what your life path number reveals about your life, read on. But, before you proceed, there are a few things you should know. First, you must follow the correct procedure to calculate your life path number. Second, each life path number is associated with certain strengths and challenges. You must understand and accept your life path number to have a positive impact on your life. When you align with your life's path, you will feel more energized, motivated, and on track. Without further ado, let's move on to the meat of this chapter!

Interpretations of the Life Path Numbers

Life Path Number 1

Traits:

Self-evidently, number 1 always comes first. This number is associated with autonomy, independence, individuality, and leadership. People with the number 1 as their life path number are known to be ambitious, bold and strong, and are naturally inclined to stick to their goals. They are born leaders who usually find success in their professions. Also known to be creative and dedicated, the Ones can sometimes be bossy and big-headed. Giving orders instead of taking them is a trait found in these individuals. But generally, they are quite charming and diplomatic. The Ones are usually interesting people to be around.

Challenges

The biggest challenge people with life path number 1 face is developing a greater sense of self-confidence. They can put a lot of importance on the desires, needs, and opinions of other people. They may find themselves too busy pleasing others instead of living the life they desire. Developing a voice of their own can be a big challenge for them. They can often be overprotective and have a dominant personality which can lead to disputes with other people. They may also be prone to loneliness or anger issues. However, with practice and focus, the Ones can overcome these challenges easily. They must remember that even the most independent ones need the love and support of their friends and family.

Life Path Number 2

Traits

The Twos are known to be balance-loving people who value partnerships and love. They are deeply caring, kind, and empathetic. Known to be diplomats, people with life path number 2 are skilled at diffusing tense situations. Their diplomatic nature may also make them good politicians. Their emotional sensitivity makes them harmonious, helping them bring together opposing forces through kindness, compassion, and empathy. The Twos can easily assume the role of a mediator and tune into their heart's desires with ease. Preaching the good and leading an honest life is a known trait of the number 2.

Challenges

The deep emotional sensitivity can make it difficult for people with life path number 2 to stand up for their needs. They can find it hard to tap into that sensitivity and use it to connect with others. Their inclination to avert conflict can make them overly dependent in their personal and professional relationships. Also, their tendency to focus on the negatives may make them feel hopeless and defeated in the face of criticism or difficulties. This fear can stop them from realizing their true potential, making them feel undervalued and under-appreciated. They must adopt a positing mindset and avoid seeking external validation. They can overcome the challenges of life path number 2 by realizing that the much-needed equilibrium already exists within them.

Life Path Number 3

Traits

The number 3 represents creativity and socializing. People with life path number 3 tend to be optimistic and fun to be around. They love communicating and being in the spotlight. Their cheerful nature can keep them highly motivated and energetic. They can accomplish great things if the fire of positivity within them is stroked. They represent self-expression and are gifted with prodigious creative skills. Be it art, oration, or writing, the Threes are destined to share innovative concepts that motivate, inspire, and uplifts others. People with life path number 3 find tremendous joy in making other people happy. Known to be avid socializers, they are great at interacting with people, networking, and even romance. In short, they are a total social magnet.

Challenges

People with the number 3 as their life path number may find it challenging to remain optimistic and realistic during tough times.

They may also find it difficult to commit or focus on a project they take up. More often than not, they tend to abandon their tasks and withdraw entirely. They may become too bothered by what others think of them. However, the Threes can easily mitigate their escapist tendencies by practicing peaceful mindfulness to rekindle their jubilant energy.

Life Path Number 4

Traits

The number 4 represents discipline, health, and structure. Those with the number 4 as their life path number are reliable individuals who adhere to principles and values. These traits make them desirable co-workers and valuable friends. They are blessed with earthly energy and have fortified roots that let them fulfill the expectations others have for them. They are known to be hardworking, practical, and responsible. The Fours believe in creating sound logical patterns, systems, or infrastructure that can support growth.

Challenges

These individuals are susceptible to rigidity and may become too fixated on rules and regulations. They may find themselves irritated by people who don't follow orders or break the rules. They may also find it challenging to balance their ambitions with their need for stability. By learning to go easy on the rules and norms, the Fours can feel liberated by finding the courage to take risks.

Life Path Number 5

Traits

The number 5 resonates with adventure and inquisitiveness. The Fives are intellectual and love movement and change. They make great educators and journalists, owing to their strong communication skills. They are often blessed with free-spiritedness and a childlike sense of curiosity and wonder. They can find pleasure in the simplest of things. Their love for freedom and movement compels them to experience the world in the best possible way. They tend to learn the lessons of life through impulsive yet brave acts. People with the number 5 as their life path number are known to be impulsive, playful, and vivacious.

Challenges

The Fives can easily feel bound, impatient, and restless due to their natural urge to discover new things. They may find it challenging to accept their interpersonal commitments and professional responsibilities. To overcome these challenges, people with life path number 5 must remember that the greatest discoveries and adventures lie in their backyard. They just need to narrow their gaze.

Life Path Number 6

Traits

The number 6 symbolizes family and responsibilities. Known to be natural healers, people with life path number 6 tend to be compassionate, empathetic, nurturing, and supportive. Their problem-solving skills, whether emotional or physical, make them great therapists. Their caring nature, gentle approach, and strong sense of responsibility allow them to easily communicate with friends and family, especially children or pets. The best part is that they display tenderness in whatever they do!

Challenges

The protective energy from the number 6 can make it challenging to remain consistent. That energy can quickly become controlling and dominating. To avoid over-protective tendencies, the Sixes must become understanding and build trust with others.

Life Path Number 7

Traits

The number 7 is associated with imagination, introspection, and investigation. People with the number 7 as their life path number have great analytical skills, detail-oriented, and keen eyes. Their mind makes them inventive and quick-witted. Known to thrive in the inner world, the Sevens are blessed with the wisdom and creativity that enables them to rarely get bored and entertain themselves endlessly!

Challenges

The Sevens may find it challenging to listen to their rational and logical side as much as their intuition and creativity. Their attention to detail makes them perfectionists, which is often disappointing because they quickly find flaws in any system. To keep things fun, the Sevens must counter their inner skepticism with a rational mind.

Life Path Number 8

Traits

The vibrations of the number 8 are associated with success, money, and authority. The Eights are blessed with authority and material wealth. They have the fire of ambition burning within them. They are known to be hardworking and good with money, naturally making them financially successful. Self-sufficiency and comfort are very important for this number. Their goal-oriented nature, broad thinking, and the will to race to the top can help them easily assume leadership roles and reach extraordinary success.

Challenges

People with life path number 8 can find it difficult to decide when to take charge and when to delegate. Their skill with money can also make them prone to tricksters and hustlers. However, this type's authoritative nature often makes them ignorant of constructive criticism. They must learn to pay heed to genuine advice.

Life Path Number 9

Traits

The number 9 represents acceptance, compassion, and understanding. The Nines value principles and are unwilling to compromise for convenience. They can be generous, idealistic, and stylish. Also known to be "Old Souls," the Nines are naturally spiritually aware who can help others achieve awareness. They are not afraid to transform and can transcend the physical realm.

Challenges

Life path number 9 presents a risk of codependency in personal relationships. The Nines tend to focus on the future most of all. They may have trouble anchoring themselves to the reality of the present. In other words, they must strive to balance dreams and reality.

Master Number 11

Life Path Number 11 can be understood as an amplified version of life path number 2. It is believed that number 11 is connected with spiritual awareness, enlightenment, and philosophical talents. Often, people with this life path number find their gifts under extreme circumstances.

Master Number 22

Also known as the "Master Builder," the number 22 revs up the energy of the number 4. By combining the believable with the unbelievable, Master Number 22 can cultivate dynamic platforms and create a long-term legacy—the power of Number 22 fuels intuitive and innovative thoughts that assist them all along with their transformation.

Chapter 8: Explore Your Personality Number

Your personality number is one of the most important numbers found in numerology. It forms a core part of the science of numerology, which helps you recognize how others perceive you and how your personality impacts those around you. These insights can shape your actions and plans to get the maximum benefits in your career, love life, business, or any other endeavor.

A personality number is an important tool since a personality is not an objective thing to point out. Even if you ask your closest friends, family members, or co-workers, you will get vastly different responses each time. This can make it difficult for you to understand the true nature of your personality, which you only show a minor part of two different people. However, by knowing your personality number and its associated traits, you can hope to pinpoint those qualities you would like to cultivate or the flaws you want to eliminate from your personality.

Let's consider how you can calculate your own personality number in just a few simple steps and work on the perception others have of you. First, write down your full name on a piece of paper since we need the consonants in your name to find your personality number. After that, you'll need a reference to the chart attached below (available online for free). Then, write down the corresponding number for each consonant in your name.

1	2	3	4	5	6	7	8	9
	B	C	D		F	G	H	
J	K	L	M	N		P	Q	R
S	T		V	W	X	Y	Z	

Let's assume a fictional name like JANE DOE. To discover the personality number for this name, we'll look at the table above and write down the digits corresponding to each consonant in the name.

J	A	N	E	D	O	E
1	-	5	-	4	-	-

Now, we simply add all of these digits to arrive at a single one, which in our case would be:

1+5+4 = 10 (double-digit so 1 + 0) = 1

Now that we know Jane Doe's personality number is 1, all we have to do is refer to the description for each number's personality type, given further below.

However, before we do that, there's one persistent issue that plagues the minds of anyone who's new to numerology and does not have a clue about master numbers or how to deal with the letter "Y." It's actually rather simple once you get the hang of it, so let's find out what all this fuss is about.

What about "Y"?

The letter Y is a special one as it is neither a consonant nor a vowel. That is why, depending on the situation, it can be treated as either a vowel or a consonant! Here are the two rules you need to follow to determine if the Y in your name should be counted as a consonant:

- Y as a Hard Consonant: Here, the Y will be considered a consonant if used in your name in place of a consonant. Some examples of this would be Toyota, Yuri, Yasmine, etc.

- Y Doesn't Sound Like a Vowel and Is Placed Near One: When the Y does not make a vowel sound and is placed near a vowel, it will be treated as a consonant. Some examples of this would be Grayson, Murray, Murphy, etc.

Master Numbers

Simply put, master numbers are special numbers with bonuses attached to the personality of those who possess them. The master numbers are 11, 22, and 33. You might be wondering about 44 or even 55, but the only numbers included in the triangle of enlightenment are 1, 2, and 3, which is why the other number combinations are not considered master numbers.

Master numbers are very rare, and consider yourself lucky if you have one of them as your personality number. However, these numbers abound with the traits present in their sums and even in their respective individual digits. This means that if your master number is 22, you will have the qualities of numbers 22, 2, and 4 simultaneously.

Personality Number Meanings

Every personality number has its own associated meanings and can help you gain useful insights into your personality. This section will look at the different numbers and what they might denote in your personality if you match any of these personality numbers.

Number 1

The Ones are aural leaders who are full of confidence and creativity. They have a knack for management, leading others, and coming up with creative solutions. They are determined, and this combined with their fearlessness, enables them to achieve anything they set their sights on.

The problem with Ones, however, is that they are also dominating and egoistic. They drive people away due to such heavy personalities that many get intimidated by. As a result, Ones can get overconfident, which can cause their downfall combined with their innate stubbornness.

Ones are not very compassionate, but they make up for it with a strong sense of loyalty. They are independent individuals who believe in taking a stand for any cause or issue they believe is worth fighting for.

The Ones can grow into exceptional leaders if they keep their arrogance and ego in check. This will lead to more people trusting and following them. The Ones will successfully lead their followers, thanks to the high standards they set for themselves.

Number 2

Number Twos are perhaps one of the most attractive personality types. They are very easy to talk to, honest yet gentle, approachable, and trustworthy people. Twos make very good friends, and their qualities make others trust them and confide in them.

One of the signature traits of the Twos is their peacekeeping attitude. They do not enjoy conflict and pacify any situation that might escalate. Their gentle and diplomatic nature ensures that they can tell people about anything they did wrong without hurting their feelings.

The Twos like to keep their feelings to themselves, so they are shy and sometimes get moody. They will put up a ferocious fight if they have to, despite their peaceful nature. The Twos can also turn cynical and pessimistic if under a lot of stress.

Overall, Twos are good at maintaining relationships and excel at keeping the romance alive. In addition, the philosophical and creative nature of Twos makes them instantly admired by other people.

Number 3

While Threes are naturally inclined to be extroverts, they are pretty good at interacting with others. Those with number three are highly intuitive with people-to-people interactions and observing their surroundings.

Number threes are adept at making conversation and attracting people towards them using their silver tongue. Threes just know when it's the right time to strike a conversation and are very opportunistic in that regard. They are highly ambitious and succeed at what they set out to do. Number threes are usually quite attractive to the opposite sex and are often blessed with extraordinary beauty or charm.

Threes sometimes come across as manipulative even with no such intentions, and you have to be careful about it. This is because they tend to be more biased towards the materialistic side of things and must control this nature to come across as a more well-rounded personality.

Number 4

Number Fours are a different breed altogether. With their gentle, caring, and pragmatic approach towards others, the Fours make for great companions and guides. Fours are very mature from a young age, and they are also dependable individuals. This makes them suited for leading a healthy family life. It doesn't hurt that they are family-oriented themselves.

The Fours seek stability and will choose a stable and dull life over adventure and freedom every time. The people with personality number 4 are very devoted to what they do, giving it a hundred percent in all aspects of their lives.

However, this stability-seeking and mature outlook on life makes them appear dull and boring. Sometimes, the Fours get too serious and have a hard time taking things lightly. This also reflects in their clothing, which is usually not flashy at all. Instead, they like wearing functional clothes, and their fashion sense is very subtle.

Number 5

Number Fives believe in living life to the fullest, and to live up to this standard, they have a deep love for traveling. Their adventurous side is only trumped by their high spirits, which can be contagious to others around them. Fives make great conversationalists as their spirit of adventure, combined with their philosophical mindset, gives them a considerable edge.

Fives don't stress out if anything doesn't go their way. They overcome obstacles easily and maintain their high spirits while doing so. The greatest quality Fives possess is their adaptability and versatility. No matter what life throws at them, they find a way to handle it in the best manner.

Fives are very lively and like indulging in the things that make life worth living. But if they go overboard, they can easily become addicted to food, drugs, alcohol, sex, or other dangerous temptations. Fives are also prone to burdening themselves more than they can handle, which they must avoid at all costs.

Number 6

The Sixes have very well-balanced personalities. They are compassionate, nurturing, and self-sacrificing. A number six will never go out of their way to hurt anyone's sentiments and are always available to help out anyone in need.

They are known for keeping secrets, which is why people seek them out to lighten their burden. The Sixes often sacrifice their own dreams, hopes, and luxuries to help their loved ones fulfill theirs.

Sixes never judge people hastily. They can see the inner beauty of the people because they are so beautiful on the inside themselves. However, a number Six can easily be hurt if someone says or does something reckless. A number Six who turns cynical will often become unkind and cold to others. This is why they need to keep their guards up.

Number Sixes also worries unnecessarily about money, and keeping their spending habits in check is bound to help them tremendously.

Number 7

The number Sevens are very knowledgeable people with a unique outlook on life. For them, the pursuit of knowledge is what matters most. Therefore, they are scholars who conduct themselves with grace and dignity.

The Sevens don't let other people's opinions affect them and have conditioned themselves to avoid harsh criticisms. Number Sevens are very intelligent and mysterious since they like keeping to themselves. This is the reason why they make great poets and writers. They don't care whether people like what they write since they don't do it for appreciation.

The Sevens are by no means shy or underconfident. On the contrary, they prefer solace rather than waste their time not thinking about the greater problems in life. They may often appear reserved and emotionless, which is why they must try to interact with others.

Number 8

Eights are a very successful breed thanks to their self-control, confidence, judgment, and instinct. Number Eights are best suited to positions of power and actively seek positions where they'll be able to lead and exert influence.

Number Eights strive to build their wealth and fame. They mostly become successful in these endeavors. However, their family life suffers due to this. The number Eights can be dominating and not give credit where it's due since they believe that they are instrumental in all of their successes.

That said, the Eights attract many influential and powerful people willing to help them out due to the charisma and confidence they exert. On the other hand, the Eights can be a bit headstrong and love to brag about their wealth. If an Eight can overcome these issues, then their personality can be a much more positive one.

Number 9

Nines are a happy mix of adventure, confidence, wisdom, and attraction. There is something about them that can't be identified but is extremely attractive. The Nines don't lack charisma or elegance and are adored by almost everyone they meet.

However, Nines don't become friends with people they meet right away. They might also come across as aloof or arrogant if they don't actively ensure they don't. The confidence runs high in Nines, but it doesn't for it to turn into overconfidence.

The Nines appreciate arts and the finer things in life. They are kind and spiritual and have premature intelligence, so many people approach them for advice. The Nines must keep themselves grounded, and everyone will easily like them.

Number 11

Number Elevens are very gentle personalities who like to maintain peace wherever they are. However, while they are equally strong, they might have a tough time showing it. Strife and conflict can have a very negative impact on the wellness of the Elevens, which is why it should be avoided at all costs.

The Elevens are very compassionate and care about the wellbeing of others as much as their own. They can come across as shy and are underestimated, but Elevens will not hesitate to shine through with their courage and fortitude when given the opportunity.

Elevens are also spiritual and know how to keep their composure. They are sometimes vulnerable to backlash from people who might see them as weak targets, but Elevens easily prove them wrong when they must.

Number 22

Number 22s want to bring change in the world, mostly for bettering everyone around them. They are compassionate and reliable leaders who keep finding new ways to influence the world for the better.

They are consistent, responsible, and dedicated to their work, making those around them satisfied since the 22s leave no stone unturned when assigned a task. They are also powerful leaders fueled by motivating their followers.

Sometimes, they might get engulfed in self-doubt, which is one of their biggest weaknesses. 22s might grow insecure about their abilities, but they must believe in themselves and understand that their dedication and personal ethics are surpassed by none.

Number 33

The 33s are nurturing personalities who like to take care of those around them. They are often seen as parental figures owing to their helpful, gentle nature. They are also very artistic and inspiring. Hence many people erect them as their role models.

However, the 33s can unnecessarily worry about anything and are also vulnerable to criticism or harsh comments. They are not very good at judging other people's character and sometimes feel betrayed by somebody they deeply cared for.

The 33s tend to involve themselves in the lives of others to improve it for the better. However, this quality can lead them to be taken advantage of due to their gullible nature.

These were brief descriptions of each personality type so you better understand how to mold your personality to avoid common pitfalls. Every person is unique, so there might be points that do not apply to you or some points we missed. Educating you about how to identify common perceptions about you is accomplished with these general points almost universally applicable.

Chapter 9: Reveal Your Heart's Desire Number

While the numbers associated with your personality work to reveal the perception others might have of you or the goal you should pursue in life, the heart's desire number, also known as the soul urge number, dictates what your deepest desires are. This number tells you what you truly feel and want, even though you might not know it.

More often than not, we choose not to confront this darker part of our personalities we don't even realize is a part of us. However, just like any other person, we too have our own hidden desires and instincts we like to keep personal and hidden from the outside world.

The heart's desire number reveals your motives and intentions in life. Knowing your soul urge number is important for you as it will show you the inclinations to which you are naturally predisposed. These greatly affect your career, family, love life, and even the kind of people to whom you are drawn. Overlooking it is a grave mistake as the heart's desire number provides one with a greater, deeper understanding of themselves.

Finding Your Heart's Desire Number

Finding your heart's desire number is similar to the procedure employed for all other numbers, except with one change. We will not be using the values of consonants but rather the vowels in our names.

There is a valid reason for that since vowels are considered the hidden aspects that provide meaning to any word. Likewise, the heart's desire number is a hidden aspect that greatly influences a person's life.

Contrary to vowels, consonants are more tangible and work as a shell that your exterior personality is akin to. This is why only vowels are used to discover this soul urge number, which is a deeper and more insightful number influencing our decisions.

For instance, let's find out the Heart's Desire Number for the name Snow White. But, first, we will write down all the vowels of this name and then associate them with their respective value, as shown in the table below:

A	E	I	O	U	Y
1	5	9	6	3	7

Using the table, we can conclude that Snow White has these values:

S	N	O	W	W	H	I	T	E
-	-	6	-	-	-	9	-	5

We can now add all of the values for the different vowels in the name:

6+9+5 = 20 (double digit so 2 + 0) = 2

The Heart's Desire Number for Ms. Snow White is 2. All we have to do now is reference this number to its description below. Once we check the qualities and pitfalls for number 2, we will easily discover our own personalities' desires, instincts, and motivations.

However, before we do that, we need to understand how Y functions in this case. People with a Y in their names must be confused about calculating their Heart's Desire Number. Let's look at how to overcome this issue.

How to Account For a "Y" in a Name

We can delve into this topic and make this unnecessarily complicated, or we can use the golden rule of phonetics to our advantage. The second option is better since it's usually correct and makes things easier.

If the Y in your name sounds like a vowel, then it is a vowel. Otherwise, it will be treated just like any other consonant. For example, in the name "Murray," the Y does not sound like a vowel-like it does in "Audrey." If the Y in your name sounds like a vowel, then assign it the value 7 and move on to the next step.

Heart's Desire Number Interpretations

After completing the above steps, you can come up with your Soul Urge Number. Now, this number is virtual if you don't have a clue what it represents. So, let's delve deeper into what the different numbers signify and which aspects of your inner self are revealed by each Heart's Desire Number.

Number 1

You are an independent person, and your desire to lead is overpowering. You don't like taking orders and thoroughly enjoying a challenging position to lead other people. In addition, you are extremely knowledgeable, which makes others want to follow you and ask for guidance.

You might sometimes become overconfident in your abilities and act arrogantly. This is something that people around you are not very fond of. However, if you can overcome this flaw in your attitude, you can become a leader who everyone willingly follows.

Your desire for independence means you take responsibility for your actions, and you believe in forging your life path, not playing by anyone else's rules. Your ambition and good judgment help you along the way by supporting your bold choices, which can be quite daring.

Number 2

You are a naturally loving and caring person who likes to maintain a sense of harmony in life. Your peacekeeping attitude is what motivates you to act as a pacifier in tense situations. You seek a balance in everything you do.

Since your emotions are what drive you, you easily fall in love. Your intuition helps you deal with people personally, which is why you excel at persuasion. Since your emotions rule you, tears can easily roll off your eyes, and you get vulnerable sometimes, which might be used against you.

You have a lack of confidence and tend to shy away from confrontation. However, if you can handle this issue of low confidence and get a hold of your emotions, you can easily succeed in life thanks to your sense of diplomacy and compromise.

Number 3

You are the person who is the life of any party or conversation. People are naturally drawn to you due to your impressive communication skills. In addition, you are very creative and artistic, which also reflects in your interpersonal skills.

The best career paths for you are those where you can freely express your creativity. Being a poet, writer, musician, or actor is what you were destined to do. In addition, you are mentally and emotionally well balanced, making you highly resilient to any blow that life throws your way.

You are optimistic, sometimes overly so, even ignoring the problems staring at you. You are also prone to excessive talking when under pressure or stressed. You often lose focus on a single thing, but you have a very good chance of success if you can mitigate these minor issues.

Number 4

You thrive with order, and you actively try to organize all aspects of your life. You are a punctual, dedicated, reliable, and trustworthy person. All these qualities ensure that you will make a good employee and a great parent.

You like to establish routines and cannot stand sudden changes to your daily life. For you, life does not get boring once you establish a regular routine. You like the safety and comfort of a regimen, and your life mostly revolves around your work. But if you are not careful, you might end up neglecting your family and social life.

You avoid taking risks due to your stable nature, and you sometimes appear to be dominating. However, your intentions are always good, and you just want to show your affection through your actions. If you can get better in touch with your emotions and express them more openly, others will be more receptive towards you.

Number 5

You are a free spirit who doesn't like being tied down in any way. Your love for exploration stems from your wanting to experience everything life has to offer. Meeting new people, visiting new places, and embarking on thrilling adventures excite you to the core.

You can be exceptionally inspirational to others thanks to your conversational skills and sharp intellect. However, your love for exploration prevents you from settling down in one place or in a relationship. You often worry about being held down if you commit yourself to someone. This is why you might start looking for a way out as soon as things get serious.

You are also adaptable and versatile, meaning you can easily adjust to new environments or people. But you are impatient and have a tendency not to see things through. This is why you should be careful in choosing what you want to pursue since a career you are genuinely passionate about will be the most suitable. You might want to look into arrangements like freelancing, remote work, and any other options that will guarantee you freedom and flexibility.

Number 6

You perhaps have the most loving and loyal attitude towards others, which is one of your core strengths. You sacrifice your comfort to spare the ones you love from having to go through any discomfort. The love and care you give others are also reciprocated since they deeply appreciate your devotion and selfless nature.

You are very devoted to family life and invest a lot of time and care to make it work. However, the overprotective nature you might exhibit towards your children can hinder their personal growth as you will always prevent them from learning lessons the hard way.

You might also suffocate others around you by constantly interfering in their lives. While your intentions will be pure and your actions come from good faith, you might get too overbearing. If you can control the urge to help everyone, then you will be much better off and successful in your endeavors.

Number 7

You are a scholar at heart who loves pondering over and deciphering the mysteries of the universe. You might be reserved and keep to yourself most of the time, which allows you to spend more time analyzing subjects that elude your understanding.

You have an insatiable thirst for knowledge, and it is never enough for you, no matter how much more you learn. You need to interact with people more and show your vulnerabilities to be more approachable. If you can adapt to new situations and take an interest in other people's lives, it will make your personality a more well-rounded and likable one.

Number 8

You live and breathe for one singular purpose, namely, to achieve success in your life. You do this because you desire power, prestige, and financial stability to be at your disposal. This is not entirely a bad thing, but you may get overly materialistic, self-centered, and dominating over others.

You have exceptional leadership skills and motivate others to give their best. You can also excel at managerial and administrative positions, but you often overlook instances where you'd need someone else's help. If you can become more attentive and self-reliant, your output will dramatically increase.

Your emotions are always in check, and nothing can faze you, but this becomes a drawback when you come across as overly stubborn and emotionless.

Number 9

You are a true humanitarian who wishes to put yourself at the service of humanity. You are often too idealistic for your own good, and you want to free the world of its sufferings and sorrows. You are a gentle and compassionate soul who believes there is no calling greater than service to others.

You have high ideals, but you are also naive and not a good judge of character. This fault in your judgment can affect you negatively and get you hurt and betrayed by people.

You must find a balance between service to others and your own comfort, as both are equally important. If you can control your emotions and let go of things, your life will prove much easier in the long run.

Number 11

You are a visionary who sees the world in a utopian state. You are idealistic and prefer to live your life this way despite the challenges. Your definition of what's right and wrong is solidly anchored in your mind, which can lead to unwanted conflict with others. And since conflict is against your nature, this can quickly demotivate you.

You probably were born in poverty and disadvantaged conditions, as is common with 11s. But this part of your upbringing taught you valuable lessons and made you stronger. You are a highly spiritual person who likes to think a lot, constantly trying to make sense of yourself, the world, and others.

If you can learn to control your emotions and accept the opinions of others, you will have a much easier time maintaining the harmony you seek.

Number 22

You are a creative and intelligent individual who wants to leave their mark on the world. You are a visionary ahead of your time and feel the need to be the best in whatever you do.

You undeniably have great strength hidden inside you. Combined with strong ambition and ideas, this will help you fulfill your dreams.

You can try to be less dominating and gentler in your approach. However, you might also get tensed due to overthinking, and it will help you if you try not to control every aspect of your life.

Number 33

You are a family-oriented person whose wish is a happy and healthy family life. You also want to be of service to others since you are full of compassion. You will be satisfied if you can manage to match your career with your desire to help out those in need. Some possible career options for you are social service, medicine, psychiatry, or similar profession that allow you to interact with people and improve their health and wellbeing.

You are loyal and caring, which makes you an excellent partner in romantic relationships. Your passion and emotions often move others, and people are inclined to handing you great responsibilities you may not want yourself.

Embracing your responsibilities and leading others will ensure that you bring change to the world you have always desired. If you run away from leadership roles, you might never bring in concrete change.

These were the associated qualities with each Heart's Desire Number. If you have carefully found your number, you are not aware of the qualities hidden inside of you.

We all have multiple qualities and issues embedded deep inside of us. Sometimes, even we are not aware of our own strengths and weaknesses. By knowing which aspects of our personalities we need to work on, we can actively resolve those issues.

This chapter was designed to ensure that you don't miss out on opportunities to improve and refine the hidden parts of your personality. After all, you cannot fulfill your destiny unless you fully know your own self.

Section Three:
How Tarot Meets Astrology
and Numerology

Chapter 10: What Is Tarot?

Tarot cards are quite the rage in the fields of astrology and numerology. Derived from the word "trionfi" (later known as "tarock" or "tarocchi"), tarot is a set of cards that have been in use since the 15th century in Europe. Today, people use tarot cards to delve deep into a person's intuition and provide wisdom and truth. In fact, it is a simple tool to learn more about one's life, personality, and achievements.

Cultural and Historical Background of Tarot

As mentioned, tarot cards were first used in parts of Europe starting from the mid-15th century by the Italian, Austrian, and French. Tarot cards were originally used as playing cards by wealthy families in Italy as they were mostly hand-painted and extremely expensive. While some enjoyed playing, others rebelled due to the toxic nature of gambling. However, it was only in the late 1700s that tarot cards were used for spiritual and divinity purposes. Frenchman Jean-Baptiste Alliette published a tarot card reading guide to tap into one's intuitive nature. He backed them up with astronomy and the teachings of Thoth, the Egyptian god of wisdom. In 1909, the cards were illustrated and developed in several versions ever since.

How Do Tarot Cards Work and How Can They Be Used?

Each tarot card carries its own unique weight and significance. Each symbolism or imagery describes a spiritual lesson and denotes a different meaning. A tarot deck comprises 78 cards: 22 of which are Major Arcana cards, and 56 of which are Minor Arcana cards. Upon drawing a tarot card, you can unleash your hidden story. It is believed that tarot cards act as a mirror to one's soul and represent their life story. Thus, when you pick and hold a card in your hand, you can reflect deep into your subconscious mind and harvest valuable insights into your life.

While Major Arcana cards represent the bigger picture, Minor Arcana cards can reveal details of one's daily life. To use tarot cards for reading, shuffle the deck and cut it in half. For beginners, starting with a one-spread reading is best. First, pick a card and turn it upside down. Then, refer to the representation of tarot cards to know what they mean. With time, you can practice different spreads (laying out the cards in specific patterns) and read your fortune or life lessons. Note that every card can be reversed (placing it upside down), which symbolizes the opposite of the actual meanings we will later discuss.

Major Arcana Cards

Major Arcana cards teach spirituality and convey lessons based on karma and eternity. The set of 22 cards represents one's life and the different phases they are likely to go through. The guidance, lessons, and perspectives these cards offer can help a person reach better awareness and live a more rewarding life. The bigger picture can be unraveled using these 22 cards. Let's take a brief look at the Major Arcana cards in tarot.

Card 0: The Fool

Mantra: New beginnings, a leap of faith, and a fresh start

Element: Air

Planet: Uranus

Chakra: Crown

Significance: Among all archetypes of the tarot set, the Fool card is extremely vulnerable due to its lack of experience and inability to distinguish right from wrong. He has not been through the ups and downs of life, thereby keeping him from deciphering his strengths, weakness, and future challenges.

Card 1: The Magician

THE MAGICIAN.

Mantra: Skill, resources, and power

Element: Air

Planet: Mercury

Chakra: Throat

Significance: This card represents uniqueness and reminds you of your talents. The skills you possess are rare, and not everyone is blessed with your same talents. This helps you stand out from others and guides you on a successful path. This card shows you can overcome adversity, and it tells you to move forward in life with your skills.

Card 2: The High Priestess

Significance or Mantra: Sacred knowledge, higher wisdom, and intuition

Element: Water

Planet: Moon

Chakra: Third Eye

Significance: Among all cards, the High Priestess represents strong intuition and awareness. If you pick this card, you must listen to your instincts and follow your inner voice. Your mind can achieve anything and can seek answers to even the most difficult questions. All you must do is look inside instead of focusing on the outside world.

Card 3: The Empress

Mantra: Femininity, nurturing, beauty, abundance, and fertility

Element: Earth

Planet: Venus

Chakra: Heart and sacral

Significance: Symbolizing femininity and beauty, the Empress card hints at compassion in your life. Her deep-seated roots with Mother Nature motivate you to absorb the positive energies around you.

Card 4: The Emperor

THE EMPEROR

Mantra: Establishment, authority, and father figure

Element: Fire

Planet: Mars/Aries

Chakra: Root

Significance: The authoritative status of the Emperor is achieved only after one has gone through hardships. Qualities like solidity, structure, and power are innately represented by this card, which tells you of your own strength. It encourages you to unravel your own inner strength and establish a powerful legacy.

Card 5: The Hierophant

Mantra: Religious beliefs, spiritual wisdom, and group identity

Element: Earth

Planet: Venus/Taurus

Chakra: Throat

Significance: As a messenger from above, the Hierophant card signifies religious and spiritual beliefs and guides people towards enlightening. Upon drawing this card, you must explore different forms of spiritual lessons you encounter and shape your current situation to expect the best outcome. In other words, pay attention to the rules to achieve the best results.

Card 6: The Lovers

Mantra: Harmony, love, relationships, bonds, and unions

Element: Air

Planet: Mercury/Gemini

Chakra: Heart

Significance: This card represents the relationships and close bonds in your life. If you pick this card during your reading session, you may have to focus more on your love life and try to strengthen your bonds. This card also represents your decisions and values, which is why you should also focus on these two aspects. When stuck at a crossroads in life, you must consider all the choices presented to you and decide after reflecting on the consequences.

Card 7: The Chariot

Mantra: Victory, success, control, momentum, and assertion

Element: Water

Planet: Moon/Cancer

Chakra: Throat

Significance: The Chariot card symbolizes determination, momentum in life, and natural drive and indicates success or victory soon. Once you learn to explore the power of your spirit and heart and combine it with your mental skills, you will be unstoppable in achieving all your goals. However, you also need the vigor to embark on the journey and triumph in the end.

Card 8: Strength

Mantra: Self-control, courage, strength, compassion, and influence

Element: Fire

Planet: Sun/Leo

Chakra: Solar Plexus

Significance: As the name suggests, this card represents the strength and courage that are probably hidden and need to be unveiled. This card represents courage and your heart's fortitude. If you are strong, you can achieve anything you want and withstand adversity alone. When caught in an intense situation, your power will help you move mountains and come out stronger than ever before.

Card 9: The Hermit

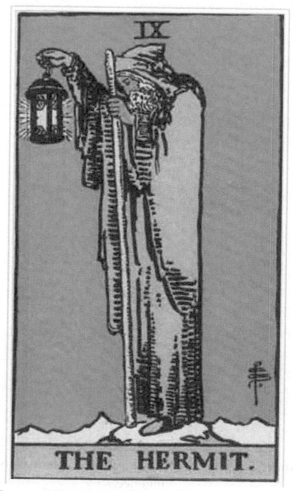

Mantra: Solitude, soul-searching, inner guidance, and introspection

Element: Earth

Planet: Chiron/Virgo

Chakra: Third Eye

Significance: When faced with a dire situation, you must be patient and listen to your inner voice by staying silent. Since the Hermit prefers to live alone, it is important to withdraw from the chaos of the outer world and figure out your life in solitude. This will enable you to anticipate any negative consequences in your life.

Card 10: The Wheel of Fortune

Mantra: Turning a cycle, karma, destiny, and good luck

Element: Fire

Planet: Jupiter

Chakra: Solar plexus

Significance: Life is an unpredictable ride. You will remain at the top at times, but some situations may suppress you. This is the significance of life. Nothing is permanent, and consequences may change with time. There is nothing too good or bad. If you are currently at the bottom, you will soon experience the better things in life. But if you are at the top, life can push you down without warning. So, be humble and willing to learn from the process.

Card 11: Justice

Mantra: Cause and effect, fairness, justice, law, and truth

Element: Air

Planet: Venus/Libra

Chakra: Heart

Significance: This card declares that karma is real, meaning every action will have a reaction. Justice is fair to everyone and does not discriminate. The decisions you made in the past can affect your current life, and your present actions determine your current state. Upon receiving this card during your reading session, note that your intuition points towards fair interaction and reinstating your actions with others. It is not too late to make a significant change.

Card 12: The Hanged Man

Mantra: Suspension, surrender, new perspectives, and pause

Element: Water

Planet: Neptune

Chakra: Third Eye

Significance: Sometimes, it is best to let go to benefit you in the long run. Even though small sacrifices may bother you at the moment, you will thank yourself for making them. If your life isn't going as planned and you pick the Hanging Man card, you must take a step to turn it around. However, not knowing where to start can halt you right from the beginning. The key is to let go of the situation to let yourself loose and avoid getting attached again.

Card 13: Death

Mantra: Beginnings, transformation, change, endings, and transition

Element: Water

Planet: Pluto/Scorpio

Chakra: Heart

Significance: This card represents the end of a phase in one's life and the beginning of a new one. Most people misunderstand this card as they assume it refers to physical death, which is entirely wrong. By hanging on to old relationships, situations, feelings, and emotions, you will not leave room for new and better things to come in your life. Make peace with the fact that every ending will have a well-deserved new beginning.

Card 14: Temperance

Mantra: Healing, balance, purpose, moderation, and patience

Element: Fire

Planet: Jupiter/Sagittarius

Chakra: Solar Plexus

Significance: Do not force change in your life, but instead, give it time to unfold in its own mysterious ways. You must master the art of moderation and be patient at the same time. Go with the flow and be peaceful along the way. Accept the things, ideas, and people coming into your life and welcome change. Condition yourself to remain flexible and adapt to new situations.

Card 15: The Devil

Mantra: Restriction, bondage, attachment, addiction, and sexuality

Element: Earth

Planet: Saturn/Capricorn

Chakra: Root

Significance: If you pick The Devil card during your reading, you may be feeling stuck. The fear and helplessness add to this chaotic feeling. Your life ahead may also seem bland due to a lack of opportunities and the unwillingness to explore your inner talents. This can also limit you from moving forward and exploring new situations because of low enthusiasm or self-confidence. While you do have the key to unlock new doors, the inability or unwillingness to do so can set you back tremendously.

Card 16: The Tower

Mantra: Sudden change, chaos, awakening, revelation, and upheaval

Element: Fire

Planet: Mars

Chakra: Crown

Significance: This card represents destruction and is dreaded by all. It showcases a person's misery and the phenomenon of their crumbling life. The person is also helpless and cannot control the situation. The Tower tells them to let it all fall to build anew. At times, all a person can do is let the weak parts tear down and start on a new basis. This restarting phase will last longer and stand more strongly.

Card 17: The Star

Mantra: Spiritual guidance, hope, purpose, faith, spirituality, and renewal

Element: Air

Planet: Uranus/Aquarius

Chakra: Crown

Significance: This card symbolizes hope and optimism. It shows how the universe is gathering all its positive energy to breathe good change in your life. It also tells you to keep the faith and let the universe do its job.

Card 18: The Moon

Mantra: Mystery, illusion, dreams, intuition, fear, and anxiety

Element: Water

Planet: Neptune/Pisces

Chakra: Third Eye

Significance: The Moon represents the subconscious that carries all your thoughts, fears, emotions, and doubts. A person drawing the Moon card in their reading is likely to feel anxious all the time, which can hinder their progress and performance. They let their fears and doubts get the best of them. Everything you see or hear may not be true, but if you focus on the positive, you can eliminate your fears and doubts.

Mantra: Vitality, youth, success, warmth, positivity, and fun

Element: Fire

Planet: The Sun

Chakra: Solar plexus

Significance: This card represents positivity and vitality in your life, which means that things are going well at the moment. Your thoughts, feelings, and path are well aligned and point in an obvious direction. You are surrounded by good people and things, which you must be grateful for.

Card 20: Judgment

Mantra: Inner calling, rebirth, and absolution

Element: Fire

Planet: Pluto

Chakra: Crown

Significance: The Judgment card represents your life as determined by your past actions and reflects the future. It tells you to check your progress and see whether or not it aligns with your future goals. Then, reflect on your actions to achieve your dreams. Your future can be changed by handling the present well. So, make it favorable and cherishable.

Card 21: The World

Mantra: Accomplishment, completion, integration, and travel

Element: Earth

Planet: Saturn

Chakra: Root

Significance: As the last card of this series, the World card represents the fulfillment and completion of your final goals. It means you are exactly where you are supposed to be in life. Your past experiences and lessons have taught you well, and you are fully prepared to enter the next phase of your life.

Minor Arcana Cards

The Minor Arcana cards represent tales and experiences of daily life based on tribulations and trials.

The main structure of the Minor Arcana comprises four suits, namely Wands, Pentacles, Swords, and Cups. They are further divided into numbers from 1 (Ace) to 10, including jacks, knights, queens, and kings.

Wands: The Wands suit represents your passion, motivation, and energy. Your ideas, spiritual status, and life purpose can be unraveled by picking this suit during your Tarot card reading session.

Pentacles: This suit depicts your material possessions and finances. The Pentacles suit can help you gather better insights into your professional career, wealth, and future opportunities.

Swords: The Swords suit represents your actions, thoughts, and words. The way you make decisions, communicate your ideas, and talk about your purpose in life all fall under this suit. It teaches you to assert your power, turn things in your favor, and communicate your thoughts openly.

Cups: This fourth and final suit represents creativity, intuition, and emotions. If you are facing emotional issues of any sort with your close ones, you are likely to get this suit during your tarot reading.

As we've seen, tarot readings can reveal a lot about your past, present, and future self. While the Major Arcana cards are mostly related to spiritual matters, the Minor Arcana cards relay aspects such as your career, business, and ambitions. The suits you pick can help you understand various areas of your life.

Chapter 11: The Fire Signs and Their Tarot Cards

The astrological connection with tarot cards can be drawn from the "Hermetic Order of the Golden Dawn," which dates back a few centuries. Although the basic learning structures of astrology were defined centuries ago, they are still intact and act as a base for fortune-telling. But tarot cards were revised during the Renaissance period, which may not provide enough leverage. However, since the same astrological learnings were used to reimagine tarot cards during the 1700s, we can draw parallels between both domains. This goes to show that the connection between zodiac signs and Tarot cards is strong and persuasive.

Fire signs (Aries, Leo, and Sagittarius) are intricately connected to their Major and Minor Arcana cards. The Major Arcana cards are associated with the layout of planets and related astrological readings. They are further broken down and placed as an elemental grouping known as the Minor Arcana group. This showcases the connection of Major Arcana and Minor Arcana groups with zodiac signs. They thrive harmoniously and share the same energy, which resonates well with their personality and upbringing.

In this chapter, we will explore Fire signs and their association with respective tarot cards.

Fire Signs

Fire signs represent warmth, brightness, and light. You need light and warmth to survive and make life more interesting and exciting. Fire signs are also vital and live to the fullest, spreading joy around them. Most crave attention but do not accept this. Some even do it without realizing it. Regardless, they always make the lives of people better and more cheerful. This is because they are extroverted and know that their bright presence can make someone's day. Fire signs stand by the idiom, "to light a fire under someone."

Fire Signs and the Suit of Wands

The suit of Wands represents qualities like willpower, action, and creativity. The tarot Wands are associated with Fire signs. This Minor Arcana card is closely related to the three zodiac signs in terms of attributes such as strength, intuition, determination, energy, creativity, expansion, and ambition. As Fire signs are full of light and wildness, the suit of Wands conforms to the zodiac signs. They are also hot, energetic, unpredictable, and wild. The way this suit represents your life and life lessons depends on how you leverage the qualities of the Fire sign. For instance, just like using fire to cook can be a productive and creative task, overuse can cause the food to burn. Likewise, the way you use your qualities will determine whether you excel in life.

The qualities displayed by the suit of Wands (corresponding to the Fire signs) are enthusiasm, personality, and internal and external personal energy. On the other hand, some negative qualities are impulsiveness, ego, illusion, and a lack of purpose. Thus, even though Fire signs are closely connected, they have their own distinct characteristics that set them apart. As such, each of the three zodiac signs expresses its traits in peculiar ways.

Aries (Mar 21 - Apr 19)

The most prominent trait of this zodiac sign is their leadership skills paired with their action-oriented personality. This zodiac sign is associated with the Ram, which is ambitious and bold.

Personality Traits of Aries

The Fire sign compels Aries to be enthusiastic and seek new activities in their life with others around them. However, they can be the victim of a strong ego and often display signs of self-obsession. But regardless of the challenges ahead, Aries will dive right in and overcome all the threats to come out victorious. Combined with their willpower and motivation, their passion allows them to excel in whatever they do, which can be attributed to the fire that blazes within them.

On the negative side, their perfectionism and relentlessness can become quite frustrating. This often leads them to work quickly and in haste. They act first and think later, which can bring about unwanted repercussions. This also teaches them multiple lessons as they move forward in life. According to popular legends, rams are extremely courageous and ready to fight in battles, which is why they were often armed. The fiery nature is apparent in Aries, but it doesn't last long and dissipates quickly.

Aries and Its Tarot Cards

Aries is represented by the Emperor and the King of Wands cards.

The Emperor

This card suggests that the Emperor will always be by your side, especially during critical times when you need him most. It says that your sign is loyal and that you will always stick close to your loved ones. Whenever your friends and family need someone by their side, you will be there and help them out. Basically, you are always on the clock, and your loved ones can rely on you through thick and thin. Since the Emperor also embodies power and authority, it asks you to dig deeper and unravel your true potential to establish a system and act as a strong support figure for your family.

Your analytical skills can also help you endorse this role and get closer to your goals. Just like Aries is placed first in the astronomical chart, the fire sign shows the first spark as the fire ignites. Since Aries are usually aggressive in nature and display leadership qualities, the Emperor perfectly suits this fire sign. This also has to do with the fact that the ram is authoritative and possesses a straightforward approach.

The King of Wands

The Minor Arcana card, the King of Wands, is also closely connected to Aries. Both are powerful, tough, and honorable. The King's throne displays power and honor, just like this zodiac sign. The King's confidence and control displayed by his wand are also seen in Aries. The fire energy, strength, and ability to conquer are other fire sign and Minor Arcana card qualities. Every motive in both domains is persistent and masculine. The dominant side of this sign also makes Aries take charge and resolve many issues in their personal and professional lives.

The King of Wands and Aries both abide by the motto "action speaks louder than words," which they prove time and again. Unlike other signs, Aries shows a strong connection with its tarot cards while retaining nuances of similarity. This Minor Arcana card illustrates the King's throne with lizards, salamanders, and lions, which signifies power. However, the King is portrayed as not sitting comfortably and wanting to move in haste, another characteristic of Aries. Overall, the throne and his ensemble represent his authoritative stance and pride in being king.

Leo (July 23 - Aug 22)

Leo has a charismatic and fiery nature as a zodiac sign thanks to its ruling planet, the Sun.

Personality Traits of Leo

Represented by the Lion, the Leo is mighty, ferocious, and the center of attention. Individuals with this zodiac sign often crave attention and being in the limelight. They can be either too dramatic or extremely loving. Most Leos possess both characteristics and balance them out. Just like a fire's flamboyant nature, this zodiac sign is also lively and willing to go to any extent to gain recognition. Like a fire that dances and shines brightly, Leos captures this essence in their personality and stays dynamic around the clock.

With the Sun as their ruling planet, a Leo personality remains the same throughout their life and changes only slightly. Their traits are apparent and stand out when compared to other signs. Leos need the center stage and have no issues stating so openly. They are not afraid to ask what they want and crackle like a blazing fire wherever they step. Furthermore, they are compassionate and warm to their loved ones. They can go to great lengths to protect their close friends and family members. Last, they possess leadership qualities and are extremely passionate, just like Aries.

Leo and Its Tarot Cards

Leo is represented by the Knight, Strength, and The Queen of Wands cards.

Strength

This card symbolizes a person's strength, both physical and mental. Like the mighty Lion who represents Leo, you can use your strength and courage to support and help your loved ones overcome obstacles. It denotes that nothing is impossible and that all you need is grit to accomplish your goals. You can also unleash your spiritual and emotional prowess to remain strong and resilient. The Strength card is illustrated with the Lion, who seems bold and courageous, similar to Leo. The colors used in this card (mostly shades of golds and yellows) are also quite enigmatic and bright, just like the personality of this zodiac sign.

The physical and mental strength of a Leo is connected with the Strength card, represented by a gentle maiden patting the Lion. Leo's passionate personality rules hearts, which can be seen from the loving bond between the maiden and the Lion. Furthermore, the regal ensemble of the maiden in a white robe depicts the zodiac sign's progressive qualities such as honor, royalty, and bravery. The crown and floral sash she wears validate this representation.

The connection can also be ciphered through the Roman numeral 8 shown atop the card. Note that the 8th month of the year, August, is majorly represented by the Leo, which corresponds to the tarot deck's 8th card, Strength. Look closely, and we notice an infinity symbol floating in the sky above the maiden. It closely resembles the number eight, denoting another linkage. Since this number also represents generosity, karmic energy, and enthusiasm, the tarot card and zodiac sign are ideal portrayals of the infinity symbol. As you can see, the Strength tarot card and the Leo sign share a unique connection.

The Knight of Pentacles

Although this Minor Arcana card shares its qualities with Fire and Earth signs, the similarities between the Knight of Pentacles and the Leo are quite apparent. The force exerted by the Earth sign and the flaming desire of the fire sign bestows the card a traditional sense that keeps it grounded. The Knight of Pentacles is the archetype of leadership skills and confidence, reflected in Leo.

Furthermore, the Knight of Pentacles is cautious of his direction and advances carefully. This helps him reach his goals with a practical approach, thereby achieving success within the designated timeframe. He is ambitious and lets others depend on him, just like a true Leo would. Note that the intense energy represented by this zodiac sign is, in a way, connected to this Minor Arcana card.

The Queen of Wands

This card comes second in the tarot deck, which proves its connection with the Leo sign due to its rank as the second astrological sign in the Fire series. Just like the King of Wands, this card represents courage, determination, and a strong-willed personality. The illustration on this Minor Arcana card depicts the Queen in a rich ensemble of bright red and yellow shades, showcasing the regal side of this wealthy sign.

With the lion heads on the Queen's throne and the feline creature by her side, the connection between the Leo and the Minor Arcana card is evident. While the Queen is courageous and powerful, she also has a kind face that makes her dependable. She will do anything for her kingdom's well-being, just like a Leo would when protecting their friends and family.

Sagittarius (Nov 22 - Dec 21)

The ruling planet of this zodiac sign is Jupiter and is often on the path of seeking pleasure and truth in equal bits.

Personality Traits of Sagittarius

As mentioned, this zodiac sign is always seeking truth, going to any length to make it happen. Even though they are joyful, they feel anxious upon remembering that nothing is permanent and that it will all end. At some point, they may delve deep into exploration, so much so they may start feeling overwhelmed. When it comes to sharing their views, they can be dogmatic. This is because the melancholy of everyday life and the fear of not finding answers can push them into a dilemma and even in terror.

Sagittarius and Its Tarot Cards

Sagittarius is represented by the Temperance and the Page of Wands cards.

Temperance

You are abundantly blessed with mediation skills, which means you can draw parallels between situations and find common ground to feel at ease. You are self-aware and possess a genuine understanding of your life's whereabouts, which can balance them out of judgments. Your patience and diligence can help you get through hardships and pave the way to brighter days. You are like a meandering stream capable of clearing its way to flow smoothly. Temperance is linked to balance and is extremely curious of its surroundings. In fact, every form of astrological relation associated with the Sagittarius represents its need to find and thrive on enlightenment. Although the Sagittarius sign has learned and gathered enough information, they continue to question their surroundings to strengthen their knowledge.

While the Sagittarius is a fire sign, they are on the verge of turning into smoke due to their curiosity and potential for stagnation. This is vaguely represented by the angel on the Temperance card who tries to balance the flowing water in both cups, the unending process of finding knowledge, contentment, and solace.

The Page of Wands

This Minor Arcana card represents impulse, enthusiasm, cleverness, and courage, much like the fire sign Sagittarius. The robes of the character on the card represent the Fire sign, which has similar qualities to the salamander on the Queen and King cards. The word "new" resonates well with the Page of Wands as they always seek new pursuits and philosophical perspectives, yet another similar quality shared by this zodiac sign.

When reading your horoscope, consider your sign and tarot card as a whole to gain a deeper perspective of your life and intuition. This will also help you be more knowledgeable when practicing tarot cards and horoscope reading. With time, you will notice the significance of the Fire signs in their respective tarot cards and vice versa. You will also get a clearer picture of your motives and direction towards a brighter future.

Chapter 12: The Earth Signs and Their Tarot Cards

As you learned, zodiac signs are divided into four elemental groups: Fire, Earth, Air, and Water. In the previous chapter, we discussed Fire signs and their association with respective tarot cards. Let's now jump on to the Earth signs, perhaps the most "down-to-earth" of all zodiac groups. Their level-headedness and practicality are desirable qualities that attract other signs to the Earth group. However, even though they are observed in other signs, it is the way they represent and showcase these qualities that set them apart.

In this chapter, we will talk about the Earth signs and their association with tarot cards.

Earth Signs

The Earth signs (Taurus, Virgo, and Capricorn) are the three zodiac groups representing individuals with the most practical approach towards their personal and professional lives. They focus more on materials and finances. Due to their nature, they are oriented towards physical health rather than mental or emotional health. All three signs are extremely hardworking and committed to their responsibilities. They are steadfast and will commit to changing their life by working hard. They can be patient, level-headed, and determined to chase their dreams and attain success.

While Earth signs are primarily stubborn, they can be equally practical as well. Certain qualities like patience and loyalty are also positive traits that Earth signs carry with pride. On the negative side, they can be inflexible and need things to go their way. They crave material things and can even get obsessed with them. This can also make them decadent and somehow lazy. When compared to other signs, they are the most grounded and realistic. While they are pragmatic most of the time, they can also portray signs of aggression and anger on bad days. When enraged, anyone should keep away from them.

Earth Signs and the Suit of Pentacles

The Pentacle suits (also known as the Coin suit), a part of the Minor Arcana tarot deck, are dedicated to Earth signs. Earth signs and the Pentacles suit represent anything related to materials, finances, and physical health. Every card associated with the Pentacle suit in the Minor Arcana deck reflects the traits of the Taurus, Virgo, or Capricorn sign. While some may represent a particular Earth sign, others provide subtle hints that make the tarot cards and zodiac signs extremely relatable. For example, the Four, Five, and Six of Pentacles symbolize money matters linked to Earth signs. While the Four and Six of Pentacles tell one to save and donate money, respectively, the Five of Pentacles hints at monetary losses in the near future.

As you can see, your card reading can also help Earth signs be prepared in financial and professional areas and make necessary changes to stay safe. Both the Earth signs and the Suit of Pentacles mirror various levels of consciousness with the creative and health aspects of an individual. The way a person creates and transforms their life also echoes with this suit of the tarot deck.

Taurus (April 20 - May 20)

The Taurus is known to be determined, strong-headed, and very stubborn in most aspects of their life.

Personality Traits of Taurus

The Ox represents the sign. Whether it's the clothes they wear or the food they eat, the Taurus likes the finer things in life. Deemed to be the artists among other Earth signs, the Taurus use their pleasures, artistic skills, and sensuality to inspire others and motivate their loved ones. They chase their dreams using this innate beauty and passion.

People can safely rely on individuals with this zodiac sign. They are stable, persistent, and work hard. However, on a bad day, they can be aggressive and lazy. They can even be possessive of their belongings and loved ones, which is a trait rarely displayed. Despite negative qualities like jealousy and possessiveness, they are loyal to their partners, friends, family members, and other loved ones. The Taurus is notorious by nature, and their flirting skills can get over the top. They pay extra attention to the ones they love and expect the same in return. All in all, they will go to any length to fulfill their dreams and live happily.

Taurus and Its Tarot Cards

Taurus is closely associated with the Hierophant, the Knight, and the King of Pentacles cards.

The Hierophant

In Greek, the Hierophant is known as "high priest" and is often called the Pope. This card is the leader of all tarot cards with its organization and holy nature. This card comes fifth in the series of the Major Arcana tarot deck. It represents positive qualities such as creativity and joy. The Hierophant is seen holding a triple specter in the left hand, showcasing domination. Basically, this card is a representation of power in the world of material things. It also preaches practicality and rules, something that the Taurus is known for.

With power, the Taurus can reach goals and chase dreams without feeling insecure or demotivated. They also govern some senses of the physical world, including pleasure and sensuality. Even though the Taurus takes their time, they can achieve great things with their inner power and creative flair. With time, they can even dominate the world. They are rightly called "the master creator." This zodiac sign is instantly attracted to individuals with knowledge and a spiritual nature. Since they appreciate discipline and hard work, the Taurus likes being validated and is therefore attracted to these qualities.

The Knight of Pentacles

All knights represent the Taurus' behavior and the life lessons they supposedly learn on their way. However, the Knight of Pentacles resembles the zodiac sign more than any other. Just like the Taurus can wait patiently to achieve their goals, the Knight of Pentacles is also steadfast and willing to wait until they see a desirable outcome. The card and the zodiac sign are down-to-earth yet stubborn. They will formulate a plan and stick to it until they are satisfied. Regardless of how much time it takes (possibly years), they will remain patient and virtuous throughout the journey.

On its tarot card, the Knight is depicted as a calm, self-assured character who seems to be perfectly in touch with the world around him. This card also stands for passion, freedom, and youth, which equates to the signs and behavior of the Taurus sign. However, the Knight can be slightly more deliberate and slower than its counterparts, especially the Knight of Wands and Swords. The Knight of Pentacles plans his moves, explaining why he is slower, just like a Taurus. He respectfully holds the Pentacle and appears to be wary of his actions. He also keeps the horse in control when seated, which shows a bright and confident demeanor.

His visual field is patiently gazed upon by the Knight, and he studies his vistas with scrutiny. He is ready to take on the world but quietly plans his moves. He patiently awaits the right moment to move ahead and conquer the world. Although he is dressed for combat, he will not take a single step until fully prepared. Furthermore, the black horse aligns with the Taurus' independent and mature self. The Knight can control the horse and battle through the hardships he faces. His perseverance and determination will keep him grounded and make his life easier.

This shows that the Taurus will take calculated risks and design a blueprint before embarking on a tough journey. This strategy will also make them more confident and mature. However, whenever the Taurus faces emergencies and attempts to sort them out, the Knight of Pentacles may act as an obstacle. In such cases, the Taurus must learn to think on their feet and make quick decisions to overcome the situation permanently.

Virgo (Aug 23 - Sep 22)

This zodiac sign is represented by the Maiden and is ruled by the planet Mercury.

Personality Traits of Virgo

As mentioned, Virgo covers the practical aspects of one's life, just like any of the Earth signs. The Virgo has an analytical mind and puts truth on a pedestal. Among other signs, they are the most practical and reasonable, which is why their loved ones often rely on them to make decisions. Their minds are naturally wired to make the most informed decisions. They can investigate circumstances with scrutiny and know that their minds can pull them out of the worst situations. On the negative side, the Virgo can obsess over the tiniest details, which can place them in a dilemma. In extreme situations, they may also ruin their life due to this obsession.

However, usually, their detail-attentive nature helps them stay aware and gather valuable knowledge. In fact, the Virgo prefer to stay this way to be able to adjust to change easily. Since they are loyal and sensible, they make excellent partners and have a strong social network. Their meticulousness helps them seek improvement in their personal and professional lives.

Virgo and Its Tarot Cards

Virgo is closely associated with the tarot cards the Hermit and the Queen of Pentacles.

The Hermit

This card can be deemed the closest to Virgo because it tells this zodiac sign's journey and highlights the most important parts. The Hermit is one of the most enlightened and spiritually aware cards in the tarot deck. Strong instincts and potent force are some qualities shared by the Virgo as well. The card states that if someone wishes to bring positive changes in their life, the key to achieving this goal lies within. They possess the power to make those changes successfully. The Virgo abides by a similar motto. They should take inspiration from this tarot card and reflect on their actions to breathe positive energy and wisdom into their life.

The Hermit also inspires this zodiac sign to share their knowledge and gain a better perspective to thrive with others. The Virgo may struggle to find their inner calling and true self. When they are on the path towards awareness and making peace with their consciousness, they may expect respect, patience, and space from the people around them. This is why the Virgo needs a partner who can understand them and respect their values. You should be able to have intelligent conversations with them and build healthy communication. The spiritual aspirations of the Hermit are lofty, and they resonate with the Virgo's spiritual side as well.

The Queen of Pentacles

While the Hermit represents the Virgo's spirituality, the Queen of Pentacles balances the zodiac sign's attributes with a less abstract approach to life. She is nurturing, resourceful, and warm-hearted, some signs the Virgo represents too. In a way, the Queen completes the other cards in the tarot deck, yet another shared attribute with the Virgo. Individuals with this zodiac sign complete the lives of their loved ones.

A major contradiction that the Hermit and the Queen of Pentacles present is the balance between spirituality and wealth. While some may seek solace on a spiritual path and become monks, others may pursue abundance and become wealthy. In the end, it all comes down to the individual's needs, aspirations, and thought pattern. For some, wealth can also be spiritual, thereby presenting a perfect amalgamation of both entities.

Capricorn (Dec 22 - Jan 19)

This zodiac sign is represented by the Sea-Goat, which is half fish and half goat.

Personality Traits of Capricorn

Commonly known as the originators of the Earth signs, the Capricorn is a hardworking group determined to stay focused and ambitious. They are proud and hold a stature in the society they live in. They prefer to have control over their life and establish a system to keep this arrangement in place. They chase the future and take the necessary steps to turn circumstances in their favor. However, this can deeply affect their emotions and sensitivity. The Capricorn will never be sidelined or stay in a single place, especially when they are not making steady progress in life. If they do find themselves lagging and lacking, they will take immediate action to turn it around.

Contrary to popular belief, the Capricorn will barely hold grudges and easily move on in life. For them, their career can surpass every other priority, even their personal life and relationships sometimes. They rarely give up and keep hard at work, building themselves a lifestyle that can make others envious. All three Earth signs are compatible and go well with one another. This is why they make great friends and long-term partners.

Capricorn and Its Tarot Cards

Capricorn is closely associated with the Devil and the Page of Pentacles cards.

The Devil

Much like the Capricorn who is fierce and speaks their heart, the Devil card is utterly savage and raw. The Devil card is intimately linked with Pan, the Greek god with a half-goat, half-man build. This connection also extends to the Capricorn, which can be extracted from Greek mythology. Both the Capricorn and the Devil want to live their wildest fantasies and go as far as possible. The Devil card feeds the Capricorn's raw desires fearing no dangerous outcome. This zodiac sign is also fearless and can go to any extent to fulfill their dreams.

Despite being tenacious and wild, the Devil is not ashamed of who he is. He lives proudly and believes that everyone must have a little bit of devil in them. In a way, the Capricorn can be just and unbiased for that reason. The Capricorn is also good in bed and desires a partner with similarly orgasmic skills. This card connects the zodiac sign with a partner who shares similar fantasies and expectations and can signify a healthy relationship for a Capricorn. If it pops up in your reading, you may be blessed with a committed and long-lasting relationship.

The Page of Pentacles

This Minor Arcana card symbolizes child-like attributes due to the Page's curious nature. He is a learner and an explorer. Once he finds something interesting, he will go in-depth and pore over the subject to the core. You can tell from the way he holds the Pentacle and gazes around with curiosity. Despite having the ability and resources, the Knight is unknot interested in ruling the kingdom and would rather explore his beautiful terrain and keep away from worries and dangers.

Chapter 13: The Air Signs and Their Tarot Cards

Air signs are the most committed and skilled with communication. The Gemini, Libra, and Aquarius make up the Air signs and keenly carry their stories through corresponding tarot cards. In the tarot deck, the Suit of Swords is the ideal representation of Air signs in terms of qualities, traits, and the manifestation of dreams. The cards also teach the air signs to act based on their current situation and condition.

In this chapter, we will talk about the Air signs and their association with respective tarot cards.

Air Signs

Air signs (Gemini, Libra, and Aquarius) are known as the doers and communicators among all signs. They possess an analytical mind and can synthesize any situation to retrieve the best outcome. They are fiery, restless, and always on the path of exploration seeking new adventures and information. You can try to stop an Air sign but will most likely fail. They are all about probing through life without catching their breath and chasing their dreams relentlessly. Since they are mostly asocial, they draw their own path in solitude without bothering others. For them, "live and let live" is the ultimate mantra.

Since Air signs are naturally intelligent and creative, they can make quick decisions that likely produce the best outcome. Even though they prefer to be alone, they have a communal sense of responsibility and do not shy away from suggesting effective solutions to better society. For them, practicality trumps emotions, and they are hardly clouded by the latter. Therefore, any kind of information retrieved and passed on by an Air sign is most probably correct and accurate. Since they live to achieve and produce new ideas, you can safely rely on them to make decisions and point out mistakes.

Air Signs and the Suit of Swords

The sword energy of the Minor Arcana cards represents Air signs, which signify action, vision, and intelligence. Since all three signs share the foundational energy of the Suit of Swords, they can easily decipher a person's inner thoughts and beliefs. This is important if the individual is uncertain about how their life is taking shape and where it is headed. Air signs are firm representatives of dual aspects, which illustrates a person's duality. Whether it's stability and intuition or intelligence and power, Air signs always manage to strike a balance between these qualities. If any imbalance is noted, the individual may benefit from too much positivity or suffer due to potential harm.

However, the Suit of Swords is not always auspicious in a tarot reading because of its proclivity for trouble. It can mean that the person is either too angry or prioritizes intelligence over other aspects, destroying their personal and social life. While the Suit of Swords primarily depicts air signs, some are also parts of the cups (discussed more below). This combined energy is often perceived as an element of curiosity and studied to extend it further.

Gemini (May 21 - June 20)

This zodiac sign is represented by the Twins, which reflects the dual personality of the Gemini.

Personality Traits of Gemini

Among all zodiac signs, the Gemini is perhaps one of the most flexible and energetic. They are so in tune with their inner selves that chaos or disorder can hardly put their livelihoods in disarray.

They will prove calm and comfortable in almost every situation. The Gemini possesses a strange sense of perception they combine with reality. Usually, they fail to distinguish between reality and the fake realms they imagine in their minds.

Usually, this zodiac sign is social and pleases others with great charisma. They are restless by nature and often look for people to share their deep thoughts and conversations. They despise schedules and fail to stick to one. Generally, they do not plan their time in the first place as they know their free-spirited nature. The Gemini do as they please and don't like setting boundaries. Therefore, it is not surprising to see the Gemini spreading their positive energy everywhere around them. Moreover, they do not hold themselves back and are not afraid to speak their mind.

Gemini and Its Tarot Cards

Gemini is closely associated with the Lovers and the King of Swords cards.

The Lovers

This tarot card is a strong representation of the Air sign as it represents their dual personality and intimacy. The Lovers exemplify "completing each other" or "sharing equal energy" to become one. The Lovers are charming and curious, which are also two apparent traits of the Gemini. This is also one reason others are attracted to individuals with this zodiac sign. The Lovers are physically attracted to each other and share the same emotional energy, making them the essential "other half." They possess every quality that a couple should have, including healthy communication, physical affection, and a flirtatious demeanor.

Just like the Gemini makes you feel extra special in a relationship, the Lovers fall head over heels for each other. They effectively redefine love and passion. Since the Gemini prefer not to stay alone, the Lovers further depict their dependent nature. They find solace in each other's arms and feel extremely comfortable, just as the Gemini does. This card speaks of love, harmony, union, and attraction, which balances one's sense of purpose and living. Whether it's in life or in love, the Gemini seeks balance above all.

The King of Swords

The King is a representation of authority and intelligence, which are two prominent qualities of the Gemini. If this card shows up in your reading, you may come to meet a person of high authority soon. Just like the Gemini, the King of Swords is on the path of seeking justice and truth. He likes to explore, much like the tarot card's counter zodiac sign. Even though the King means well, not everyone construes his intentions in a positive light. The card illustrates the King with a blank face where he lacks expression and is seen watching his land with curiosity.

When drawing this card, you might have already established order in your life or are working hard to get your life together. This quality can also be seen in the Gemini. They follow a specific method and draft a protocol to safeguard their situation. Due to their practical nature, you hardly see them getting emotional. In fact, they shape their emotions into realistic and practical aspects, which according to them, makes situations easier to control. This makes them rational and far-sighted by nature.

Libra (Sep 22 - Oct 23)

The Scales symbolize this zodiac sign, which stands for harmony and balance.

Personality Traits of Libra

Libras represent strong social connections and strive for love and cooperation from their friends and family. They are appreciated for their just and fair-minded attitude, which helps them make better decisions. They are intelligent and interesting beings who offer plenty of knowledge to those around them. However, the other signs should be open to seeking and receiving the wisdom of the Libra. Individuals with this zodiac sign are charming and often work on pre-established schedules. They want things to be in order and always seek balance in all aspects of their life.

The Libra knows how to compromise and can help resolve issues caused by misunderstandings or misjudgments. They know how to make peace with others. They are calm and give time to their partners and friends to speak up and resolve arguments. For this reason, Libras are known to make amazing friends, partners, and leaders. They learn from their own mistakes and apply those lessons in their personal and professional lives. While most Libras are exciting and likable, some may disappoint you. However, they often come clean due to their level-headedness, which makes them more reliable overall.

Libra and Its Tarot Cards

Libra is closely associated with the tarot cards Justice and the Queen of Swords.

Justice

As the name suggests, this card advocates for justice and fairness, just like Libra. It illustrates a judge holding scales in the left hand, which is the prime symbolization of balance most Libras seek. It showcases the intention of individuals who often employ their expertise and intuition to make important decisions and take necessary steps. As the 11th card in the tarot deck, Justice represents strong intuitive power, just like the number 11. The number is so powerful that it is commonly known as the "Master number" in the astrological world.

In parallel, the number 11 can be seen in the pillars illustrated on the tarot card, which strengthens the connection. Excessive usage of any aspect can cause an imbalance, which can frazzle the Libra. The Justice lady holds a double-edged sword in her other hand, which signifies protection against ambiguity or confusion. Any sort of conundrum can easily be cut with the sword. You can also relate the illustrated sword with the Suit of Swords, which represents all Air signs.

The Queen of Swords

The lady illustrated on this card represents solitude, something most Libras often seek. The Queen favors emotions over practical matters and prefers to live alone. She is also looking to solve all the problems that lie ahead, which explains her curious gaze. Her rationality and practical response can likely help her solve matters with her judicious skills. If you get this card in your reading, your intuition is pointing at your rational skills and encourages you to use them to make more informed decisions. It states that if you look deep enough, you can easily take charge of your life and find answers to your problems.

The Queen illustrated on the card appears emotionless yet still demonstrates a mild, curious gaze with a sword held upright. Her ensemble seems conservative, and her pose looks serious. Yet, she has integrity and stands with the truth. She probably doesn't need the support of a loved one as it can trigger her emotions. In fact, she would rather handle the situation and life challenges with tact and grace. Despite being critical and just, she will compel you to look deep inside and appreciate your own qualities.

Aquarius (Jan 20 - Feb 18)

This sign is represented by the aquatic animal, the water-bearer, and is ruled by the planet Uranus.

Personality Traits of Aquarius

Their quirky nature and eccentric personality often garner plenty of attention. Aquarians perceive themselves to be just and forthright. However, they can get absorbed in deep thinking, which is why they often get distracted. They are the prime example of mankind and abide by the law of the community. If you need someone by your side in times of need, an Aquarian will always reach out to help. However, they lack the ability to console others and provide reassurance. Since they focus more on the community instead of single individuals, they do not always expect to feel better in the company of an Aquarian.

Aquarians are often seen as detached from the world due to their own thought patterns. You need evidence and fact-based data to persuade an Aquarian to accept your viewpoint. Since they are known for going with the flow, changing their mindset can be quite a challenge. While deep thinking and self-reflection are positive qualities, usually, the Aquarius can prove annoying when they fail to listen to others and think about random subjects.

Aquarius and Its Tarot Cards

Aquarius is closely associated with the Star, the Knight, and the Page of Swords cards.

The Star

This card illustrates a woman holding a cup and pouring water into another water body deeply connected to the Earth. It represents nourishment and hope. It compels the sign to look forward to the future and be patient. The woman places one foot in the water body, which relates to the individual's intuition. To counterbalance this, she places another foot on the land. This means that the individual is stable yet intuitive at the same time. Since the Aquarius is represented by water and air, this reference can help better understand the connection.

While the air element demonstrates the woman's intellect, the water depicts her emotional side. Furthermore, the Star represents the sign's traits of staying inspired and finding guidance while seeking solace in an oversaturated world. Aquarians prefer to stay alone and hardly blend in with the community, which can be seen from the single large star on the tarot card. Individuals with this sign are highly intuitive and can easily find their inner calling. They are guided by their gut feelings and listen to them carefully. Some highly depend on their intuition when making important decisions while dismissing external or practical opinions.

The card also shows a bird behind the woman known as the Sacred Ibis of thinking and thoughts. The bird is the representation of the element that sprouts our mind's tree. This also shows that the Aquarius is intelligent and can carve their own path in life with their strong intuition. In essence, the Star and the Aquarius zodiac sign share a sense of inspiration, societal improvement, and thriving on their intuition.

The Page of Swords

This Tarot card depicts a young man standing on a mountain peak with a sword in his hands. He is looking in the opposite direction and appears ready to use the sword. He looks young and prepared but is not exactly ready for combat. He wants to fight for his principle and beliefs, reflected in his confident, fearless look. However, it is not the right time for the Page to fight the world as he is not yet fully grown. If this card shows up in your reading, your mind and body are not prepared to deal with the challenge that lies ahead. You must be patient and let time take its course. Step back and experience the journey taking no risk. If not, you will waste your energy and time without gaining a favorable outcome.

All in all, Air signs adhere to community beliefs and carry a strong vision to make a difference in the world. However, certain life challenges can temporarily hinder their personal and outer world perspective, which can be resolved or at least handled by reading the corresponding tarot cards that pop up on their spread.

Chapter 14: The Water Signs and Their Tarot Cards

As you learned in the previous chapters, specific elemental groups are closely associated with a certain set of tarot cards. While some share qualities and traits with other signs, most adhere to specific signs, making tarot card reading easier. In the last group in discussion, the Water signs correspond to the emotional side of the tarot, which is the Suit of Cups. Since Water signs rule over their emotions, this suit perfectly embodies the traits of the three zodiac signs, namely Cancer, Scorpio, and Pisces.

In this chapter, we will talk about the water signs and their association with respective tarot cards.

Water Signs

Pluto, the Moon, and Neptune rule water signs (Cancer, Scorpio, and Pisces). Among all, individuals with the Water sign are the most sensitive and delicate through their emotions. At times, rational thinking can be quite challenging as they favor emotions over practicality. This is a major disadvantage for those who need to make informed decisions. Although individual characteristics vary from sign to sign and person to person, all Water signs can be labeled as creative, sensitive, and intuitive. In addition, they are compassionate beings who can easily make friends and stay loyal to their loved ones. Their sensitive and benevolent nature pulls them closer to their social group, which is why they are often the stars among their friends and family.

Furthermore, the water signs are extremely creative and often engage in artistic ventures. Not surprisingly, they make fantastic poets, writers, actors, and artists. Their strong psychic abilities and intuitive power are quite impressive. They can care and nurture, which is why they make great partners and parents. Their emotional side also makes them capable guardians who can take care of children with utmost diligence.

Water Signs and the Suit of Cups

As mentioned, Water signs and the suit of Cups are linked to each other. For them, love, relationships, feelings, connections, and emotions trump other qualities. The suit of Cups abides by a similar principle. Since water is agile and fluid, it can easily flow through or on any surface. It can take the shape of the container it is poured in and act. It can be molded as needed yet still be gentle. Regardless of how you treat water, it can either work for you or against you. For instance, it can show its power through massive, raging waves crashing on the shore or flow gently in the form of a brook.

Just like the Water sign, the suit of Cups can represent healing, fluidity, and cleansing. It is feminine, subtle, and powerful. Just like a woman, this suit declares its ability to adapt to change and take responsibility. It flows, nurtures, receives, and purifies. If you get the suit of Cups in your reading, you must be prepared to think rationally and with your head instead of your heart. Put your emotions aside and handle the situation with an analytical mind.

Cancer (June 21 - July 22)

This zodiac sign is represented by the Crab and ruled by the Moon.

Personality Traits of Cancer

The most prominent signs of Cancer are sensitivity and emotional attitude. They may seem firm and stubborn on the outside but are rather warm and soft on the inside. However, you must get very close to them to know their real side. They are notorious for being moody and wandering out of focus. The Cancer is self-aware but can still project a layered personality. For them, current emotions and sorrows will dictate the course of their lives. This can also affect the lives of their loved ones at all times. However, they will try to understand others and decipher their sorrows to make their loved ones feel lighter and better.

By contrast, they will barely open up to others. They carry this fear of being exposed or vulnerable, which is why they prefer to stay shut. They do not want others taking advantage of their pain and weaknesses and therefore stay isolated. Even if they are not well, they will act as if they are and convince others. This often pushes them into a downward spiral.

Cancer and Its Tarot Cards

Cancer is closely associated with the Chariot and the King of Cups cards.

The Chariot

The connection between Cancer and the Chariot fascinates tarot readers and astrologers because they display contradictory qualities. While the Cancer is known to be nurturing and kind towards their peers, the Chariot displays signs of progress and growth. Even though these two sets of qualities are not exactly opposite, they do not sit well with each other either. The Chariot card's representation of evolution and movement signals the individual towards needing to work on their intuitive growth and reflect on their movement. With this, the person can truly experience evolution and move forward in life.

The Chariot tells a person to dig deeper and find their true purpose to experience transformation. Just like the zodiac sign, the Chariot also asks us to tug on the strings of our hearts to strengthen intuitive power. If you get this card in your reading, you are probably going through a stagnant phase with no clear way out. However, you can pull yourself out of such a plateau by working on your beliefs and channeling your inner forces.

The King of Cups

As you learned, all the cards representing the suit of Cups show water in their illustrations, which showcases their connection with Water signs. One such card, the King of Cups, shows an emperor sitting on a throne that rests on a sea. The high waves cover the base of the throne by crashing into each other. The card also depicts a ship and a dolphin behind the throne. The waves and the sea, which symbolize a person's unconscious mind, seem quite turbulent. It means that the person should find the real reason behind their current hardship.

The King of Cups has Cancer as his zodiac sign, another connection between the two entities. The cards represent qualities such as love, romance, and financial independence, and a Cancerian can also display these qualities. In addition, they can take responsibility and handle crises with maturity. The King of Cups is also considerate and wary of other people's feelings. He is calm on the outside and soft on the inside. However, he can be moody at times. Some successful career paths include chef, minister, priest, doctor, or businessman.

Scorpio (Oct 23 - Nov 21)

This Water sign is deeply sensitive and also ruled by their emotions. Interestingly enough, they are represented by the Scorpio, which is a land animal.

Personality Traits of Scorpio

The Scorpio is perhaps the most peculiar and misunderstood among all signs. With their intimidating stance, they are often perceived as arrogant and mean. However, this need for having their own space is often misinterpreted. They are intimate, loyal, and make great friends. Having a Scorpio in your life is, in fact, a blessing. The Scorpio rules in social settings thanks to their strong and charming personality. Their presence is quite powerful, which is also why they can be intimidating. This is also due to their mysterious nature and penchant for puzzles.

The Scorpio seeks intimacy in all forms due to its emotional nature. Since they are serious and possess ruling abilities, they also make great and efficient leaders. They are also intense, which adds to the leadership. At times, they can come across as mean or rude. However, they just mean better for you and wish to see improvement in your life. They are also determined and can make the most out of the bare minimum. If they seek to achieve something, they will never return empty-handed. The Scorpio prioritizes their goals and goes to any length to fulfill them.

Scorpio and Its Tarot Cards

Scorpio is closely associated with the tarot cards Death, the Knight, and the Queen of Cups.

Death

Since the scorpion (Scorpio sign) is known to be a deadly animal, it is always connected to the Death card in the tarot deck. This is why most people who get this card in their reading often panic. While most relate this card to physical death, it actually emphasizes the true meaning of the life-death cycle and how this endless loop sustains human life. Basically, it means that every dark night is followed by a bright day and that the bad situation you are in will soon give way to happier days. This can also mean the opposite, in that nothing is permanent, and you must stay prepared for changing circumstances.

The Scorpio sign also depicts sexuality, a symbol of new life. This can be linked to the Death card that symbolizes rebirth. It is believed that individuals who draw this card in their reading should listen to their unconscious mind and spirit as it is asking them to find a higher purpose. Interestingly, the month of Halloween also coincides the Scorpio's birth month. Even though Halloween symbolizes death, most people celebrate it with joy and life.

The Knight of Wands

This card illustrates a knight in full armor ready to enter the battlefield. In the same way, the Scorpio is impulsive and ready to bite, so the Knight is also prepared to defeat his enemies. His ensemble comprises a bright yellow robe with flames over this armor. This is linked to the fiery nature of the Scorpio, who can bite to kill his enemies and protect themselves. The card also shows him holding a sword in this right hand that is raised high. This demonstrates the Knight's enthusiastic nature and swift movements. He is ready to move forward and conquer the land before him.

Like a Scorpio that glides in haste, the Knight is also believed to be full of energy and advance without thinking twice. Sometimes, this can be dangerous. If you get this card in your reading, it means you might find a new idea that might change your life. However, you must not make hasty decisions during execution as it can lead to failure. Prepare a solid plan and take it one step at a time. This card also tells you that you have enough courage and willingness to succeed in life and achieve your goals.

The Queen of Cups

This card illustrates a queen sitting on her throne, staring at a cup she is holding in one hand. She is deeply engrossed, trying to figure out the thoughts hidden in the cup. Since the cup is closed, this can be linked to a person's unconscious mind that is often shut and needs to be opened with effort. One's unconscious mind carries the secrets to their wellbeing and abilities needed to succeed. However, if you fail to open it, you can never uncover these secrets. The card also tells us about the physical realm, the importance of books and research, and magnetism. Moreover, you can also interpret the significance of abstract ideas, attraction, and romance through this card.

Just like the King of Cups is believed to have Cancer as his zodiac sign, the Queen of Cups has Scorpio as hers. This woman is a symbol of power and imagination. She has creative skills and psychic abilities. On the negative side, she can be secretive, suspicious, and aloof. Just like life should be taken seriously at times, the Queen keeps hers in control and does not take it for granted.

Pisces (Feb 29 - March 20)

The final sign of the zodiac calendar, Pisces, is symbolized by a pair of fish. This sign is known for its laid-back attitude, unlike other Water signs.

Personality Traits of Pisces

While Pisces mostly adhere to their principles and strongly express their feelings, they can sometimes be moody and care less about letting out their emotions. They are empathetic by nature and do their best to keep others happy. They are selfless and ready to help others without giving a second thought. Their creative skills and imaginative thought pattern set them apart from the rest. This is why they can easily build things from scratch and innovate. However, if things don't go their way, they can become moody or desperate, affecting others around them to varying extents.

If someone hurts them more than once, the Pisces will isolate themselves and fear showing their emotions. When expressing their feelings, they are careful and try not to hurt others. This makes them one of the most thoughtful zodiac signs. At times, they will even go out of their way to place other's needs before theirs, which is why they often lack in some areas. By contrast, Pisces can be easily influenced and swayed. No matter the nature of their goals, they will employ every tactic to achieve them once they set their minds.

Pisces and Its Tarot Cards

Pisces is closely associated with the Moon and the Page of Cups cards.

The Moon

The two main qualities that the Moon stands by are idealism and subconscious thinking. It basically means that the things you see are not always real. This card delves deep into the subconscious mind of the Pisces and describes their secretive side. It illustrates a moon looking down on the earth along with a dog and a wolf (representing the Pisces' tame and wild side, respectively). Two tall towers symbolize unity, just like the pair of fishes. While the card advocates for the practical life that most of us live, it hints at a life that can be more meaningful and mystical. We simply need to find our path and take the most meaningful road to living life to the fullest.

The Page of Cups

We can see a young person holding a cup on this card, ready to make an important announcement. This symbolizes eventfulness and news. The cup depicts a fish popping out with waves in the background. It means that the individual is either blessed with or on their way to formulate a new and life-changing idea. This new perspective should be leveraged to bring a positive change in your life. This also relates to future planning and making informed decisions to lead a comfortable life. The person on the card is believed to be kind, gentle, and creative, just like the Pisces.

Chapter 15: Master the Minor Arcana with Numerology

Now that we understand the relationship between the Major Arcana and numerology, we will explore how the Minor Arcana deck is also linked. With this knowledge, you can interpret your life decisions, personality, and intuition at a deeper level. This methodical approach is believed to be effective and mostly accurate. However, since the Minor Arcana comprises numerous cards, narrowing down your readings can be overwhelming. This is where the power of numbers can help you.

Let's take a quick recap to understand the classification of the four suits of the Minor Arcana cards based on respective elemental signs.

The Four Suits of the Minor Arcana

Suit of Wands

Sign: Fire

Quality: Momentum, energy, inspiration, and enthusiasm

Your soul's movement and energy are represented by the Suit of Wands and correspond to the Fire sign. It indicates that your actions must be supervised to pursue the right direction and experience positive change. You must find your true calling to stay driven and content. You possess the flame and passion needed to achieve your dreams, yet the only hindrance is the inability to find these qualities. While these qualities can help one attain contentment, they can also destroy them if. Learn how to use your inner power to leverage them for you, not against you.

Suit of Pentacles

Sign: Earth

Quality: Physical, wealth, material, manifestation, and career

All matters related to money, materials, resources, and the physical world are hinted at by the Suit of Pentacles and the Earth sign. Just like the earth nurtures and supports the growth and livelihood of living beings, your inner strength can help you take control of the world around you. If you search deep enough, you can find the changes needed for gaining resources and fulfilling your dreams in the physical world. However, if the person is not grounded, they can become greedy and possessive, which must be avoided at all costs.

Suit of Swords

Sign: Air

Quality: Mental, truth, communication, thoughts, and intellect

The Suit of Swords symbolizes the mind and mental energy. Whether you are indecisive or unable to utilize your mind's capabilities, this suit indicates the need to consider your options and take a clear step. Just like a double-edged sword, one's mental capabilities and power can either make or break them. Learn how to use your mental power to fulfill your dreams instead of destroying yourself. Use the movement of air as an inspiration, moving unnoticed but forcefully.

Suit of Cups

Sign: Water

Quality: Emotions, intuition, creativity, and relationships

The Suit of Cups encompasses relationships, emotions, love, and passion. As the water flows in a gentle yet constant motion, your emotions can also guide your way. If you get this suit in your reading, you may be thinking with your heart instead of your head. It can also mean that the decisions you make in serious situations may not be the best, and you that must think analytically to achieve the best outcome.

This classification will help you grasp the correlation between the Minor Arcana cards and the numbers they represent.

The Minor Arcana Tarot Cards and Numerology

You can use this interdependence to memorize the meanings of the cards with ease. The Minor Arcana deck comprises 56 cards with the numbers 1 (the Ace) through 10 (each with four suits). These 40 numbered cards are divided into four suits, and the rest are labeled as Court cards.

Let's explore the numbers of the Minor Arcana and their correspondence with the four suits (Cups, Pentacles, Swords, and Wands).

One-Ace

Qualities: Opportunity, new beginnings, potential, new ideas, and birth

As mentioned, the Ace is just starting their journey and taking the first step. While they may appear hesitant and lack self-confidence, they possess the courage and ability to attain great heights at first sight. They have a fresh perspective that is difficult to find in others. If this number pops up in your Tarot card reading, it can mean that the Ace can find you before you begin the climb.

At times, Aces can intimidate with their youthful stance and raw energy. If they get a new idea with potentially life-changing prospects, they will summon their powerful energy to get the best outcome. Even if you don't yet have an idea, this number asks you to delve deeper and find your calling. Your new idea is buried deep, and you just need guidance to unravel it. You possess the potential to trigger and experience positive change with a shift in your perspective. The way you take advantage of opportunities depends on you. More important, you must take care of your ideas, as new beginnings can often overwhelm you.

Two

Qualities: Partnership, balance, duality, attraction, waiting, and choice

---

140

Characteristics like union, pairing, and tie-ups are firmly represented by number two in the Tarot deck. Whether it's a new relationship, marriage, or business partnership, you might have recently entered or will soon enter a new important affiliation. It signifies the action of two opposite forces trying hard to become one. The notions of union and harmonious existence might affect your wellbeing. However, you must be wary of the complexities that may occur because of said affiliation.

By contrast, this partnership or union can prove to be so perfect and balanced that moving on can be quite challenging. You are comfortable and advance at your own pace, hindering your progress and having you plateau. This can also affect your decision-making and paralyze your analytical skills. However, usually, this union simply implies that the new beginnings perceived with the Ace are in place and that you need more time to plan ahead. You will also face choosing between potential partners and including the most competent one on your team.

Three

Qualities: Growth, creativity, group, increase, expression, and fruitfulness

Number three also represents group work and the idea of growing together. Your ideas and plan are in motion, and you steadily move ahead. At this stage, you may have more people joining your group and working towards progress. It also refers to the emergence of new ideas that can strengthen the existing plan. Your group is taking actionable steps and celebrating your evolution. While most readings are positive, some pairings of the suit and number three can indicate different outcomes. Since the number three is chiefly associated with the concept of completion (the holy trinity and the first polygon), it can indicate some sort of attainment in your life.

Note that the number three can be tricky and produce distinct meanings based on the suit you pull out. For example, while the Three of Swords can depict misunderstanding and sadness, the Three of Cups can mean joy and celebration. These are the two ends of the spectrum, and your reading will largely depend on the element you get.

Four

Qualities: Stability, structure, manifestation, security, organization, and foundation

Number four hints that you must expand your current idea or project to keep yourself growing. Usually, the foundation has already been laid. However, hindrance or slow progress can mean that the execution could be slow or poor. This often leads to disappointments as the outcome is unforeseeable. If you get the number four in your reading, it is a sign from the universe to push and progress to achieve expected results continuously.

Basically, your inner power, skills, and hopes have already manifested themselves in the practical world, and you just have to keep growing. You will face numerous challenges and crucial decisions, most of which will pertain to the plan in progress. Even though the number four chiefly indicates peace, certain situations can trigger this force to turn into stagnation. Reflect on your work and comprehend the changes that need to be made to keep evolving. After all, you don't want the time and effort you invested in yourself to be for nothing.

Five

Qualities: Conflict, change, instability, challenge, fluctuations, and loss

Right now, you may face several uncertainties that can create fluctuations or instability in your life. Usually, the number five signifies temporary chaos and minor setbacks. However, your project, phases, and outcomes can get permanently damaged if you don't take it seriously. You must learn to deal with the uncertainties and carve your own path towards progress. Note that most people start overthinking in times of chaos, which should be avoided.

If you haven't yet faced any setback, be prepared to face one if this card pops up in your tarot reading. The hindrance or obstacles can occur in any form, whether it's tiffs with your partners, loss in your business, or personal issues that can jeopardize the bigger picture. It is also a great time to learn from the past and turn your mistakes into lessons. However, this phase is temporary. To bounce back, you must take immediate action and stay positive. Be calm and find your way out to overcome this temporary disruption.

Six

Qualities: Harmony, cooperation, communication, recovery, peace, and adjustment

Number six is rather solution-oriented and brings peace. It indicates that you have successfully dodged the temporary hardship and are making progress. You are at peace with your partner and are working harmoniously on your project or new ideas. You may also be joining forces or bringing new members into your venture. Regardless of the direction, the union will help you achieve a desirable goal, which all parties covet.

If you are in a staggering phase, the new union will help set you straight again. You will receive plenty of guidance and empathy to overcome your issues. In essence, the number six highlights a person's needs and their desire to find true companionship. No matter the suit you get, the number six will ask you to seek help. It is time to move on from conflict and implement permanent solutions. This number also indicates the need to let go of both internal and external strife. There is always light after dark and clear skies after storms.

Seven

Qualities: Knowledge, assessment, reflection, discovery, spirituality, and independence

Number seven indicates introspection and the need to dig deeper. Stop whatever you are doing and step back. Are you on the right path? Are your life and plans going as expected? Should you make any improvements? If yes, reevaluate your trajectory and change the order of execution. At this point, you are also assessing your mistakes and learning from them. This will ensure that you do not repeat them and instead use them to pursue your path.

Even though you may feel lonely, you must reexamine your condition to fulfill your pursuit. Contemplate your authentic desires and pause if you have to. Take as much time as you need, but always come back stronger. Everyone needs a break, especially after chasing their dreams relentlessly. You have worked hard and can now afford to relax for a little while. Even during a pause, you find better ways to ameliorate your life, which is still a form of progress.

Eight

Qualities: Action, mastery, accomplishment, fortitude, and courage

Once you have experienced the phase of reflection and contemplation, it is time to integrate your actions into your true pursuit. Number eight indicates courage, momentum, action, and mastery, which means you must fight and accomplish your goals. You have the courage and skills to fulfill your destiny. All you need is some motivation and positivity, which number eight brings to the table. Furthermore, it states you are close to success and can almost taste it. You just have to cover the extra mile to make it happen.

The eight also indicates completion and achievement. You have already tasted success or are on the verge of experiencing it. It does not always mean fame, worldly success, or monetary rewards. Sometimes, it refers to the person's emotional wellbeing. In the end, you are bound to keep growing and experience a successful outcome. You may not see or feel it coming, and you may get the opportunity when you least expect it.

Nine

Qualities: Attainment, fruition, fulfillment, self-knowledge, and awakening

As you near completion, you are steadily transitioning into a stagnant or stable phase. Most individuals confuse this phase with reaching the finish line, whereas it is merely a transition in reality. You feel you have successfully completed your project, but you are not there yet. You are simply changing and evolving to be prepared for success. In a way, the contemplation and momentum the number eight inspire are slowly turning into progress, guided by the number nine.

In certain astrological readings, nine is indicated as a state of completion in place of the number ten. At this stage, you can clearly see the bigger picture and are close to the finish line. In fact, you can see it and are rapidly moving towards it. However, if you are tired and need to pause, consider taking a break to relax. You are close to the end, and it will eventually arrive. Use this time to gain knowledge, work on yourself, and foster self-awareness.

Ten

Qualities: End of a cycle, completion, renewal, or endings

By now, you have attained completion and reached the end of the cycle. Whether it's a worldly project or your emotional progress, you have successfully culminated on top. Most individuals at this point are content, both emotionally and spiritually. If you get this number in your tarot reading, you have most likely completed the circle.

As time passes, you will start the process and do it all over again. You can build a project that is completely different from the one you lived in the past. However, it is necessary to rest before you take the new path to avoid draining your energy.

To get an accurate tarot reading, combine the qualities of the numbers with the Minor Arcana card traits that show up in your spread. For example, if you get the Four of Pentacles, relate the number four to stability and the suit of Pentacles to finances. You are therefore blessed with financial stability. Similarly, the Five of Cups can mean a downfall or strife in your relationship because the number Five signifies conflict, and the suit of Cups depicts relationships and love.

Chapter 16: Understand the Major Arcana with Numerology

In its true essence, the tarot is much more than a set of cards. Although it may seem like a parlor trick clouded in magic and mystery, tarot can help you dive deep into the realms of human consciousness and recognize past and present patterns, along with your probable future. As we've seen, the tarot is divided into two different arcanas. The major arcana reveals and sheds light on the intricate aspects of your life experience using numerology, symbolism, and elements.

Most tarot enthusiasts begin by understanding the meanings associated with the major arcana cards. The major arcana correspondences can be an effective way to learn the meanings of each card. Once you grasp the key traits associated with each major arcana card, you can learn more about them in-depth. You can learn major arcana astrology, major arcana numerology, major arcana elements, and more, depending on the technique you use to read tarot cards.

This chapter will focus on the major arcana meanings hidden in the 22 tarot cards. Each card symbolizes a different experience of your psyche that ultimately leads you to understand the universal subconscious. The tribulations and trials that the major arcana cards entail can inspire and unsettle the reader. It goes without saying that the numerical figures, characters, and glyphs connected with the major arcana cards can be overwhelming for novices. This is why it's best to approach tarot as a story that depicts the Fool as the central character.

The Story of the Major Arcana Cards

The Fool (Number 0)

The story begins with the zero, the carefree Fool, unfolding the mysteries of the major arcana as he advances through the journey, unaware of what lies ahead. The Fool appears in the tarot deck wearing a white tunic and holding a flower in his hand. He is often depicted as standing at the edge of a precipice. You might see him as unaware or dim, but you'll be surprised when you understand his personality and actions. In tarot, the Fool resembles the power of the present moment. The dominant theme of the Fool card is mastering life's journey. Besides his political prowess, the Fool excels at directing others and can accumulate great wealth. He is fearless, open, and innocent, which makes this adventurous journey of self-discovery possible.

The Magician (Number 1)

When the Fool sets on his journey, the first person he encounters is the Magician, representing pure masculine energy and leadership. The Magician, being number 1, is a natural leader, unique, assertive, yet often stubborn. This tarot card represents intellectual development, problem-solving skills, independence, and endless creativity. The Magician is highly inventive, impulsive, and entrepreneurial. He has a conscious mind and pioneering instincts. This card symbolizes a strong willingness to assert personal views out in the world and the ability to harness one's talents towards the betterment of self.

The High Priestess (Number 2)

Next, the Fool encounters the High Priestess, sitting patiently in front of Solomon's temple. Known as the guardian of the secrets of divine power, the High Priestess embodies pure feminine energy, equilibrium, and immense knowledge. The mysterious, powerful, and magical forces of intuition are embodied in the High Priestess. These intangible forces enable her to explore the realms of magic. She may struggle with decision-making and self-confidence and is often oversensitive. This card in tarot represents mild and peaceful energy. The High Priestess is socially aware, loves balance, and is an excellent peacemaker.

The Empress (Number 3)

The Empress is considered the earthly counterpart of the feminine High Priestess. Like the number 3, she represents communication, divine feminine bonding, and harmony. As the mother of the Fool, she is known to be nurturing, loving, and kind-spirited. She represents abundance, fun, and optimism. Known to be a natural entertainer and a skilled orator, the Empress is expressive and can easily strike conversations. Sometimes, she suffers from extreme self-indulgence, craves opportunities, and may lack focus. However, the Empress finds solace in her vivid imagination, creativity, and unwavering optimism.

The Emperor (Number 4)

The Emperor is the earthly embodiment of the masculine Magician and the Fool's father. This tarot card represents law and order. The Emperor is hardworking, focused, and disciplined by nature. To protect his realm and the softness of the Empress, he builds walls and creates firm boundaries from the external world. The Emperor is a creative builder who thrives on planning and systematic approaches. Known to be very practical and a natural supervisor, the Emperor shares his knowledge with the young Fool to help him find security and establish boundaries.

The Hierophant (Number 5)

The young Fool leaves the safety of his home, empowered by the knowledge of his parents. When he starts exploring the structured world, the Fool encounters the Hierophant. This card symbolizes freedom and adventure. The Hierophant is known to have a restless mind that questions everything and learns from experiences. This impulsive spirit dislikes monotony and thrives on constant change. In addition, the Hierophant is blessed with great sex appeal and loves physical indulgence that involves all human senses.

The Lovers (Number 6)

As the Fool continues on his journey, he meets the Lovers. The Lovers card represents responsibility, beauty, honesty, harmony, generosity, and symmetry in tarot. From them, he realizes the power of choice and that his own doings will shape his future. The Lovers card also symbolizes protectiveness, fairness, peace, and love. The number 6 is associated with discernment, protectiveness, and intolerance of hostility. In short, for the lovers, the heart is where the home is. The Lovers are known to prefer a domestic life and are community dwellers. They crave love and attention, are naturally artistic, and love attractive surroundings.

The Chariot (Number 7)

Educated by the Lovers, the Fool is now ready to apply his knowledge to the real world. To embark on this adventure, however, he must pass the Chariot. It represents graduation, a sign that the Fool has sufficient knowledge to face real-world challenges. In tarot, the Chariot card is associated with the mind. It represents dreams, philosophy, and intuition. The number 7 is sacred and represents spirituality and deep thinking. The Chariot is anti-social and a natural loner who prefers isolation. It is contemplative, analytical, and studious. However, the chariot's excellent mental powers enable it to appreciate details.

The Strength (Number 8)

After graduating, the Fool faces his first challenge in the form of Strength. The Strength card in the tarot represents materialism. In parallel, the number 8 is associated with wealth and abundance. The Strength card also embodies ideals of stability, safety, and security. This card is associated with leadership, financial balance, spiritual growth, and courage. A balance between spiritual and mental is what keeps this card satisfied. This card represents large reserves of strength and energy. It is also known to have exceptional organizational skills capable of managing large businesses.

The Hermit (Number 9)

Tested by the challenges of Strength, the Fool finds himself spiraling into the world of the Hermit. Finding himself alone with his thoughts, the Fool learns about introspection. The Hermit card represents wisdom and is known as a universalist. The number 9 is associated with compassion and innate wisdom. The Hermit is blessed with abstract thinking and formidable energy. Often viewed as naive, the Hermit must share wisdom with others and learn to say no. Known as a humanitarian, he is idealistic, merciful, and tolerant.

The Wheel of Fortune (Number 10)

Once detached from the outer world, the Fool understands that life is a game to be played and a set of riddles waiting to be solved. These twists and turns are a result of fate and choices. This is when the Wheel of Fortune appears as if a manifestation of the Fool's newly found knowledge. This card in tarot represents new beginnings. The number 10 in numerology is associated with influence, opinion, and spirituality. The Wheel of Fortune is a clear thinker and possesses great pragmatism and leadership skills. It represents the change in fortune, connection with consciousness, and a new cycle of energy.

Justice (Number 11)

As the Fool gets accustomed to the ever-changing nature of fortune, he is led to the Justice card. Here, he learns how decisions are made and implemented. The Justice card represents a master's intuitive visionary. In numerology, the number 11 is called a master number and is associated with enlightenment. The Justice card is idealistic, naturally perceptive, and quite creative. It draws energy from cosmic forces and is a natural educator. It has a keen sense of justice and a great curiosity for the metaphysical. The Justice card is a natural catalyst, has boundless creative potential, and is known to be positively decisive.

The Hanged Man (Number 12)

The Fool soon learns that life is not so black and white when he encounters the Hanged Man. He finds himself between two worlds, trying to adopt a fresher perspective. In tarot, the Hanged Man card symbolizes the law of reversal. It also represents a period of waiting or suspended decision-making. The Hanged Man observes the world from a different perspective, can look beneath the surface, and believes that reality is an illusion. He is the epitome of wisdom and has tremendous inner strength. Known to be deeply serene, the Hanged Man is spiritual, analytical, and can tolerate diverse beliefs. The number 12 is associated with the importance of natural and universal laws.

Death (Number 13)

His uncomfortable encounter with the Hanged Man makes the Fool realize that whatever he accepted as blind truth was the ideology of his former tutors. This is when the Death card appears to release him from the Emperor's teachings, Empress, Hierophant, Lovers, Justice, and every other notion accumulated since childhood. In tarot, the Death card represents karmic rebirth. It suggests constant change, destruction, and reconstruction. This card is all about regeneration and transformation. The number 13 is associated with psychic abilities, transmutation of energy, and limitless creativity. The Death card also symbolizes "all-or-nothing" energy.

Temperance (Number 14)

The experience with Death changes the Fool forever. His understanding takes the form of Temperance. The angel of the Temperance card provides the Food with a deeper understanding of spirituality. The Fool finds his emotion stabilized and the extremities of life connected through a middle path. In tarot, the Temperance card represents moderation. The number 14 is associated with vivid sexual energy and imagination. The Temperance loves adrenaline and excitement. It learns by experience and loves a fast and furious life. Temperance needs to beware of extremes and learn about caution and the importance of slowing down every now and then

The Devil (Number 15)

The clarity that comes with the Temperance reveals the blind spots of the Fool. These hidden spots take the form of the Devil. With the Devil's appearance, the Fool's subconscious urges manifest themselves in the form of attachment and addiction. The Devil card represents discernment and circumstantial bondage. It is naturally magnetic and strong-willed. The number 15 is associated with ambition, perseverance and also symbolizes responsibility. It is largely associated with the home and family.

The Tower (Number 16)

The amount of stress, manipulation, and tension that arises due to the Devil are short-lived. The awe and shock of the Tower awaken the Fool. The Tower card resonates with the notion of awakening. It displays an expressive, perceptive, and often forceful personality. The Tower may face challenges such as material losses due to emotional issues, temporary setbacks, destructive temper, and impatience. It can easily assess circumstances and is blessed with clear-sighted intellect.

The Star (Number 17)

The Fool's inner world walls are shattered by a lightning bolt from the heavens, allowing the Star to be reborn. Perhaps one of the most hopeful and magical moments of the Fool's life, the Star's divine assistance blesses him with new and healthy ideas. In tarot, the Star card represents success. It symbolizes the desire for truth, determination, and insightfulness. The Star's auspicious vibrations and fine thinking help the Fool find wise ways in the material world. The Star is often associated with executive leadership abilities, high focus, and the Aquarian influence.

The Moon (Number 18)

The level of transcendence that the Fool finds with the Star has a dark side. From the shadows, the Moon appears. It reminds the Fool of the cycle of women and the tides of the ocean. The psychic and profound Moon embodies all that is mysterious and uncontrollable. The Moon represents shadow development in tarot and is associated with natural healing ability, intense emotions, imagination, and sensitivity. This card is also associated with emotional instability, inexperienced energy, anxiety, and nervousness. The Moon is intuitive, receptive, highly influenced by the subconscious, and can develop high focus.

The Sun (Number 19)

As the Moon starts to set, the Fool can feel his journey ending. His feelings are confirmed as the Sun rises with the promise of returning home. The Sun card epitomizes independence in tarot and is perceived as an excellent speaker and a gifted leader. The card is associated with high intellect, art, and science. The Sun must master emotions, control impulsiveness, and restrain from self-pity. The card is the sign of life and light. The Sun is blessed with divine guiding power.

Judgment (Number 20)

As the Fool returns to his ancestral castle, he is ready to reveal everything he learned throughout the journey. This is where the Judgment card is revealed. In tarot, the Judgment card represents cooperation, collaboration, and decisions. This card is the power behind the throne and is naturally diplomatic. One must learn to master emotions, adapt to diverse perceptions, and distinguish between what is true and false.

The World (Number 21)

Eventually, the Fool ends his journey as the final inner works are completed. The World welcomes the Fool. While it represents the end of one's journey, the World hints at the start of another adventure. The endless cycle of life is perhaps the deepest level of wisdom that the Fool learns from his journey of self-discovery. The World card, in tarot, represents cyclical integration and is associated with a positive attitude, freedom, and liberation. The number 21 is a fortunate number that represents a positive outlook on life. It symbolizes the union of love and wisdom. The World can often be greedy or selfish. However, it is just another opportunity for the Fool to discover new ways of learning and growing.

Chapter 17: The Major Arcana and the Planets

In tarot, every astrological sign corresponds to a major arcana card. Throughout this chapter, we will discuss the ten major arcana cards ruled by planets and how these cards embody the characteristics of the astrological signs. This chapter will also help you gain insights into your Sun, Moon, and Rising sign using tarot. By the end, you must gather valuable knowledge that will help you outline your personality using the connection between astrology and tarot.

In astrology, the signs and meanings associated with the planets originate in Roman and Greek mythology. These correspondences are a great tool for learning about the key traits and notions associated with each planet and zodiac. Knowledge of the planets can be used in tarot reading. If you are new to tarot, this chapter will enable you to grasp the connection between the planets and the major arcana cards.

Major Arcana Cards and Corresponding Planets

The Sun

The Sun symbolizes conscience, fame, identity, individuality, life, positivity, success, and victory. The positioning of the Sun, and the zodiac signs at the time of your birth, determine your Sun sign. In tarot, the Sun card represents happiness, success, and recognition. It is believed to be a good omen and a form of divination. The Sun card helps predict the positive things, success and achievements, which will come to you in the future. The Sun symbolizes good health and positivity.

The High Priestess - The Moon

The Moon corresponds to the High Priestess. The Moon is traditionally associated with femininity, dreams, and creativity. In many cultures, the Moon symbolizes feelings, emotions, reputation, psychic abilities, and the human subconscious. In tarot, the High Priestess card is associated with emotions and psychic ability. While the card represents intuition, it also symbolizes cheating and secrets. You'll find that the High Priestess is connected with darkness and night, not unlike the Moon. This is why they are often associated with occult abilities, infidelity, and hidden information. Since the Moon is visible at night, it is mostly connected to dreaming, creativity, and imagination. The Moon also symbolizes crabs, oceans, and water.

The Magician - Mercury

The planet Mercury corresponds to the Magician card. The Magician represents diplomacy, enterprise, and knowledge. As a good and witty orator, the Magician excels at communication. This ability to speak logically and thoughtfully can make the Magician a good showman and a good conman. In Greek mythology, Mercury is believed to be the god of thieves and symbolizes social networking and communication. The key traits associated with Mercury are knowledge, networking, and travel. The planet Mercury is known as the planetary ruler of the rising sign and symbolizes how you connect with others.

The Empress - Venus

The planet Venus corresponds to the Empress card. Venus is one of the most beloved Greek goddesses. She is worshipped as the goddess of love. In mythology, Venus's symbols include girdle, Myrtle, rose, and shell. Venus represents love, relationships, and romance. In astrology, Venus represents beauty, desire, fertility, harmony, love, and sexuality.

Interestingly, the Empress in the tarot represents harmony and fertility, just like Venus. The Empress card usually predicts the start of a new relationship, pregnancy, and is associated with children's birth. Venus appears in the form of the Empress in tarot, and it is a card that represents balance.

The Tower - Mars

Mars appears as the Tower card. It is known as the planet of aggression, anger, determination, drive, masculinity, war, and will. Mars corresponds to the Tower in tarot and represents destruction, negativity, and ruins. Although Mars has some positive attributes, they are often read quite negatively. Swords, shields, and spears are symbols of Mars. Dreaming of these things can be signs of future conflicts, troubles, or arguments. Mars can be used to reflect your level of aggression, how brave you are, and how quickly you can sort out your problems.

The Wheel of Fortune - Jupiter

The planet Jupiter corresponds to the Wheel of Fortune card. Jupiter is believed to be the planet of luck. If the planet appears to be well placed in someone's chart, it means they are naturally fortunate and blessed with good things. However, it doesn't mean they will find them effortlessly. Instead, they will be nudged in the right direction by the universe. Just like Jupiter, the Wheel of Fortune is associated with fortune and luck. The card also symbolizes confidence, charity, and expansion. The planet Jupiter, just like the Wheel of Fortune, represents leadership, authority, and power. Besides the prediction of luck, Jupiter can also help reveal destiny and fate.

The World - Saturn

The planet Saturn appears as the World. Saturn corresponds to the World card and represents limitations, restrictions, and responsibility. In mythology, Saturn represents the things that must be done, whether you feel like doing them or not. Traditionally, Saturn symbolizes authority, a sense of duty, and responsibility. Helped by Saturn, you can reveal your shortcomings, whether you are truly content with where you are in life. It can also highlight the responsibilities you have that you shun away. Similar to Saturn, the World card represents a significant change in your life when starting a new phase and leaving the old one behind.

The Fool - Uranus

The planet Uranus corresponds to the Fool. Uranus is associated with change, individuality, originality, and technology. The planet Uranus represents the beginning of the age of technology and the industrial revolution. In tarot, the Fool advises others to implement change in their lives. The Fool is depicted as someone who is airy and difficult to pin down. The Fool card tells you that you don't want to be shackled to something forever. Just like the Fool, the planet Uranus showcases a dislike for responsibility and someone who finds joy in doing their own thing.

The Hanged Man - Neptune

The planet Neptune symbolizes dreams, intuition, and spirituality. In tarot, Neptune corresponds to the Hanged Man card. If Neptune is well placed on someone's chart, it means they have the power of prophecy and deep psychic abilities. However, Neptune can also represent clarity. Although it is primarily associated with positive qualities, if Neptune is badly placed in someone's chart, it can mean that the person may face difficulty in making decisions. The Hanged Man card represents spiritual awakening, dreams, and intuition, just like the planet Neptune. Like Neptune, this card symbolizes uncertainty and a poor sense of orientation.

Judgment - Pluto

The planet Pluto is known as the planet of change, renewal, rebirth, and transformation. In Roman mythology, Pluto was believed to incarnate Roma, god of death, which is fitting since death is the bringer of renewal and rebirth. Since Pluto was only discovered recently, it represents new beginnings and major life changes ahead. In tarot, Pluto is believed to rule the Judgment card. They both represent life-changing opportunities and intense transformation.

Understanding the Sun, Moon, and Rising Signs

In astrology, the zodiac signs along with celestial bodies communicate a unique signature, known as a birth chart. This unique cosmic signature is a map that reveals the positions of the planets, the sun, the moon, and the stars at the time and place of birth. The Sun, Moon, and Rising signs are the three primary planetary points that reveal your everyday personality. Another interesting thing to note is that each astrological sign corresponds to a major arcana card in tarot. This section will discuss what your Sun, Moon, and Rising signs say about you and which major arcana cards correspond to the astrological signs. Are you ready for this intentional journey of self-exploration? Without further ado, let's begin by understanding the Sun, Moon, and Rising signs.

Sun Sign

Almost everybody knows their Sun sign as this is the most discussed aspect in astrology. The Sun sign can be found within a specific zodiac in your birth chart. It speaks of your identity and how you express yourself. It represents the powerful energy that urges you to seek your true self and express it in the best possible way. It also represents the way you express your individuality and how you portray yourself to the world. In other words, your Sun sign is who you are at your core.

Rejuvenating your energy, socializing, and involving yourself with people can prove very useful. If your Sun sign is Cancer, Pisces, or Scorpio, you will experience deep motivation through emotional desires and feel recharged by being meditative and mindful. If your Sun sign is Capricorn, Taurus, or Virgo, you will feel recharged by being productive and engaging with the physical world to stimulate your senses. These signs are very practical in life and are deeply motivated by materialistic needs. If your Sun sign is Sagittarius, Leo, or Aries, you feel recharged by pursuing your ambitions and through physical activity. Your aspirations and goals keep you highly inspired. Last, if your Sun sign is Aquarius, Gemini, or Libra, the best way to recharge is to socialize and express yourself intellectually.

Moon Sign

Your Moon sign reveals everything that you feel. It is associated with your inner emotional self and how you deal with your feelings. The Moon sign also represents your intuition, subconscious, and spirituality. This aspect of your life is generally hidden from the outside world and may be evident only to you and those closest to you. It can be understood as your subconscious side that drives your emotional reactions. This sign can help you understand how to recharge and nurture your emotions healthily. It helps you feel the emotions of joy, pleasure, sorrow, and pain.

If the Moon in your birth chart is positioned in Cancer, Pisces, or Scorpio, you will feel in alignment with the universe and your inner self while experiencing deep emotions. These signs are sensitive to changes and may emotionally react when going through change. If your Moon sign is Sagittarius, Leo, or Aries, you will feel the most aligned with yourself when doing something with confidence. Showing strength and refraining from self-doubt can be satisfying for these signs. Experiencing a change in life can be exciting for you and motivate you to act. If your Moon sign is Capricorn, Virgo, or Taurus, being productive and getting closer to goals can make you feel the most aligned with your inner self. These signs react to changing circumstances with stability and steadiness. If your Moon sign is Aquarius, Gemini, or Libra, you are most in alignment with your inner self when you interact with others and express your ideas. These signs react to change with proper evaluation and discernment.

Rising Sign

Last but not least, the Rising sign is the sign that was present on the eastern horizon at the time of your birth. Also known as the ascendant sign, it reveals how you reflect and project on the outside world. This is how you appear to other people and how the outer world perceives you. Your Rising sign can be understood as your apparent style and social personality. It represents your inner and your outer world.

If you have Cancer, Pieces, or Scorpio as your Rising sign, you make many decisions based on your emotions and are easily influenced by your environment. It is common for people with these signs to be empathetic and sensitive. If your Rising sign is Aries, Sagittarius, or Leo, you possess great energy and vitality. You are confident, goal-oriented, yet often too blunt. Having Capricorn, Virgo, or Taurus as your Rising sign means you are factual and have a steadfast approach to life. Finally, if your Rising sign is Aquarius, Gemini, or Libra, you are friendly, inquisitive, and verbally expressive.

Major Arcana Correspondences of the Sun, Moon, and Rising Signs

Now that we understand the meanings associated with the astrological signs and discovered your three big signs (the Sun, Moon, and Rising), it's time to apply this knowledge to tarot and discover more about yourself in depth. In this section, you will learn about the tarot cards corresponding to the zodiac signs. Each astrological sign has a corresponding major arcana card. For each of your Sun, Moon, and Rising signs, you will be able to find the tarot cards associated with them and better understand what your cosmic signature says about you.

Aries - The Emperor

Like the authoritative Emperor, Aries represents a fierce leader, impulsive yet balanced. Both the Emperor and Aries tend to be independent but are embracing at the same time.

Aquarius - The Star

Aquarius shares the eccentricity of the Star. The creative and innovative Aquarius is capable of forward-thinking. Their aspiration inspires others. Spiritual exploration comes naturally to the Star and Aquarius.

Cancer - The Chariot

Cancer corresponds to the Chariot. Like the Chariot's forward motion, Cancer represents the willpower to keep moving in the right direction. The Chariot and Cancer symbolize control, emotions, and victory.

Capricorn - The Devil

The hardworking Capricorn is paired up with the Devil. Capricorns can be willful and work hard to achieve their goals. However, they are prone to becoming workaholics, giving in to worldly temptations or other addictions.

Gemini - The Lovers

The dynamic Gemini love to follow their passion, just like the Lovers. Gemini, like the Lovers card, represents exploration and self-love.

Leo - Strength

The powerful and commanding Leo corresponds to the Strength card. This card symbolizes taking control over your power and strength. Both represent exuberance and immense strength, which must be tamed and controlled.

Libra - Justice

Just like the Justice card, Libra represents maintaining balance, encouraging fairness, and being decisive. Both symbolize healthy communication.

Pisces - The Moon

Pieces correspond to the Moon card in the tarot. Given the deep and imaginative nature of Pisces, it pairs well with the mysterious and intimidating Moon. The key quality of both Pieces and the Moon is to listen to one's intuition.

Sagittarius - Temperance

The patient and moderate Temperance card is paired with the fair and open-minded Sagittarius. The Temperance card, just like Sagittarius, displays generosity, sincerity, and friendliness.

Scorpio - Death

Scorpio corresponds to the Death card. Their shared qualities represent endings, transitions, and cycles. They welcome change and not afraid to replace things with new ones.

Taurus - The Hierophant

The grounded and patient Taurus corresponds to the Hierophant card. This card symbolizes conformity, institution, and tradition. Mentorship is a key quality that links Taurus and the Hierophant.

Virgo - The Hermit

The practical Virgo is paired with the Hermit card. Deep introspection is a quality found in both the Hermit and Virgo. They are creative, rarely tempted by the outside world, and content in their situation.

Chapter 18: Tarot Spreads

In simple terms, a tarot spread is defined as the number of chosen cards and the way they open before you. They reveal the answer to the question posed and give you the ability to interpret those answers. From a tarot spread, you can learn how to see current circumstances clearly, get insights about past influences and what the future might hold for you. In a way, the tarot cards will form a map to help you make the right decisions no matter what occurs or when without pointing you in a specific direction. This chapter analyzes the most common tarot card layouts, including the one-card spread, the three-card spread, the Celtic cross spread, and the zodiac spread, teaching you how to master them.

Learning the art of tarot reading by yourself will bring you immense benefits, as it is free and only requires a little practice. First, you will need to understand the meaning of the different Major and Minor Arcana cards. Then, look at the cards and hold them in your hand as often as you have a chance. The more you use and handle your deck of cards, the more you charge them with your own energy, making your readings more specific and reliable. Once you grasp their essence, with some creativity, you can form any tarot spread. Consulting the subject of your interest will create the right atmosphere only for the reading, which will enable you to connect with your energy. Burning some incense, lighting up a few candles, or even playing soft music are all superb, effective ways to set the mood for a tarot reading. Whether you are a beginner or an advanced reader, these methods can help you open your mind and spread your energy outwards.

The One-Card Spread

One-card tarot spreads are ideal for simple, quick readings. It allows you to connect to each card more deeply by doing only a few short readings a day. If you need an answer to a specific question or some general guidance for the day ahead, one card may be all you need to help you out. This is also the best way to introduce novices to this type of fortune-telling.

To begin, take your deck of cards and choose one of the 22 Major Arcana cards randomly. Without looking at it, leave the card facing down at the beginning of the day, and turn it over at the end of it. Reflect on your day, linking your experiences to the card you drew. Try to remember this match and your mood for future readings. It is recommended to repeat this practice for 22 days and then repeat it for the same duration while also trying to guess the card you have drawn.

Once you have learned how to match your experiences with each card, you will be ready to ask some questions from your cards. Remember, start with a question that requires a simple "yes" or "no" for an answer, after which you can transition towards more complex ones. Advanced spreads can take quite some time to master, but once you practice the one-card pull long enough, complicated spreads will be easier to master. It is vital to clear your mind for a more accurate reading and only then begin to shuffle your deck. While you shuffle the cards, think of the question you seek an answer to. Choose any Major Arcana card whose back catches your attention and try to interpret it. If the card you have chosen is the World, the Sun, the Magician, the Temperance, the Strength, the Star, or the Chariot, then the answer to your question is "yes." By contrast, drawing the Devil, the Hanged Man, the Hermit, the Tower, and the Moon, will signify "no." If the card that came up is the Lovers or the Wheel of Fortune, your question doesn't have an answer, as these two represent indecision. Try formulating the question differently or seeking an answer again later in the day. With practice, you can determine a card for each day of the week, month and year.

In your reading, you may inquire as to the experience that awaits you on that day. If you have a challenging day ahead of you, a one-card spread can show you what strengths you muster to help you out. You can use any occurrence to help yourself and others. This is a good way to learn what you are being called to share or express each day, as it can strengthen your communication with others. It can also help boost your confidence by discovering which part of you needs more acceptance and love and where you are on your healing journey.

The Three-Card Spread

Like the one-card spread, the three-card tarot is also ideal for simple questions, although it is less beginner-friendly. Since you will need to select three cards from the deck and assign three meanings to them, you should already be familiar with what the cards represent. The most practical way to interpret those three cards is by considering them an answer related to your present, past, and future. When you select your cards from the deck, lay them face down with the future card placed in the middle, as this one is heavily affected by the other two. The card on your left should be your past card, and the one on the right should signify the present. Always begin your reading with your past experience and finish it with future answers.

Your Past

Your past card can grant you the opportunity to reflect on your past and discover anything that may be holding you back from realizing your full potential. Sometimes, we are confronted with intense emotions or lessons we don't take time to examine closely. Whether it happened a week or a year prior, there could be something keeping you unsettled. In fact, your past has a significant influence on your energy, and you will need to resolve it before you can successfully move forward. This is precisely why you must begin your reading with your past card. Only after leaving behind your past ordeals can you focus on your present and, most importantly, on your future. It is best to concentrate more on your experience the week leading up to the session for a more accurate reading.

Your Present

After laying your foundation by understanding the past, you can now turn over your present card. With this card, you will be able to evaluate your current situation and mood, which can also give you valuable insights into your mental health. While the past might be affecting your present, the solution for older problems is often found in present times. For example, you may have a deep, unfulfilled desire you were not even aware of until you got in touch with your inner emotions. Whatever caused you to feel exhausted can now be resolved by resting. The first part of your resolution will be revealed to you through your present card, which will show you how to start your journey. The solution is probably already there in your subconscious, waiting to be discovered. Here, make sure to direct your energy towards only a couple of days after the reading.

Your Future

The last card you drew indicates your future. Most specifically, it can shift your focus on an event that may happen the week after the reading. After identifying your problem and its solution from the previous cards, the future card can show you how to achieve it. Overcoming traumas and other negative emotions is only possible once you can identify the right things. When we work towards a certain goal, we often focus on the things we cannot do well rather than the ones we can. By showing you what served you until then, the future card can prevent you from wasting time finding the actions needed to carry on. If you put more effort into taking the most effective steps only, you will be more likely to succeed. However, these steps will be useful only if you consider the first two cards carefully and interpret them correctly. Otherwise, your future may turn out to be different, despite what its corresponding card holds.

The Celtic Cross Spread

Celtic Cross Spread

After practicing basic tarot spreads, you will also learn how to perform more advanced readings, such as Celtic cross spreads. Since it provides you with detailed analysis and interpretation techniques, its main purpose is to answer a specific question. More often than not, our emotions stem from several issues. Celtic cross spreads use ten cards from your deck, and by reading them one by one, you can interpret and focus on one problem and solution at a time.

Place your first card vertically on the middle of the table and put the second one on top of it horizontally. The next four numbers should be placed around the first two and be read clockwise. Cards number 7-10 should be placed in descending order, on the right to the rest of the cards. Arranging the cards in a face-down position and revealing them as you proceed can be helpful if you are learning this spread. However, you will soon learn that placing them all facing up from the beginning can be just as efficient.

Interpreting the Cards in the Celtic Cross Spread

1. **The Person in Question:** Usually, this is the person who seeks answers and is being read for. If this person cannot relate to the meaning of the cards, the answer may have been meant for someone close to them, like a friend or relative.

2. **A Potential Situation:** This card reveals meaningful circumstances in a person's life, whether or not it is related to the question they have asked. In any case, a challenge or obstacle will turn up, along with a possible solution.

3. **The Basic Foundation:** Related to the potential situation and is often a possible event from a distant past. This influence helps determine the main problem and the resolution.

4. **A Recent Event:** While it generally represents the influence of the near past, this card might have links to the previous one. The current problem may be caused by an old trauma or be completely unrelated.

5. **The Near Future:** This card shows how the potential situation will evolve in the next few weeks or months. It can also reveal a totally unrelated event and bear great significance for the person inquiring.

6. **The Present Problem:** If you would like to know whether the situation is about to be resolved, this card can help you figure it out. Whether the expected outcome is positive or negative, you will see where you stand in the present.

7. **Other Influences:** This card reveals how the people you surround yourself with influence your situation. Their energy can have an impact on the possible outcome of your issue. However, knowing this can help you take back control.

8. **Internal Resolution:** Because your emotions have an enormous impact on your actions, revealing them might help you find a resolution sooner. Here, you will see if there is any conflict between your conscious and subconscious desires.

9. **Conflicted Emotions:** Whether or not they are deep-rooted, your fears and hopes can be conflicted, preventing you from finding an efficient solution to your problem. You may hope for one outcome and dread it at the same time.

10. **Possible Outcome:** After analyzing all other cards, this last one may present the final piece of the puzzle. If you interpreted the previous cards correctly, this one should show you a long-term solution, extending as far as a year in the future.

The Zodiac Spread

The Zodiac Spread

If you have little experience with simple tarot layouts but aren't ready to try a Celtic Cross spread yet, consider exploring the Zodiac spread. Despite using 12 cards, this spread is easier to comprehend than the previous one. It's generally an excellent spread to use for holistic readings when you have more deep-rooted questions to explore. Given that the Zodiac spread provides answers for general, albeit important, questions, this reading is best conducted on occasions when you find yourself at a crossroads in your life.

While there are many ways to perform and interpret a Zodiac layout reading, most use twelve cards, each representing a house of the zodiac map. After clearing your mind, infuse your energy into the cards while shuffling them, and you should visualize your question. Lay the first card on your left, at the 9 o'clock position, and follow with the rest going counterclockwise until you reach a full circle. Occasionally, a 13th card is added to the middle of the spread. However, this can make the reading slightly more complicated. So, if you are new at this, it is recommended that you start with the 12-card layout.

The 12 houses of the Zodiac tarot spread are as follow:

1. **The First House:** This house represents your state of being and general outlook on life. Besides showing you how other people see you, including your physical appearance, this card can also give you insights into how you view yourself.

2. **The Second House:** This card shows your rapport to your professional life and self-worth and can help you set your priorities more clearly. It can also reveal if you have a hidden potential you can explore to earn more money.

3. **The Third House:** This house can help you explore your general surroundings, such as your workplace or social settings. Additionally, it covers your relationships with people you meet daily but who aren't close to emotionally.

4. **The Fourth House:** This house shows your connection with the people close to you. Your partner, children, or parents will show up here, as will the stability of your relationship with them.

5. **The Fifth House:** The house of your creativity reveals what you enjoy in life. It also shows how you use your creative side to resolve problematic situations that arise in your life.

6. **The Sixth House:** This card can highlight negative areas in your health and indicate the need for change. Whether you need to pay attention to healthier nutrition, better rest, or personal hygiene, you can find the answer here.

7. **The Seventh House:** This is a house of partnership, both legal and personal. It can be used to find a suitable partner, whether for a romantic interest, in business, or just a friendship.

8. **The Eighth House:** This is the card that reveals all your secrets. Everything will show up here from the grief about your family members passing away or something unexpected you would rather not talk about.

9. **The Ninth House:** This card can reveal your true potential and all the ways you can grow as a human. It covers things like how you can earn more money, but it can help realize other dreams, such as traveling.

10. **The Tenth House:** Like the previous card, this house also helps you realize your full potential, only in more professional settings. It can show you what career goals you should set for yourself and the kind of public image you should display.

11. **The Eleventh House:** This is the house of generosity towards the people in your life. It focuses on showing you how much empathy you have toward others and how they see you as a result.

12. **The Twelfth House:** All negative emotions you haven't dealt with (but that still lurk in your subconscious) will be revealed in this house. The card also shows how these thoughts limit you from being the best version of yourself.

Conclusion

As you know by now, astrology is a fascinating subject that holds the power to change a person's life. The position of the stars and alignment with certain planets highlight an individual's life, personality, wellbeing, inner thoughts, and intuition. Astrology implies that an individual is attuned to the universe and survives in harmony. Now that you have learned everything about Astrology and its implications in zodiac signs, tarot, planets, and numerology, it is time to experience the effects and bring positive change in your life.

To wrap up, let's briefly look at the subjects we covered throughout the book and apply them to begin seeing positive changes.

Planets and their respective signs play a significant role in our lives by unraveling our true personalities and guiding us on the path towards enlightenment. The way the planets are positioned is expressed through Natal charts. They are also called Birth charts and reveal your hidden tendencies and desires. The ten planets in the realm of astrology are the Sun, the Moon, Mercury, Venus, Mars, Jupiter, Saturn, Uranus, Neptune, and Pluto. Each one represents a zodiac sign, namely Aries, Taurus, Gemini, Cancer, Leo, Virgo, Libra, Scorpio, Sagittarius, Capricorn, Aquarius, and Pisces. These 12 zodiac signs are further divided into four elemental groups, i.e., Earth, Fire, Water, and Air.

Sun Sign Astrology takes the position of the sun into account when determining a person's sign. The location of the zodiac sign is deciphered to find their sun sign. The twelve zodiac signs mentioned above are divided into specific months based on the sun's position. Each of the zodiac signs has distinct ruling planets as well. Furthermore, each sun sign falls under a part of every season, which are labeled as modalities. Regardless of the season or time of the year, certain zodiac signs share similar traits as they fall under the same modality. These Sun signs also display four personality type variants: sanguine, choleric, melancholic, and phlegmatic.

Moon Sign Astrology is often disregarded because of the burden imposed by the Sun signs. However, like every celestial body that plays an important part in astrology, the moon also rules and controls some zodiac signs. The moon represents an individual's hidden intentions, deep-rooted emotions, and innermost feelings. In other words, these are the feelings that one is unable to process and express. If you feel misunderstood, your moon and sun may be failing to cooperate. The sensitive side of the zodiac signs is interpreted by the moon's energy on respective groups, which gives rise to the emotional zodiac signs.

Numerology is the study of numbers with significant values that distinctly examine the characteristics of individuals. They are also used in the world of astrology to derive new concepts and ideas. Your primary traits, thoughts, feelings, and soul's calling all point to a specific set of numbers, which are significant to your being. These are then called your "lucky" numbers. While all zodiac signs are assigned certain numbers based on collective traits, each person can have a different number that best describes their essence. You can study the numbers and compare them with your own personality based on Odd, Even, and Master numbers.

Your Personality and Heart Number can be figured out using the science of numerology and considering your personality. Refer to the table and guidelines again to discover your personality number based on your name. These numbers represent your true personality, traits, heart, and inner calling. The power of numbers is such that they can reveal your outer behavior and your heart's desire. Interpreting your personality and heart numbers will help you realize your true purpose and put you on the right path. More importantly, it will provide courage and motivate you to achieve your goals and fulfill your ultimate purpose.

Tarot card reading is the art of reading and deciphering a set of illustrated cards representing a person's true personality, hidden intentions, and life path. A standard tarot card deck contains 78 cards divided into two groups, i.e., Major Arcana and Minor Arcana cards. While the Major Arcana cards symbolize a person's personality and major traits, the Minor Arcana cards reveal their encounters and experiences in day-to-day life. This helps them understand the bigger picture while acting towards positive change incrementally. The Major Arcana set is a deck of 22 numbered cards, and the Minor Arcana set contains 56 cards divided into four suits, the Wands, Pentacles, Swords, and Cups. You can master the art of tarot card reading by practicing different spreads, different ways of laying Tarot cards, and opening them for reading.

The Four Signs and Their Tarot Cards represent respective zodiac signs and reveal hidden truths. As you learned, the four signs are Fire, Earth, Air, and Wind, and they are assigned a set of cards that closely resemble them. Each card is depicted as one of these natural elements and resonates with certain zodiac signs. You can compare and relate your zodiac sign with its tarot card to analyze your personality on a deeper level. While some Tarot cards overlap with certain zodiac signs, most of them are assigned to dedicated Major and Minor Arcana for better understanding.

Tarot and Numbers are also closely connected, and their influence is intertwined. Each Major and Minor Arcana card is dedicated to specific numbers that are placed in order. If you need to strengthen your tarot card reading practice, read and interpret the numbers to reinforce your art.

Here is a glyph dictionary reference for zodiac signs and planets for a better understanding.

Zodiac Signs

♈	Aries	♎	Libra
♉	Taurus	♏	Scorpio
♊	Gemini	♐	Sagittarius
♋	Cancer	♑	Capricorn
♌	Leo	♒	Aquarius
♍	Virgo	♓	Pisces

Planets

☉	Sun	♃	Jupiter
☽	Moon	♄	Saturn
☿	Mercury	♅	Uranus
♀	Venus	♆	Neptune
♂	Mars	♇	Pluto*

While astrology has the power to alter and enhance one's life, the only catch is to learn the right way to do it. You now have all the knowledge you need to begin your spiritual exploration journey. If you have benefited from this knowledge, please share it around you with friends and relatives, helping your loved ones seek this positive path as well. Good luck! As established, this information can help you lead a happy life and get in touch with your true calling.

Part 2: The Zodiac Signs

Amazing Facts about Each Sign and Everything You Need to Know about Lunar Houses, Birth Charts, and Sun, Moon, and Rising Signs

Introduction

No matter how different our journey in this life is, we all seem to have one life mission in common: finding ourselves. Astrology has been a great tool that has helped countless people find themselves.

If you have been doing some astrological research recently, you know by now that you are not just your Sun sign. This mirrors the experience you may be going through right now. You might be familiar with your more obvious qualities, but there is so much more to you than what's on the surface.

Astrology reveals what is beneath the surface and so much more. It explains why you have these surface-level qualities to begin with. This book will introduce you to the natal chart, its content, and how to understand and interpret it. This is a great start for every beginner astrologer. You will find that once you have learned how the natal chart works, you'll have started the subject with a strong foundation in understanding astrology.

This book takes an in-depth look at every part of the zodiac signs. You will become familiar with their energies and how they manifest in your life. You will also understand the true functions of the Sun and Moon placements.

People unfamiliar with Astrology have sometimes oversimplified and exaggerated the Sun's function and purpose. There is a common misconception that all you need is to know about your Sun sign to make everything fall into place. The more you read this book, the more you will see for yourself how inaccurate this is.

The more you learn about zodiac signs, the more you will learn about the planets they are connected to. Remember, everything is connected in Astrology, so you cannot study one thing without the other.

This book also covers rising signs in great detail, and you will never have to be confused about rising signs and their function again. By the time you are finished, you will find you have acquired a rich understanding of rising signs.

You will also be introduced to the function of houses in the natal chart. You will understand the life aspects they represent and the energy they carry. You will also find easy-to-follow instructions to guide you as you intercept these houses for yourself.

This book will also introduce you to lunar houses and their functions in astrology. Beginner astrologists often find this topic a bit daunting to understand. Still, this book makes it easy to offer a clear explanation of lunar houses and gives examples of how they manifest in one's natal chart reading.

One thing that you are advised to keep in mind is that every zodiac sign matters. It is not enough or sufficient to study your Sun's sign. Every sign is included in your natal chart, and they are associated with different planets.

So, to have a rich understanding of astrology and read your natal chart, you need to study every astrological sign to understand how they affect you and manifest in your life.

Section One: The Basics

Welcome to part one of this book. In this section, we'll introduce you to the foundations of astrology and explain things so you get a clear understanding of how astrological bodies work and how they affect you.

Firstly, we will deal with the history of astrology, its evolution, and how it generally works. One of the main reasons people question or consider astrology to be pseudo-science is that they don't know how it began or how long it has existed. Chapter 1 will give you a solid basis of astrology's origins and how different societies, in different timelines, all observed the same factors and reached the same conclusions.

Secondly, you will learn about the natal chart in depth. The following chapters will break it down so that you understand how it works and how you can read it for yourself. Chapter 2 discusses the houses and planets found in natal charts, which are necessary for any successful reading.

Chapter 3 will teach you how to read the natal chart and eliminate any confusion you may have regarding how to read it. You will find that everything has been broken down into categories so that it is easy to follow and understand.

Chapter 4 will discuss "The Big Three" in astrology; if you have heard this term, you will know what this entails. This chapter details the sun, moon, and rising sign placements.

Finally, we will end this section with Chapter 5, which will discuss Vedic lunar houses and how they relate to a natal chart reading.

Chapter 1: How Astrology Works

The universe has a multitude of ways to communicate with us, and astrology is one of them. As Dane Rudhyar, a French author and astrologist, puts it, "Astrology is a language." If you understand this language, the sky speaks to you."

People are often astounded by astrology; believers and non-believers don't understand how it works. Many people find it absolutely foolish to look into astrology, let alone study its origins. To them, it is merely entertainment or a complete waste of time.

There is a plethora of evidence that the universe does speak to us if we only listen. If we don't, we are left oblivious to the magic surrounding us. All you need is to keep an open mind and heart to understand; the rest is easy.

Origins and History

The earliest astrological studies date back to Ancient Mesopotamia. One would naturally assume that early astrology would be primitive, but the Mesopotamians proved otherwise. They were the people who developed the Zodiac, and they also read omens and predictions based on the planets' movements in the sky.

The earliest astrological studies date back to Ancient Mesopotamia.
CC0 Public Domain https://pxhere.com/en/photo/1367444

Mesopotamians recorded their astrological predictions on clay tablets; usually, these tablets predicted important events based on planetary placements. For instance, in the second tablet, Mesopotamian astrologers recorded an omen about the fate of the world based on Jupiter's movement. It predicted that winds would cease to blow when Jupiter was facing west, and famine would spread. During this time, the King Ibi-Sin of Ur will be imprisoned. As history would have it, the King of Ur was indeed captured and taken by the Elamites.

Around the same time, the Ancient Egyptians were also observing the heavens. They studied the stars and noticed that certain constellations were bigger and brighter during certain months. Based on this, they assigned each constellation to a specific month and gods.

For instance, Virgo was known as Serqet and named after the goddess, Selkis. They also studied other stars and named them. All of this can be shown in the Dendra zodiac, a disc containing ancient Egyptian astrological knowledge.

Ancient Egyptians also developed Decan astrology, which is a system that gave every constellation 30 degrees, also known today as houses.

These two civilizations paved the way for others to follow and revolutionize astrology. Other civilizations preserved the ancients' pattern and added updated observations to it. Planets were still named after gods, constellations were linked to myths, and the art of studying the heavens was revered and respected.

This is also evident in Greek astrology. After Alexander the Great's conquests, Ancient Greece was introduced to Mesopotamian and Ancient Egyptian astrology. They merged the zodiac with Decan astrology and developed Hellenistic astrology.

Hellenistic astrology involved the planets, zodiacs, houses, elements, polarity, and modality. All of these factors are still used to this day in Western astrology.

They also gave constellations their modern names and studied the planets and constellations in depth. The astrological information that we now know originally came from the Greeks.

Later, they rose to power, and so did astrology. It was studied in universities and was consulted by prominent roman figures. The Romans associated the planets with a few of their gods. Mars was named after the god of war, Jupiter was named after the god of the sky and thunder, etc.

To this day, astrologers who use the western method work with the same calculations, approach, and information cultivated by the previous civilizations. As accurate as Western astrology is, it is not the only method astrologers use.

It is believed that Vedic astrology originated between 1500 and 2000 BCE. There had been trading between ancient India, the Mediterranean, and Egypt over the course of many centuries. There are a lot of similarities between both cultures; for instance, they believed in the afterlife, Sun and Moon gods are the most prominent, among many others.

One could argue that these similarities were caused by their trade. While Vedic astrology is not a replica of Ancient Egyptian astrology, they do have similar methods. For instance, Vedic astrology integrated Egypt's Decan system.

The Vedic natal chart is uniquely created; it is not similar to Western astrology but includes the zodiac with the same names. It is mainly used to understand one's karmic life. Vedic astrology explains that the planets' positions in one's natal chart determine their karma in this life based on their past life. Like Western astrology, the Vedic natal chart is also used to predict life events.

It is estimated that more than 2000 years ago, Ta Nao, the Emperor founded Chinese astrology. According to historians, Chinese astrology was officially developed in the 5th Century. The mythology behind Chinese astrology tells a story of a race charged with strategy and betrayals.

One day, the emperor divided the yearly calendar and assigned one animal to one month. He called on the dragon, rabbit, rat, cat, tiger, monkey, dog, pig, rooster, horse, ox, goat, and snake and announced the race. The animals that won the race earned a place on the calendar and the Chinese natal chart.

This natal chart has its own zodiac and element system, like Western astrology. While Western astrology has elements like fire, earth, air, and water, Chinese astrology has fire, water, earth, wood, and metal. It also has gods associated with specific elements and planetary placements. It is said that the gods in one's natal chart help predict events based on how strong their presence is in the chart.

In the 8th Century, Arabs developed their astrological system. Like the Chinese, they developed their own zodiacs, too, except theirs is weaponry. So, Cancer is Knife, Pisces is Axe, etc. They also developed their own Lunar houses. They are known as Manazel, and there are 28 of them, unlike Vedic Lunar houses, which are only 27.

Principles

History has repeatedly shown that astrology has been an essential part of humanity's life since the dawn of man. It is an ancient practice that bestows wisdom and reveals the pathway to divine knowledge.

Humans have been studying astrology over the course of many centuries and noticed patterns that quickly changed to principles or philosophies behind this pseudo-science. One of the main philosophies is that planets and stars affect humankind.

The reasoning behind this concept is simple. Astrologers reckoned that since everything is energy, humans are bound to be affected by it, especially when it is concentrated in planetary bodies. The amount of energy they hold is quite overwhelming to humans, and their energy will be affected and influenced by it.

Another principle comes from the Hermetic philosophy: "That which Below corresponds to that which is Above, and that which is Above, corresponds to that which is Below, to accomplish the miracles of the One Thing." Today, this concept is known as "As above, so below." This philosophy goes hand-in-hand with astrology because it simply means that you will mirror the planets' positions, and they will mirror you.

While these concepts break down astrology and explain it in a sentence or two, many people are shocked by them. When people are first introduced to astrology, they begin to fear it because they think they do not have control over their lives. It is as if what was once believed to be true is not anymore. That fear of losing control or having no free will is, of course, frightening.

However, this is where the third principle comes in, "The stars don't compel, they impel." In other words, the planets and constellations do not draw your life for you and certainly don't make decisions for you.

On the other hand, the planets influence specific energies toward you; it is up to you to decide how you want to live and react to these energies. Now, the planets may send certain people or opportunities to you, but they do not make you accept or deny them.

How Can Astrology Improve My Life?

The amount of knowledge and understanding that astrology provides is unmeasurable. Astrology is the study of spirit, along with the joyful and challenging times that it will go through during its stay on Earth. These experiences teach and purify the soul, and that is the perspective that astrology gives.

It is like you have a time machine; you can look into the past, present, and future and ultimately understand where you came from, who you are, and who you will be. This gives you a perspective and teaches you to trust your journey, even when you are going through difficult times. The universe has a special place for you. Otherwise, why would you be here?

There are other benefits, such as:

- Insight into your career
- Insight into your psychology
- Insight into your romantic relationships
- Insight into your social circle
- Knowing your gifts and talents
- Knowing your strong points
- Learning about your Finances
- Learning about your Karma and your Karmic debt
- Learning about your Roots
- Looking into your past life
- Looking into your sex life
- Meeting your shadow self
- Predicting major life events
- Predicting the future
- Receiving Medical information
- Remembering your past
- Understanding how the surrounding forces impact you
- Understanding how your brain works
- Understanding your main challenges
- Understanding your subconscious

Chapter 2: Signs, Planets, and Houses

In astrology, everything is connected, and understanding this interconnectedness eases the learning process. There are three main factors that you need to familiarize yourself with first.

The natal chart is divided between zodiac signs, houses, and planets. Each planet has its own energy, and you are affected by all of them. However, the same planet can impact you and another person differently, so how does this happen?

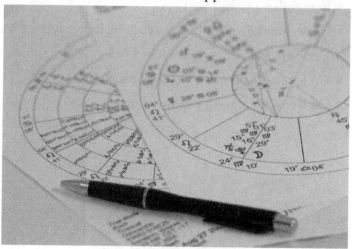

The natal chart is divided.
CC0 Public Domain https://pxhere.com/en/photo/682838

Planets have placements unique to your natal chart. For instance, you can have Mars in the first house in Libra, while another person has Mars in the 7th house in Aries. Both of you have different Mars placements, which will influence you and your life entirely differently.

These different outcomes result from planetary placements in particular houses and signs. The Zodiac signs and houses shape the planets' energy in your life, and so these planetary placements play out differently in every person's life.

In this chapter, you'll get to understand the energies of each house and planet. This will give you a solid foundation as a novice astrologer, and it will help you as you expand your astrological knowledge.

Zodiac Signs

Astrological signs have been passed down from one civilization to the other since ancient Rome gave them the names you are familiar with today. Zodiac signs are constellations that appear in the sky throughout the year. The astrological calendar begins with spring, so when it is Aries season, the Aries constellation appears in the sky, and so on.

The Zodiac signs are divided into 12, which fit the 12-month calendar. Astrologers believe every month has its own energy, which is different for each zodiac sign. This is one of the basics every student needs to know to begin to understand the signs.

Ever since astrology has gained popularity, people have been fixated on their sun signs and ignored the rest of the signs. This is not a practical way to go about learning astrology because each sign plays a role in everyone's life.

These signs are fixed in different places in each natal chart and assigned to certain houses. Your natal chart may or may not contain a planet depending on what was happening in the skies at the date and time of your birth. The chart tells you that you are affected by each of the 12 signs, not just your sun sign. This is why it is vital you learn about each of them and understand their characteristics so that you have a better understanding of how these energies manifest in your life.

Planets

Planets have great energies that shape and directly influence human lives. Everyone has all the planets in their natal charts. However, their unique placements manifest differently, and this is why people's lives and paths are unique to them.

The planets play an important role in astrology.
CC0 Public Domain https://pxhere.com/en/photo/905924

Planets move at different speeds, the ones that move quickly e are known as inner planets, while slower ones are called outer planets.

Inner Planets

☉ Sun

This star represents your core personality, ego, individuality, vitality, energy, creative expression, and authority figures. This star has high masculine energy, representing a strong presence in your life or your own masculine energy. Your confidence is a manifestation of the Sun's placement; wherever your Sun is, so is your confidence.

☾ Moon

This luminary body represents your emotions and feminine energy and reflects a deeper side not always evident on the surface. The moon represents your inner life, sensitivity, vulnerability, intuition, subconsciousness, and feelings. Astrologists believe the moon represents the mother, so this means that the moon gives you information about your mother's true identity and your relationship with her.

Many people identify more with their moon sign than with their sun sign, which makes a lot of sense because they are experiencing their inner self more than their personality.

☿ Mercury

Mercury represents the mind - the more analytical and practical part of the brain. It represents communication, technology, transportation, and general mental faculties. Astrologists take a deeper look at Mercury when they want to understand how someone's brain functions. This is especially useful when a client is complaining about mental challenges they are having difficulty overcoming or healing. This is why studying this planet's placements and understanding the energies that affect it is crucial.

♀ Venus

Venus, the planet of love and divine feminine energy, represents romantic and platonic relationships. It represents intimacy, giving and receiving affection, as well as money, art, and beauty. This planet also portrays hedonism, sensuality, and female sexuality.

This planet is intensely studied when one wants to know more about the kind of partners a person is attracted to and the nature of their love lives. Your social life is also reflected in this planet's placement, so study it carefully for essential knowledge regarding your romantic standing.

♂ Mars

Of course, Mars is one of the more obvious masculine planets. This planet represents force, energy, drive, bravery, impulsiveness, violence, war, aggression, and sex. This planet embodies male sexuality and libido levels for both genders.

Mars is an active expression of your drive and energy, so whenever you feel you lack drive or are going through an energy dump, look at your Mars placement and study it. There is much information to be revealed depending on this planet's position in your chart.

Outer Planets

♃ Jupiter

Jupiter is known as the planet of good fortune. This planet's placement is the "X' on the treasure map for you. This is where you can find your natural good fortune or where good luck will find you. This planet represents religion, philosophy, wealth, travel, the higher mind, higher education, intellectualism, and wisdom.

♄ Saturn

Known as a great teacher, Saturn represents discipline, responsibility, life lessons, restrictions, commitments, weaknesses, and fear. This planet tends to be feared and disliked. Still, when objectively examined, one will find that it only instills a sense of responsibility and fearlessness within each person. This planet's placement informs you of your greatest fears and weaknesses and how to overcome them.

♅ Uranus

Uranus is known as the planet of sudden change. This planet represents uniqueness, rebelliousness, chaotic change, nonconformity, innovation, independence, and anything unconventional. This planet also represents the eccentric side of your identity and how you express it creatively.

♆ Neptune

Neptune represents delusions, dreams, the subconscious, magical energies, psychic abilities, a sense of oneness, music, and art. It also represents the harsher things in life, like isolation, confinement, addiction, and anxiety. Please note that Neptunium placement does not always denote its dark energies. Specific placements bring out darker energies, so study them carefully before you make any assumptions.

♇ Pluto

Pluto is an intense planet, and rightfully so, since it reflects heavy energy. It represents death, rebirth, transformation, manipulation, the occult, sex, abuse, hidden knowledge, and secrets.

Death is now always literal with a Pluto placement, it mainly signifies the death of a phase or a part of yourself that needed to undergo an immense transformation, so you can become a more authentic version of who you are.

Houses

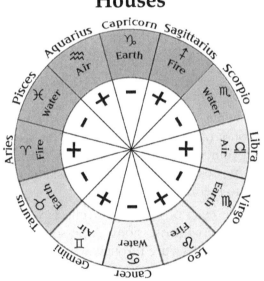

Signs, houses, and their modalities.

The inner part of the natal chart is divided into 12 sections. These sections are called the houses. Each has its own themes, characteristics, and energies, which will inform you about various sides of your life.

Together with the signs and planets, they paint a fuller picture of different aspects of your life. They do not necessarily contain a planet, but they still give you an idea of certain events when you combine them with the sign they are assigned to in your natal chart.

First House

Aries and Mars rule the first house. The section is known as the "house of self," and it is vital to learn about it. This is where you look deeper into your sense of self and where a rich journey of self-discovery can begin.

This is a critical house because the ascendant, also known as AC, falls on the cusp of this house. Briefly, the AC is how you are presented to the world and how others perceive you.

When people first meet you, they do not meet your sun sign but the ascendant's sign. The qualities of your AC's sign are the ones that shine out of you before any other qualities you may have.

Planetary placements in this house have a strong effect. Astrologists say that the qualities of any sign and planet in this house are amplified. For example, suppose you are a Virgo rising with Neptune in the first house. In that case, your sense of self and how you are presented will be an amplified expression of the energies of Virgo and Neptune.

Second House

Taurus and Venus rule the second house. This house is also known as the house of value or ownership. This section allows you to get an idea of your materialistic values. You can learn about your attitude to your possessions regarding their status in your life and your attachment to them.

The sign on the cusp of this house reflects your mentality and behavior toward material possessions. A person with Taurus in the second house might feel secure through acquiring materialistic gain. Another individual with Libra in the 2nd house might have a balanced approach regarding their possessions.

The planets residing in this house speak of your level of prosperity. An individual with Jupiter in the second house might have material blessings in their life. Others with Saturn in this place might need to reevaluate their perspectives on possessions before they can obtain them.

Third House

Gemini and Mercury rule the third house. It is also known as @the house of communication". This part of your natal chart reflects your communication style and the left side of your brain. It also represents relationships within your immediate environment, such as your siblings, aunts, and uncles. Your school is also part of your immediate environment, so experiences with your peers at a young age were affected by signs and planetary placements in this house.

Signs and planetary placements shape your communication and expose you to certain energies you need to learn and grow from. For instance, someone with Cancer in the third house is compassionate and empathetic towards others. However, their sensitivity grows a shield that protects them from being hurt too often. This type of person might be thought of as aloof and cold.

Fourth House

Cancer and the Moon rule the fourth house. It is called the "house of home and family." It's exceptionally important when you are learning about your upbringing and how your family and house shaped you. The Imum Coeli, or IC, is on the cusp of the fourth house. Together, they give shape and information about your relationship with your parents, particularly your mother.

This house stands for home and family. Many traumatized adults cannot recall much about their childhood, so they do not know how to heal. This house will tell you how you were brought up, what your environment felt like, and how it shaped you.

To get a better understanding of how energy manifests in this house. Picture a Capricorn on the cusp. This denotes a cold environment. Parental figures might have neglected you because they were fixated on their status or work.

Fifth House

Leo and the Sun rule the fifth house. It is known as the "house of pleasure." This house represents creativity, joy in life, and children. It represents the areas where you shine or stand out, like the sun. It is about creative production that releases joy. This is why children are connected to this house.

Your artistic sense is found in your fifth house. Still, you do not have to be necessarily artistic in the traditional sense. You could be artistic in the activities you find joy in, even if they are not literally artistic. Someone could be artistic in their cooking, another in the way they redecorate, etc.

Placements in this house can exacerbate this section's energy or dim it based on the planetary placement. Both planets and signs can show you what is special about you and how you express yourself creatively.

Sixth House

Virgo and Mercury rule the sixth house. The "house of service" is another name given to this section. This house stands for health, work, and service. It represents a mind-body connection, responsibility towards yourself, and the dull life tasks that need attention.

When we use the word service, it does not solely mean the act of service towards others; it is also service towards ourselves. The sixth house looks at life with a more practical eye-view and asks how things could improve, whether you think you are doing right by yourself or not. It wants you to be practical and have more accountability so that you can be your purest form.

This part can show you the nature of your job or your behavior in the workplace. It can give you some insight into the kind of people you will be meeting professionally or paint a picture of your relationship with them.

Seventh House

Libra and Venus rule the Seventh house. It is also known as the "house of relationships." Of course, from the name, anyone would think that it is romantically centered. However, this would be considered an oversimplification.

This house is about relationships in general, the type of people you attract or who are attracted to you. Your behavior in these relationships is the thing you need to outgrow. The descendant, opposite the ascendant, falls on the cusp of this house.

The descendant or DC represents the opposite qualities of the AC. It represents the qualities that you want to embody or the qualities that people see in you. These qualities could also be the things you love about other people and may indicate the qualities you would like in a partner. The DC also reflects qualities that you dislike about other people. So, you need to look deeper into it to understand its yin and yang energy clearly.

Together, the seventh house and DC could give you information about your romantic life but remember that it is not just about your romantic relationships.

Eighth House

Scorpio and Pluto rule the eighth house. It's also known as the "house of death," which might sound scary, but the house does not signify *literal death*. This house is about transformation, sex, death, rebirth, the occult, and that which is shared.

Death and rebirth here indicate transformation. Death is not always literal in this house. A lot of people go through many cycles of death and rebirth throughout their lives because they are actively changing. The act of shedding their skin is part of their lives. Of course, it is never easy – and it is intense – but these are the energies of this house.

The eighth house involves other people's money, property, and taxes. This could manifest in many ways; there really isn't one way of looking at it. It highly depends on the planetary placements that you have in this house.

Ninth House

Sagittarius and Jupiter rule the Ninth House. It is also known as the "house of life." This house represents travel, a superconscious mind, religion, philosophy, and in-laws. The ninth house represents the more abstract side of your brain; things like psychology, philosophy, and religion are addressed in this house.

Individuals such as foreigners, grandchildren, and in-laws are represented in this house. Placements here can give you a lot of information about all the previously mentioned topics.

Certain planets can tell you about foreign love or marriage. Others can indicate a lot of traveling for you or reflect your intellectual journey. Study your ninth house sign and planet placements carefully here to understand more about these parts of your life.

Tenth House

Capricorn and Saturn rule the tenth house. This house is also known as the "house of career." On the cusp of the tenth house is the Medium Coeli or MC, which is opposite the IC. It represents career, achievements, public image, and social status.

The MC is the highest point of the natal chart. Together, the tenth house and the MC give you plenty of information about your destination in life and the highest point you could potentially reach.

The MC represents the qualities you will likely be remembered for. It also reflects the characteristics that you would like to be admired for. Any placements in this section are elevated. So not only will you reflect these energies, they will also radiate off you, and everyone will take notice.

Eleventh House

Aquarius and Uranus rule the eleventh house. The "house of friendship" is one of the names attributed to this section. It represents unity, community, group activities, friendships, situations beyond one's control, and adopted or stepchildren.

As you may have noticed, the eleventh house is more concerned with group consciousness than the other houses. It's here where your sense of compassion and selflessness are expressed. Placements here reflect who you are in a group dynamic, the kind of group activities you enjoy, and your concern for humanity.

Twelfth House

Pisces and Neptune rule the Twelfth House. This house is also known as the" house of endings." It represents the subconscious, the unknown, hidden traits, secrets, isolation, karma, and limitations.

The twelfth house is one of the more complex sections of the natal chart. There are a lot of energies that reside within this house, and they remain unseen for a significantly long time. This is where you will find the battle between the ego and spirit. Your spirit might long for its natural state while the ego fights the idea of its own demise.

Astrologists and reincarnationists believe that one's past life karma is reflected within this house. Planetary placements could reveal a lot about your karmic debt. They can also give you information about your subconscious, habits, and the parts of yourself that remain in the dark.

Chapter 3: How to Read a Birth Chart

The natal or birth chart is a simplified system that allows you to interpret and understand the energies that will shape and affect your life. In this chapter, you will learn how to read a Western birth chart since other systems operate differently.

If you are reading this book, you likely believe in the universe's energies. There are a lot of unseen forces affecting us daily. This is where the birth chart steps in; it tells you which energies you have been affected by since birth.

It is filled with an abundance of details that may be overwhelming at first. However, the more you expose yourself to its system and learn about planetary placements, the easier it is to interpret.

The Birth Chart

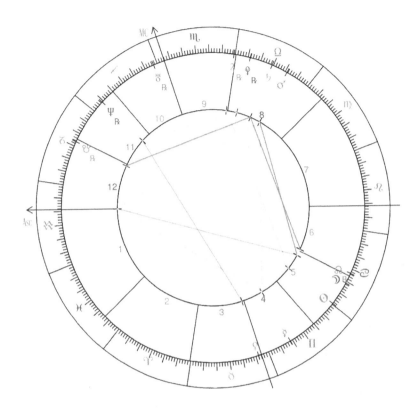

Sample birth chart.
Mom, CC BY-SA 3.0 <https://creativecommons.org/licenses/by-sa/3.0>, via Wikimedia Commons: https://commons.wikimedia.org/wiki/File:Natal_Chart_--_Adam.svg

The birth chart holds knowledge that is sacred about you and your personality. All the information that you might need, you will find there. Think of it as your personal astrological fingerprint. Your Natal Chart tells you who you are, how others perceive you, and how you perceive others.

It has information on your love life, creative expression, fears, hopes, destination, and life path. It can tell you about your children, even if you do not have any yet. It can also explain your relationship with your parents, siblings, and other family members.

There are really no limits to what a Natal Chart can tell you. If you find yourself lost or unsure of what is wrong with you, you can refer to your Natal Chart to understand more.

The Natal Chart is a circle that is divided into three sections. The first section has the 12 zodiac signs spread all around it. The second layer has the houses; each house corresponds with a certain sign. The third layer contains planets. Every planet is placed somewhere in your natal chart based on the time and place of your birth.

You can read your Birth Chart on various websites; one of them is https://www.astro.com/horoscope. Before accessing your Natal Chart, you will need to have your time and date of birth to get accurate results.

Aspects

Aspects are another important factor to consider when you are reading your Birth Chart.

Aspects reveal how a planet reacts to another planet's energy. In your birth chart, you will find that most of your planets have aspects within each other. You will not necessarily find aspects between every planet, but you will find some.

The table below features the main aspects of astrology, and these aspects are considered to be the strongest ones. When astrologists check a client's natal report, they check these aspects first because they fill in a lot of gaps about the person in question.

Aspect	Glyph	Degree
Conjunction	☌	0°
Sextile	✳□□	60°
Trine	△	120°
Square	□	90°
Opposition	☍	180°

Aspects are mainly divided into two categories, malefic and benefic, or harmonious and challenging. As you read more about aspects, you will understand more about their harmonious or challenging natures. Now that you have familiarized yourself with the main aspects and what they look like, it is time that you understand what they mean.

Conjunction

A Conjunction is created when two planets are under the same zodiac sign. Ideally, they should be at 0°. This aspect is really interesting. According to astrologists, Conjunction between planets means that both of them are affected by one another. In other words, when two planets are in conjunction, they blend together. You can think of it as two planets forming a new planet, with their energies mixed.

This aspect is neither harmonious nor challenging. It is just a strong aspect, and its *benefic or malefic nature* solely depends on the planets involved.

For instance, Mercury conjunct Venus is an example of *a benefit conjunction*. Here Venus makes Mercury sociable with harmonious and smart communication skills. People with this aspect are often clever, attractive, artistic, and have great minds for business affairs.

On the other hand, Mercury conjunct Saturn is considered to be *a malefic aspect*. In this pattern, Saturn makes it really difficult for the mind to get past negative thinking. These people may frequently get stuck in a negative space in their lives. They find themselves dealing with self-destructive behavior, dark thoughts, and heartache. They may suffer from loneliness, separation, anxiety, and depression.

However, a malefic aspect is usually there to teach you something, especially when it involves Saturn. With this aspect, for instance, Saturn wants to make you become proactive, organized, and productive. It wants you to discipline your mind into occupying itself with work that would benefit you as a human. Usually, after humans learn the teachings of Saturn, the effect ceases to be malefic.

Sextile

A Sextile is created when two planets are positioned at 60°. This is considered a harmonious aspect, even when heavy planets are involved. The magical thing about sextile is that it brings out the positive energies of planets and the signs involved.

This means that if there is a sextile between a heavy planet like Pluto and the Sun, this person has a natural magnetism and a powerful character. They have this deep urge to do something great with their lives, and more often than not, they do. They can regenerate and transform frequently throughout their lives, and it's not limited to one aspect of life; they can also transform something in their career or community.

So now you see how sextile functions; no matter how heavy a planet is, a sextile will always bring out the positive elements, and they will bless you. Look out for any sextiles in your birth chart and see the harmonious factors in your life.

Trine

Another harmonious aspect is the Trine. This happens when planets are positioned at 120°, and Astrologists consider this to be even more harmonious than a sextile. This aspect gives you the full range of the positive qualities of the planets and the signs involved.

For example, people with Moon trine Uranus are very comfortable with themselves. They do not feel the need to change and accept themselves as they are. People find them fascinating. They love learning and have a sharp intrusion. They were probably raised in an unconventional home, but it worked out for the best in the end.

Square

One of the most challenging aspects of astrology is the Square. This aspect is created when planets form 90°, and this aspect creates tension, competition, and resistance between planets. Naturally, you are affected by these energies, and it can get quite uncomfortable.

Picture an individual with Sun square Saturn. They most likely had a critical father, who destroyed their self-esteem. This individual will suffer from low self-esteem issues, especially in their 20's. They will have to overcome many challenges to get past their critical self and heal themselves.

Opposition

Another challenging aspect is opposition. This aspect occurs when planets form 180°, and Astrologists say that this aspect is akin to a seesaw. When two planets are in opposition, their energy tends to swing back and forth.

For instance, a person with Venus opposite Moon might find it difficult to show emotion in relationships, even though they love their partner. They have a lot of love inside them but tend to pick toxic partners.

Unfortunately, the two bodies do not have a harmonious aspect that would bring out the kind of energy that would benefit this individual. So, this person will keep going back and forth between Venus and the Moon.

Interpretation

In chapter 2, you learned about planets and houses. The whole idea is that you cannot fully understand one without the other. Remember that the planet's location defines how it will manifest in your life.

Below, you will find a Natal Chart with different planetary placements and a few empty houses. This is designed to help you understand how to interpret a random birth chart before you read yours.

Before reading this birth chart, you might want to make a list of all the houses and the kind of life aspects they affect. Then write down the planets and signs that are connected to these houses, and doing so will help you narrow down things when interpreting this chart.

General Pointers

This table includes aspects that you may inquire about. You will find everything arranged per category. Here is how to use it; let's say you want to know about your personality; you will look for your Sun sign and the house it is in.

If you want to know how people perceive you, you will look at the ascendant's sign, which is located in the first house. Now, the rulers of the first house are Aries and Mars, so you can also check their placements to know more.

Another example is if you are checking the 5th house because you want to know about your future kids or your creative expression, then look at the 5th house sign and planets if there are any. You can check the Sun sign and its placement since it is the ruler of the 5th house.

Please note that it is normal to have empty houses in your chart. These houses may not contain a planet, but they are not completely empty. Check the sign of this house and interpret it. Match the themes of the house with its sign, and you will understand its effects.

Category	Planet	House	Sign
Personality, appearance, and drive	The Sun Mars	First House - AC	1. Sun Sign 2. AC's Sign 3. Aries
Others - relationships/ partnerships	Venus	Seventh House - DC	1. Venus' Sign 2. Libra
Personal Property & financial security	Venus	Second House	1. Venus' Sign 2. Taurus
Other people's property, sex, & death	Pluto	Eighth House	1. Pluto's sign 2. Scorpio
Communicatio n & Left brain properties	Mercury	Third House	1. Mercury's sign 2. Gemini
Abstract Mind travels, higher education & philosophies	Jupiter	Ninth House	1. Jupiter's sign 2. Sagittarius

Roots, emotional, & family life	The Moon	Fourth House - IC	1. Moon's sign 2. Cancer
Reputation & Career	Saturn	Tenth House - MC	1. Saturn's sign 2. Capricorn
Pleasure, creativity, & children	The Sun	Fifth House	1. Fifth house's sign 2. Sun Sign
Friends & communities	Uranus	Eleventh House	1. Uranus' sign 2. Aquarius
Health & Service	Mercury	Sixth House	1. Mercury's sign 2. Virgo
The Subconscious & the Hidden	Neptune	Twelfth House	1. Neptune's sign 2. Pisces

Personality

Let's say that you are inquiring about yourself in terms of who you are, how you are perceived, etc. The first thing you will do is check your Sun sign. Why? Because your Sun sign tells you about your personality.

In the case of this chart, this individual's Sun sign is in Leo in the 12th house. Let's break this down. A person with a Leo Sun sign tells you they are creative, loving, generous, and need to be in the spotlight. However, that would be an oversimplification of things. To understand more about the Leo Sun sign, have a look at chapter 15.

Sun sign in the 12th house means that this person is introspective, highly compassionate, shy, introverted, and intuitive. This individual struggles to see their talents – or hides them from the world. They might like to be center stage, but they are afraid of the attention that they may get.

Now that you have checked this person's personality, you can move on to other things like their emotions, brain, love life, desires, and energy.

Emotional Life

For their emotions, look for the moon. The moon here is in the 5th house in Capricorn. The Moon in Capricorn means that this individual may seem emotionally detached and cold, but in reality, they are not. Their pragmatism and calculative mentality might make them seem cold. Still, they feel a sense of security when they can look at the situation objectively.

This also tells you that this person is highly responsible and needs to assess their goals and follow through with their plans to feel a sense of achievement. They are reliable as friends and can emotionally support their loved ones by assessing the problem and figuring out a solution. Their emotional well-being may depend on their status in the world, this can be challenging, but Capricorns are naturally driven.

The Moon in the 5th house describes an individual who is youthful at heart. They love children and have a good relationship with them. Their interests, hobbies, and creative expression may change frequently, but that is just who they are. This person might be slightly cold emotionally yet have a dramatic emotional life. They take their romantic relationships seriously but must cultivate a better emotional environment for themselves and their partners.

Now that you know how to interpret a birth chart, it is time to try it yourself. Using the same logic, interpret Mercury, Venus, and Mars placement. Note where these planets are, which signs they are under, and which houses they are in. Based on your assessment, connect these planets, houses, and signs. After you are done, write down your interpretation and check if it matches the energies of these planets' placements.

Planet	Sign	House	Interpretation
Mercury			
Venus			
Mars			

Tips and Tricks

The deeper you study astrology, the more you will learn. It will never cease to fascinate you, but since you are in the beginning stages of your journey, here are a few tips and tricks to kick off your journey.

Chart Ruler

The planet that has rulership over your ascendant sign is your chart ruler. What does this mean? This simply means that the planet that rules your AC's sign is the same planet that affects you most.

For example, if your rising sign is Taurus, then Venus has rulership over your chart since it rules Taurus. How does this affect you? To start off, you feel Venus' power the most and are strongly affected by its energy.

This shows in your behavior, mentality, interests, and how you carry yourself. On another level, whenever this planet moves, you feel its effects. In this case, this is called Venus in transit. You will need to check where Venus is stationed in terms of the sign, house, and any planets that it has aspects with.

Born Under a Retrograde, or Two

Retrograde means that the Earth is moving faster than other planets, so they seem to be going in a backward motion, even though they are not. This phenomenon frequently happens throughout the year, so it is quite possible that you were born under a retrograde, if not multiple ones.

Now, why is this important? People born during a retrograde tend to be affected differently than those born under the same planets when they were not in retrograde.

For instance, people who were born under a Mercury retrograde can be shy growing up, but they come out of their shells during their early 20s. These people might have difficulty listening to others and have a habit of projecting their thoughts onto people's words. They are also described as introspective and humorous.

How can you check if you are born under a retrograde? Easy, all you need to do is look up planets in retrograde during your birth year. Take notes of these planets and look them up to better understand yourself.

A Natal Chart for Two

A birth chart is not the only thing you can look up to learn more about yourself. You can read numerous charts depending on what you want to find out. In this case, there is a type of chart known as the Synastry chart. This chart involves you and another person, and through it, you find out how you react to one another, how your energy collides and clashes, and, more importantly, how you feel or feel about each other, given a certain time.

Looking up a Synastry chart is easy; all you will need to do is find a website that provides charts of all kinds. The challenging part is finding out the birth time of the person you are inquiring about. Only when you have the full information can you accurately check your synastry chart with said person.

Chapter 4: The Big Three: The Sun, Moon, and Rising Signs

Ever since astrology has gained popularity, people have been fascinated by its Sun signs, thinking that it alone describes their individual characteristics. This is a common misconception, and it is fairly common for people to only check their Sun sign.

This is not to say that learning about your Sun sign is a waste of time, it is far from, but you are only scratching the surface.

To gradually understand who you are through the eyes of astrology, this chapter will discuss 'the big three,' also known as the sun, moon, and rising signs.

These celestial bodies describe the three main aspects of your personality but remember this is not everything you need to learn about, so stay with us for more in the following chapters.

The Sun

In astrology, the Sun sign represents your core personality. You can learn about your overall personality and ego through it. The Sun rules the 5th house, so you can learn about your creative drive and style between them.

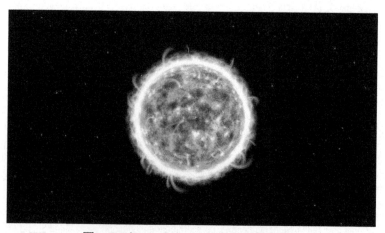
The sun sign represents your core personality.
https://unsplash.com/photos/tLFHQIqALz0

This luminous star is associated with masculine energy, so your zodiac sign can describe your own masculine energy and the masculine figures in your life. One important thing to remember is that checking your Sun sign is as important as checking its house; otherwise, you are getting an incomplete picture of yourself.

Check out which season you were born in to know which Sun sign you are. For instance, if you were born between the 23rd of September and the 23rd of October, you are a Libra. Another easy way to do this is to put your data on an astrology website and check your Sun sign in your natal chart.

The Moon

The moon sign is all about your emotional, inner life. It represents your sensitivity, intuition, vulnerability, fluctuating moods, and divine feminine energy. It also represents your mother, specifically the type of relationship you have had with her.

The moon is also connected to the subconscious since it rules the inner and emotional parts of yourself. This is why it is considered more important than the Sun sign in Vedic astrology.

The moon's phases are something you have to consider when studying your natal chart. Look up which phase you were born under to understand more about yourself and your emotional makeup.

The Rising Sign

The rising sign, also known as the *ascendant*, takes place on the cusp of the first house. The ascendant represents how the world sees you and how you see the world. It is the part of your personality people meet first before they get to see all of you. Think of it as your public mask that covers your inner self.

Calculating your rising sign is easy. All you need to do is enter your birthdate, time, and country into an astrology app or website. After you get your results, check the zodiac sign that is in the first house. Now that you found your rising sign, check this list to find out what it means.

Aries

Aries is a fiery sign ruled by Mars, so if Aries is in the first house, chances are you emulate the sign's fiery attitude and have that independent flare around you. People may view you as an energetic and fun person to be around. You also inspire people with your innovation, bravery, and charisma. You may appear stubborn and have child-like energy at first, but the more people get to know you, the more sides they see to you. However, you are prone to butt heads with others and can be a bit argumentative.

You are also known for bringing competition everywhere you go, which can be both healthy and unhealthy. Your child-like curiosity brings people closer to you and helps them to see life from your angle. It is truly something special to be able to give that gift to someone else. That is why people like spending time around you, ascendant Aries; you open up new sides to the world and possibilities they haven't seen.

Taurus

Ruled by Venus, the planet of love and beauty, Taurus ascendant is very attractive, to say the least. You present yourself as easy to talk to, and you have peaceful energy about yourself. People can relax when they are around you because they can sense calming energy radiating off them.

You also have a good sense of style, and you show it. People admire everything from your clothes to how you have put them together. Being a Taurus rising, you also admire anything that looks aesthetically pleasing. Beauty is important for you, so your books might be arranged in a certain color scheme. The same applies to your clothes, furniture, and anything else that is susceptible to your sense of style.

Despite your calmness, you are a headstrong person who is too fixed in their ways. People also experience your defensiveness when they attack or offend something or someone you like.

Gemini

Gemini risings are radiant and full of energy. Ruled by Mercury, they love soaking up knowledge and sharing it with everyone else. They are naturally sociable individuals who love conversing with everyone, whether they are in their social circles or not.

People see you as a curious and knowledgeable individual. To others, you are the kind of person who people can strike up a conversation about any topic, and you always have something to add. People close to you see you as moody and can't predict when the shift will happen, but they have become used to it.

Being a Gemini rising means that you are a shapeshifter. It is not that you like change; it is that change is a necessary element for your well-being. This does not mean that you like instability; on the contrary, stability is important to you. However, you like it when there is a change in your surroundings. For example, you do not need to change your main group of friends, but you like to have new people to talk to whenever possible. The same applies to everything else, your taste in clothing, materials that you read, the food you eat, etc.

Cancer

Cancer rising are seen as sweet and caring individuals. Your friends know you are sensitive and emotional, much more so than you let on. You might show the world that you are tough and unbothered, but that could not be further from the truth. You are thoughtful, caring, and affectionate.

People see you as someone who values comfort and needs their alone time frequently. That is because you are sensitive, so you pick on various energies throughout the day. Naturally, after the day is done, you will want to sit alone to recharge.

You are most likely the secret keeper in your social circle, and people come to you when they need to be comforted or taken care of. You have this maternal energy that makes people feel safe around you.

Being a Cancer rising means that you worry about safety and stability. You might spend your time worrying about money or working a lot, which is why you appear hardworking.

Leo

Ruled by the Sun, nothing can take the spotlight away from you. You are seen as a shining individual; whether it is through your talents, intellectualism, or looks, whatever it is, it is working for you.

People see you as a loving and protective person. They might get tired of how much you monopolize the conversation, but your friends might see it as a lovable quirk. You have a strong sense of self, drive, and willpower. You are naturally optimistic, and people love that about you. Your optimism is contagious, and people might feel lighter around you because of your positive outlook.

Perfectionism might set you back a bit because, deep down, you are afraid of failure. Rest assured, Leo, rising; you have nothing to be afraid of. You can accomplish whatever you set your mind on, so redirect your attention from fear to your goals.

Virgo

Mercury rules Virgo risings; this makes you seem very organized and have a fixed mindset that is not susceptible to change. People might find you a bit too fixed in your ways, but that is the same quality that makes them know they can depend on you.

Virgo risings are helpful by nature, and you might always be ready to go to the aid of anyone in need. You have a crystal-clear picture of how to help others. You tend to be the person who helps other people get their lives together because of your sense of structure and organizational skills.

Speaking of organization, people see you as an organized person. This does not mean that you always are, and it just means that things about you give people the sense that you are organized, even if you are not.

Represented by the goddess Astraea, Virgo risings ooze strong feminine energy. It may show in their appearance, body language, or how they connect to their emotions and care for others.

Libra

Ruled by Venus, Libra risings are physically attractive. People think you are put-together, stylish, and pretty, and this is because Libra is all about balance, beauty, and art. Speaking of which, you are most likely to be artistic or just have this artsy flair around you. You are someone who appreciates art and knows its value.

People might come to you when they need a mediator because you are a natural communicator and a peacemaker. You know how to view a situation from different perspectives, which makes you objective. People tend to trust your judgment because they know you will be compassionate and fair.

Anyone who has talked to you long enough will believe you are an intelligent and composed individual. They also think you are a bit talkative and might be attracted to co-dependent relationships. Whether this is true or not, Libra risings are known to be drawn to companionship, so make sure you lead a healthy relationship built upon strong boundaries.

Scorpio

Pluto rules Scorpio risings; this gives you an intensity that can be both enticing and intimidating to others. You have this allure that fascinates people when they meet you. Your mysteriousness and quietness lure people right into your charm.

As a Scorpio rising, you need to know that your energy is not for everyone. Some will find you mesmerizing, while your reserved demeanor will put others off. As intense as you are, you are also very sensitive. Scorpio's element is water, so you have a rich inner emotional life that runs deep. This gives you an emotional depth that can make you an exceptional understanding and emphatic individual.

Since your rising sign is a water element, your intuition is strong. Your sensitivity does not just make you emotionally sensitive; it also strengthens your intuition. You might find that you notice and sense things that other people miss.

Sagittarius

Sagittarius risings are known for their optimism and their sharp intellect, and this is because Jupiter rules you. This planet makes you feel like life is always a half-full cup, and this attitude enriches your intellectualism.

People see you as an optimistic person, even when it is not on purpose, and they enjoy conversing with you on philosophical topics because your mind is not afraid to venture into unconventional topics and theories.

Your friends might see you as an adventurer in the literal and figurative sense. They feel like you are always up for any spontaneous endeavors. You might be the person who suggests going on a trip or going on an unplanned car ride to a different city. You also might be the person who travels with their minds a lot, so you venture into topics that others might not think deeply about as much as you do.

People see you as a person who is full of energy; you are like the life of the party all the time. They also see you as a goal-oriented person, so whatever you aim for, you usually reach.

Capricorn

Saturn rules Capricorn risings, so you might have an unintentional serious resting face. People might think you are solemn and reserved when they first meet you, but that quickly changes when they are exposed to your sun sign.

Capricorn risings are known for their work ethic, maturity, and strong sense of responsibility. People know that they can depend on you and love this quality about you. You understand what it takes to build an empire or be a cooperative team member, and your work colleagues respect this about you.

Your friends see you as a dependable friend who has got their backs. They are also more than familiar with your sarcasm and dry sense of humor. They might feel worried about you sometimes because of your working hours, but they understand your maturity and dedication when it comes to achieving your career-oriented goals.

Aquarius

As an Aquarius rising individual, you are someone who looks unique and original. You also present yourself as innovative with an inquisitive mind. Everyone who meets you thinks that you are a humanitarian, and they are right. You care about unity, justice, and everything that is good for the earth and the collective humanity.

Emotionally, you may appear cold and distant at first, but that quality quickly changes when people know you on a deeper level. If you have an emotionally warm sun or moon sign, then you are definitely not cold and aloof.

Uranus rules your rising sign, so you might be leading an eccentric lifestyle. This eccentricity may show in your walk, body language, clothes, views, and philosophies. Not everyone will appreciate your originality, but the right people do, so keep them close.

As an Aquarius rising, you might deal with emotional commitment, whether it is towards things like subscribing to a gym or romantic relationships. Uranus is all about change and the unexpected, so commitment can make you feel as if you are stuck, which is a feeling you loathe.

Pisces

Pisces risings wear their hearts on their sleeves. You are empathetic, sensitive, and sweet. People do not need to talk to you for too long to see these qualities. Those who spend time around you notice you often spend most of your time in your head. You have this dreamy, ethereal quality about you, and it shows.

Your rising sign is ruled by Neptune, the planet of art, illusion, psychic abilities, compassion, and spiritual enlightenment. That said, as a rising sign, you appreciate and embody these qualities.

You are a water sign ruled by Neptune, which means that you have an exceptionally strong intuition. You are sensitive to everything and everyone. You also feel vibrations, the earth, and the universe, and your compassion and empathy are for people, animals, and plants. People might feel like you are almost always drained, but the more you practice protecting your energy, the more energy you will have.

Chapter 5: The Lunar Houses, or Nakshatras

The lunar houses, also known as the lunar mansions, are part of the eclectic plane. As the moon orbits around the earth, it crosses different constellations, and these constellations are known as the "lunar houses."

It is the same concept with the sun and constellations. The earth orbits around the sun, crossing one of the twelve constellations every month. The moon does the same things as well, with a few exceptions.

The moon orbits the earth much faster than the earth orbits the sun, so naturally, it crosses the constellations faster. Also, the constellations it meets differ from the twelve ones we know.

The moon orbits the earth faster than the sun.
https://pixabay.com/es/photos/luna-luna-llena-mar-cielo-2762111/

Ancient civilizations studied the lunar houses and incorporated them into their interpretations. To this day, people still use lunar houses to learn more about themselves and the world.

Lunar houses are used in Vedic astrology and are known as the Hindu nakshatras. They are also known as Manazil al-Qamar in Arabic astrology and Chinese sieu in Chinese astrology. There are 28 lunar houses in Arabic and Chinese astrology but only 27 nakshatras in Vedic astrology.

In Vedic astrology, the moon represents our intuition and our inner selves. The moon is the lord of these 27 lunar mansions, representing different parts of ourselves. The word Nakshatras represents our life force. This means that you can check the factors that affect your life force. These factors could be anything from the weather to emotional and mental well-being.

Each Nakshatra has four Padas; each Pada represents the four elements. So, the first Pada is called Agni and represents fire, Prithivi is earth, Vayu is air, and Jai is water. Now you might be wondering, how are these Nakshatras and Padas connected to the twelve constellations?

Well, the 360 degrees of the sky are divided between the twelve constellations, each of them covering 30 degrees. Now, each 27 Nakashatra covers 13 degrees and 20 minutes of the 30 degrees. Then each Pada covers 3 degrees and 20 minutes of the 13 degrees.

In Vedic astrology, your sun sign and Nakahsatra are calculated per the Sidereal zodiac, not the tropical zodiac. Western astrology uses the tropical system. However, this system was accurate when it was first created. This means that it was only accurate about 2000 years ago. On the other hand, the Sidereal zodiac calculates the current location of the stars.

This calculation is a bit confusing. Luckily, you do not have to calculate the stars yourself. All you need to do is search for a Nakshatra calculator and then insert your data. The website will ask for your name, birthdate, time of birth, and the country and state you were born in. Make sure you have accurate information so you can receive accurate results.

There are 27 Nakshatras, and each of them has four Padas. This can be difficult to navigate and keep track of. This is why this book covers each Nakshatra and thoroughly explains each Pada. You will find that each chapter covers the lunar mansion it is connected to; this way, you can keep track of all the mansions.

The Nakshatras: Characteristics of Each

1. Ashvini

Degree: 00° oo' - 13° 20' Aries.

Name: The Horse Goddess

People who are connected to this mansion are natural healers. They are skilled with energy healing, herbs, and medicine. They are children at heart and love exploring new places and going on adventures. They are prone to boredom, so they pack their schedules with tasks and activities. They are a bit impulsive and irresponsible at times. They can also feel agitated and become arrogant when their life does not go according to their plans.

2. Bharani

Degree: 13° 2o' - 26° 40' Aries.

Name: The River of Souls

Natives born with mansions in their charts are passionate, sensitive, and artistic individuals. They have a binary mindset, and it is either black or white with them, which is why they sometimes tend to go to the extreme sides of the spectrum. Their views might also be idealistic too, but that is because they always strive to reach perfection. These individuals have a spiritual side to them that they do not show. They will go through transformative phases and realize how powerful their willpower is.

3. Krittika

Degree: 26° 40' - Aries - 1000' Taurus.

Name: The Star of Fire

These individuals are loving nurturers and natural leaders. They can be strongly committed to an idea or principle and lead by example. For instance, honesty is very important to them, but they do not see how harmful it can sometimes be. They can be honest, but they can also be sensitive with their honesty. They can be intense at times, especially when overwhelmed by emotions. This can make them impulsive and irrational at times. During this lifetime, they will learn to control their temper and act instead of simply reacting.

4. Rohini

Degree: 10° 23' - 23°- 20' Taurus.

Name: The Red Goddess

People born in this mansion are sensual, attractive, and lovers of all that is beautiful. They are softly spoken, and they know how to charm others. They are also artistic; they love to look at art and maybe artists themselves. They enjoy everything comfortable, luxurious, and different. They may need to watch out for being too materialistic.

5. Mrigashirsha

Degree: 23° 20' - Taurus - 06° 40' Gemini

Name: The Star of Searching

These individuals are travelers. They don't like to stay in the same place for too long, and they do not associate with what is conventional and stereotypical. They are also always chasing knowledge, which makes them well-read intellectuals, and they don't necessarily have firm beliefs because their perspective is always changing.

6. Ardra

Degree: 06° 40' - 20°00' Gemini

Name: The Tear Drop

People born under this star are bold, smart, curious, and determined. Astrologers have noticed that these individuals reap many rewards in their life, but it only comes from their commitment and patience. Their impulsiveness and impatience might step in the way of their success. This is why these individuals must contain their temper and learn to wait. These people are often writers, speakers, or work in the media,

7. Punarvasu

Degree: 20° 00' - Gemini - 03° 20' Cancer

Name: The Light Bringer

Individuals born under this star are sensitive, creative, artistic, and attached to their families. They like to stay in the comfort of their own house most of the time so that they can enjoy their own company. They love reading poetry and traveling. These individuals tend to have a spiritual perspective on life. However, they still worry about the smallest of things.

8. Pushya

Degree: 03° 20' -16° 40' Cancer

Name: Nourishment

These individuals are wise and mature. They have their own moral compass and follow it throughout their lives. They are communicative and know how to use their words. They are humanitarians at heart. They will likely incorporate their creativity with their charity work and other humanitarian activities they might pick up.

9. Ashlesha

Degree: 16° 40' - 30° 00' Cancer

Name: The Coiled Serpent

This star represents Kundalini, which is the divine energy that is within everyone. People born under this star might unlock their kundalini without even trying. They are independent, brave, and incredibly intuitive. They gain their wisdom by looking into the darkest parts of themselves and accepting themselves regardless.

10. Magha

Degree: 00° oo' - 13° 20' Leo.

Name: The Forefathers

Natives born under this star have an air of royalty surrounding them. During their lifetime, they will feel as if they have a connection to their ancestors. They may or may not be able to channel them, but they will want to follow in their footsteps any way they can. These people are generous and loving but must be careful with their earthly desires.

11. Purva Phalguni

Degree: 13° 20' - 26° 40' Leo

Name: The World Tree Goddess

The goddess associated with this star is the goddess of love, romance, and marriage. This makes the people connected to her affectionate, loving, and looking for their significant others. These people attract good fortune, and they are generally blessed. They tend to over-indulge in anything that makes them feel good, creating unnecessary trouble for them.

12. Uttara Phalguni

Degree: 26° 40' Leo - 10° 00' Virgo

Name: The Marriage Goddess

These people have magnetic personalities. They are spiritual and believe in unearthly concepts. People view them as loving and compassionate beings, which is true. They care about justice and might be attracted to fight for their and other people's rights during their lifetime. One thing that they need to pay attention to is their need to be with someone. They must learn to be with themselves first before being with another.

13. Hasta

Degree: 10° 00' - 23° 00' Virgo

Name: Skilled Activities

These natives are intelligent, creative, and caring. They are interested in metaphysics, psychology, art, and the spiritual realm. Their personalities are difficult to understand, but people will love them anyway. They might be a bit indecisive and find it difficult to commit to one belief because they constantly change their views.

14. Chitra

Degree: 23° 20' Virgo - 06° 40' Libra

Name: The Jewel

These people need to shine in the world. They believe in their mental capabilities, creativity, and their potential. They do not want to leave this world unseen and unheard. They are not the most flexible people; sometimes, they don't understand why everybody can't be like them or do what they do. They are deep thinkers and analyzers. They may want to be careful of ego and arrogance; they must always find their balance.

15. Swati

Degree: 06° 40' - 20° 20' Libra

Name: The Wind God

These individuals love learning and creating art. They are independent beings who will not tolerate being confined to anything. They naturally shine in the world, but their humanitarian work makes them shine from within. They sometimes feel lost in the world, which is why they go down many paths until they find their own. They need to honor themselves to reach inner peace.

16. Vishakha

Degree: 2o° 00' Libra - 03° 20' Scorpio

Name: The Moon of Power

These natives are brave and ambitious. They can be competitive at times, but they do it healthily. These individuals are goal-oriented, so it is fair to say that they are dedicated and committed to achieving them. They may burn themselves out in the process, so they need to be more balanced with their routine and habits. They have this serious outlook on life that takes away the fun elements that make life tolerable.

17. Anuradha

Degree: 03° 20' - 16° 40' Scorpio

Name: The Moon of Friendship

Natives born under the star are friendly, sociable, and confident. They are highly sensitive and feel everything. This will affect their emotional well-being, which is why they need to tend to themselves before anyone else. They love traveling and exploring foreign places. They are also passionate lovers and know how to be gentle with their partners. They might take an interest in statistics or accounting because they love numbers.

18. Jyeshtha

Degree: 16° 40' - 30° 00' Scorpio

Name: The Wisdom Crone

Natives born under this mansion are talented, skilled, and crafty. They are likely to struggle with self-esteem issues, which destroys their confidence. They are interested in the occult, mysticism, and wisdom that can only be found in the dark places in life. They have strong personalities and can be arrogant at times.

19. Mula

Degree: 30° 30' - 13° 20' Sagittarius

Name: The Root of all things

These individuals are philosophical, passionate, and brave. They like to go with the flow and do not like their lives to be controlled by others. They like to watch things run their course. Their philosophical perspective on life will help them achieve the kind of balance that will ground them.

20. Purva Ashadha

Degree: 13° 20' - 26° 40' Sagittarius

Name: The Moon of Early Victory

Natives born under this star will be very successful during this lifetime. They are strong debaters and communicators with powerful personalities. Astrologers say that they will reach success early on in their lives. They are also intuitive and full of empathy. People like talking to these natives because they feel seen and heard by them. Their spirituality helps them through the difficult phases in their lives.

21. Uttara Ashadha

Degree: 26° 40' Sagittarius - 10° 00' Capricorn

Name: The Moon of Later Victory

These individuals care about humanitarian work. They have a lot of enthusiasm for life, but they can also be lazy and indifferent at times. They need to find their balance if they are to accomplish their goals. During this lifetime, they will have strong bonds with others and find lifelong friends.

22. Shravana

Degree: 10° 00' - 23° 20' Capricorn

Name: The Moon of Listening

These individuals are lifelong students and teachers at the same time. They are likely to pick a career where they can constantly absorb new information. They will also collect many books during their lifetime or have a large e-book library. They are sensitive souls who care about other people. They are also likely to achieve success later in their lives.

23. Danishta

Degree: 23° 20' Capricorn - 06° 40' Aquarius

Name: The Drummer

These natives have liberal views and need their freedom and personal space above everything else. They like to be in control; otherwise, they feel unsafe in the world. They would like to be powerful people in the world and associate themselves with powerful individuals. This could make them arrogant and abuse their power if they let themselves.

24. Shatabhisha

Degree: 06° 30' - 20° 00' Aquarius

Name: The Divine Healer

These individuals are self-healers. It is as if they are channeling that Chiron energy and have become wounded healers like Chiron. This means they can improvise with others and give them the tools to heal themselves. Other than their healing capabilities, they are intelligent beings interested in metaphysical and psychological studies.

25. Purva Bhadrapada

Degree: 20° 00' Aquarius - 03° 20' Pisces

Name: The Fire Dragon

People born under this star are unique and a bit magical. They have an eccentric outlook on life, which gives them their mystical flair. They will go through transformative experiences that will change them for the better. They are visionaries and often have unusual ideas for improving the world. They are capable of so many things, but they need to be more compassionate with themselves if they are to make their dreams come true.

26. Uttara Bhadrapada

Degree: 03° 20' - 20° 16' Pisces

Name: The Dragon of the Deep

These natives are introverted, quiet, and keep to themselves. However, these are the kind of qualities that will make them reach their awakening and experience their inner wisdom. They can be a bit secretive, but that is their nature. These people will make good writers and communicators.

27. Revati

Degree: 16° 40' - 30° 00' Pisces

Name: The Moon of Splendor

People born under this mansion are sensitive, intuitive, and love nature and animals. They are also a bit artistic and enjoy creating art. They might have been born into a difficult environment and might have been disappointed by people at a young age. They are highly spiritual, though, and their spirituality helps them through difficult times.

Section Two: The Earth Signs

Each zodiac sign has an element that shapes thinking processes and mannerisms. These elements are divided into four sections –each contains three zodiac signs.

Earth element contains Taurus, Virgo, and Capricorn. These zodiac signs are completely different from one another, so naturally, they behave differently. However, the one thing they have in common is their element, which means they also share a few traits.

Earth signs are more rooted in earthly things, hence the name. They are not especially known for contemplating abstract or spiritual thoughts. Still, they spend time thinking about things that are taking place in the present.

To paint a clearer picture, earth signs find pleasure in food, sex, vanity, relationships, and possessions. Each earth sign relates to these things differently. A Capricorn might not care about perfectionism the same way a Virgo would or take much pleasure through the five senses as a Taurus would. A Virgo might not take as much pleasure in food as a Taurus, but it still matters.

Earth signs are known for their loyalty, perseverance, dedication, modesty, being grounded, and goal-oriented people. They are also notorious for their stubbornness, materialism, possessiveness, and indulgence.

To reiterate, not all earth signs fully project these qualities. They do have these qualities, but the intensity varies from one sign to another. It also depends on the level of awareness that the person has. With enough awareness, these qualities could be heightened or diminished.

Chapter 6: Taurus, the Materialistic Bull

Taurus symbol.
Phantom Open Emoji maintainers and contributors, CC BY 3.0
<https://creativecommons.org/licenses/by/3.0>, via Wikimedia Commons:
https://commons.wikimedia.org/wiki/File:Phantom_Open_Emoji_2649.svg

Date: April 20th - May 20th

The bull is a fairly relaxed animal that likes eating and sunbathing in a field. The only time a bull is aggravated is when it butts heads with another bull; other than that, it is a pretty relaxed being.

People with strong Taurus placements are very much the same. This is why the bull is the assigned symbol for this constellation. Sun, Moon, or Rising Taurus individuals exude these qualities.

They enjoy life through their five senses, and they are relaxed most of the time. They are humble, and they don't necessarily like getting into fights.

When they fight with someone, they are usually headbutting, and it is probably because they are being stubborn.

There are different legends behind the image of the bull and Taurus, and one dates back to ancient Babylon. In the Epic of Gilgamesh, the goddess Ishtar was fighting Gilgamesh and Enkidu, so she sent Heaven's bull, or Taurus, to kill Gilgamesh. However, Enkidu pulls the bull apart and throws its body into the sky – creating the Taurus constellation.

In Ancient Greece, Zeus took on the form of a beautiful white bull to approach princess Europa. The Phoenician princess rode the bull, and once they landed on land, Zeus transformed into his original form and professed his love for her. When Europe died, Zeus sent her to the sky, creating a constellation of her riding the bull.

Key Phrase: "I Have"

This constellation is mainly concerned with two things, financial security, and ownership. Not to mention that it rules the second house, which is the house of possessions. With these characteristics, it makes sense that a Taurus' key phrase is "I have." They are also possessive over their humans as much as they're possessive of their own property. So, there is depth to a Taurus' possessiveness. It goes for material and nonmaterial things, and it mainly stems from wanting security.

Strengths

- Appreciates art
- Artistic
- Dependable
- Financially secure
- Friendly

- Humble
- Loyal
- Patient
- Sensual
- Thorough

Weaknesses

- Explosive anger
- Hedonism
- Indulgent
- Materialistic
- Stubborn
- Uncompromising

Pet Peeves

- Being rushed
- Interruption
- Impracticality
- Sudden change

Ruling Planet

Venus, the planet of love and harmony, rules this constellation. Taurus individuals tend to be fine-looking, have comforting voices, and always have style. They care about the materialistic side of life. Their priorities will involve earthly things like money, ownership, food, and company with loved ones.

Taurus individuals are not vain; however, they do find their sense of security in worldly things. So, they may seem to be fixated on this aspect of life, but they still have depth to their character.

They also have a penchant for being around aesthetically beautiful places or pleasing settings. They appreciate art and can relax and enjoy life in places stimulating their five senses.

Sun Sign

Taurus Sun sign people have grounding personalities. They are humble and kind and like helping others out, mainly because they are the kind of people you can depend on. Not to mention how responsible and dependable these individuals are.

They are generally patient, but a Taurus Sun can get angry and aggressive when someone has stepped over the line. They are not very confrontational, but once they have accumulated enough transgressions from one person, their anger is explosive, and they might yell or be aggressive with this person.

Financial security is vital for their well-being. They need to know that they have good financial backup whenever they need it. They also care a lot about the safety of their family and the people they love, so they may offer advice on financial planning or suggest investment in profitable markets.

These individuals are stubborn; you can't change their minds easily. Earthly pleasures bring them gratification, so they may indulge in food or entertainment, especially when stressed.

Moon Sign

Moon Sign Taurus is full of love and has this nurturing quality. They are understanding, caring, and give amazing hugs. These individuals may feel anxious about their safety in the world. Financial security is one of their goals, and they work hard to achieve it. These individuals may find security in property and investments.

Moon Sign Taurus is artistic. They are probably talented when it comes to the arts. They appreciate all kinds of art and are probably attached to music. They also might find their creative expression in painting, singing, or playing an instrument. There are a lot of Taurus Moons who like to make pottery, which makes sense since they are an earth sign, after all.

Rising Sign

The rising sign takes place in the first house. Taurus rising individuals are attractive. People see them as calm, collected, and serene. Of course, this does not mean that they are actually this calm, but they appear as such in front of others.

They are very well-dressed, and their style is chic and elegant. People like how their voice sounds, and they have a nice laugh. Taurus rising might like a good debate, but they may appear stubborn at first or throughout the debate.

Taurus in the first house are kind and helpful, and people appreciate these qualities about them. They offer a nice, calming presence in any situation, and it is as if they can ground you just by being around you.

Taurus through the Houses

Second

Taurus rules the second house; naturally, the energy is amplified here. Taurus, in this house, is fixated on financial security, and they get it from materialistic possessions. They are likely to invest in real estate or any lucrative investment that promises money in return.

Their financial fixation brings out their dedication and sense of responsibility; on the other hand, it can make them rigid and anxious about their financial situation. They are naturally talented in their profession of choice, and they are likely to succeed in whatever professional endeavor they seek. These natives are fond of food and art, so they are likely to indulge and spend money on them.

Third

Natives with Taurus in the third house often communicate slowly and process life and conversations according to their own pace. Life is understood more when it speaks to their senses. A third house Taurus is more likely to remember an experience if it stimulated their senses.

They are likely to be dependable with their siblings, aunts and uncles, and close friends. These natives have a natural ability to create. Not only will they spend hours honing their craft, but they will also easily incorporate it within their schedule. Debates with these individuals can be a bit frustrating because they are unyielding and too stubborn to change their outlook.

Fourth

Fourth house natives were probably raised in strict households. Their parents were probably traditional and concerned with financial security. They might have been too stuck in their ways to appreciate how the fourth house native's creativity and uniqueness. On the other hand, their parents might have been caring and loving. They were devoted to keeping the child safe and financially secure.

These natives are especially caring for their loved ones, usually in a nurturing way. They are also sentimental, so they are most likely to collect items and place them around the house. They need to keep up with their habits and are unlikely to drop an activity they've incorporated into their schedule.

Fifth

Fifth house Taurus express themselves through their art. They could be naturally talented singers and musicians. They feel joy or gain pleasure from the material world. They're likely to indulge in anything that brings them pleasure. They're also likely to spend a lot of money, so they might have to deal with financial fluctuations every now and again.

These natives enjoy attending concerts, theater, and visiting museums. They are also romantic, sensitive, and selfless with their romantic partners. Although, at times, they can be unintentionally dismissive because they have a self-gratifying complex. These natives need to be careful with hedonism and indulgence because they can quickly lose track of their reality and cause damage to everything they hold dear.

Sixth

These natives are compassionate and resourceful. They might have a few health challenges throughout their lives. This could be caused by their fixation on work or service for others that they neglect themselves and their well-being.

Sometimes sixth house natives forget to feel and express gratitude because they strive for perfectionism. Often, this quality shows up in their work, and there is no doubt that their work is of high quality. However, they can project their perfectionism onto others who do not see the beauty in their efforts.

Their spirituality can also take a hit, so they often need to remind themselves that there are other things they need to tend to. As dedicated, reliable, and compassionate as these natives are, they sometimes forget to apply these qualities to themselves.

Seventh

People with Taurus on the cusp require a partner with more Taurus-like qualities. They do not necessarily have to be Taurus, but they ideally should have some of their characteristics. An ideal partner for this native is someone who is stable, reliable, dependable, and financially secure.

These individuals can be a bit vain when picking their partners, so they must be careful with whom they choose to be intimate. They can also come off as a bit controlling, which does not always work in partnerships.

These people tend to have a good sense of balance in their partnerships, whether it is within a romantic or professional partnership. They might not be the most flexible, but they are not too rigid in their ways that they would upset the balance because they are more comfortable with their stubbornness.

Eighth

Natives with Taurus in the eighth house are good with finances. They like investing, but they are notorious for going through financial fluctuations. They like spending and making money, so money comes and goes with this person. They know how to make money out of thin air, but they either use their talents and profit from them or juggle multiple jobs at a time.

Accepting change does not come easy to these individuals. They have slow periods of transformation because they don't process everything they are going through. Their emotional health is often neglected because these individuals have a difficult time processing and feeling intense emotions.

These individuals have a hard time letting things or people go. They have a difficult relationship with death. They are a bit controlling, so they have difficulty understanding that someone has died or simply left their life.

Ninth

People with Taurus in the ninth house tend to have a strong practical approach to life. They might display rigidity when confronted with different philosophies and faiths. They understand and accept different views but rarely consider changing their beliefs or questioning them.

You might spend a lot of money when you are traveling, and you might have a knack for creating money abroad or from foreign clients. You might be a well-read person, but you would not consider yourself a philosopher. In fact, there is a high chance that you think philosophy and similar topics are a waste of time.

Tenth

These natives have an intimidating reputation. Not everyone will like them, but they are mostly well respected within their community. People with Taurus in the tenth house might enjoy a career in decorating, cooking, design, business, fashion, or managing finances.

With this placement, their reputation for being reliable and dependable precedes them. They are almost always well put together; people admire their sense of style. They are also friendly with people and rarely pick up fights unless someone has crossed the line with them.

They are friendly with professional colleagues but find it difficult to cooperate in group projects. Their stubbornness can prove fatal in the workplace. They always seem to be in conflict with their boss or colleagues, especially when they are part of a professional group project.

Eleventh

These natives are full of love and care, especially towards their friends. Their friendships tend to be stable and sturdy. They are the kind of people who have managed to stay friends with their childhood friends. They are generous with their time, emotions, and love.

These natives care about the well-being of the earth and their fellow humans, so they are most likely to donate to charities and help strangers. They have a sense of unity with everyone and everything in the universe, making them feel whole.

Twelfth

These natives tend to be shy and hide their talents from the world. They might have difficulty finding their creativity and take even longer to figure out their creative expression.

They may be a bit closed off and a bit introverted, like spending time alone in the safety and comfort of their home, or t be dealing with greed as karma, so they need to develop strict boundaries with themselves, as well as how to master their hedonism.

They also need to learn to be more flexible and present with others. They might seem happy and open, but in reality, they are preoccupied with their own safety, especially with their financial security.

Taurus and Lunar Houses

In Vedic astrology, this constellation is connected to the following lunar houses, Krittika, Rohini, and Mrigasira. These three Nakshatras, or lunar houses, are believed to be in the Taurus constellation.

Krittika

Second Pada

Second, Pada individuals are concerned more with earthly matters, which makes them a bit materialistic. Vedic astrologists say that people born in the second pada seem indifferent when talking to others, they might care about the person or the conversation. Still, one can never tell that they do because their eyes are not expressive enough. Vedic astrologists also add that second pada individuals have a natural talent in psychic abilities or utilizing their intuition when reading tarot or interpreting someone's natal chart.

Third Pada

Third, Pada natives are responsible for their work and those they care about. They might have an idealistic outlook on life that may hinder their progress. Their idealism might lead them to perfectionism, making them lose their sense of reality. Vedic astrologists say that these natives may have a lazy posture and a mature gaze when talking to others.

Fourth Pada

Fourth, Pada natives have emotional depth. They are intelligent, caring, sensitive, and creative. They are interested in education, so they are likely to feed their intellectual thirst by reading or pursuing higher education. They are also interested in learning more about their philosophies and faiths. Vedic astrologists claim that fourth pada natives might be teachers, soldiers, policemen, surgeons, fighters, warriors, housemaids, or the head of an orphanage.

Rohini

First Pada

First, Pada individuals seem calm, serene, and gentle. They are talented when it comes to business and finances. They are also charming enough to get out of tough situations. They also have a natural ability to express their feelings clearly. They respect others, which makes other people respect them as well. However, they are prone to frustration because they expect quick results. They also tend to be quite materialistic.

Second Pada

Second, Pada natives have a wide connection, thanks to their large social circles. They are mainly concerned with their financial security, which brings about dedication and a sense of responsibility in their profession of choice. They are also experts in planning, they know how to reach their goals, and they do not mind how long the road takes. Vedic astrologists say that these natives will likely profit from artistic endeavors, nursing, or business.

Third Pada

Vedic astrologists say third Pada natives will likely succeed later in life or at least after their 30s. They are well-balanced all-rounders and are talented in business, finance, and anything artistic in nature. They may not have a good relationship with their mother, but this is also fixed later in life.

Fourth Pada

Fourth, Pada natives focus on home security and nurturing their loved ones through financial security. They love the art of trading, and they are good at it. They are also interested in religious texts and maybe a bit religious. Their income is most likely to come through short travels, and they are more talented in business than in the arts.

Mrigasira

First Pada

First Pada individuals have sharp mental faculties. They are intelligent and have piercing gazes. They have gentle faces and sharp nails. Vedic astrologists say they will have an average marriage and are more likely to have daughters. They are also curious and enthusiastic, especially in their professional field.

Second Pada

Natives born under this Pada have a good sense of humor. They are also artistic and may be talented singers or musicians. They are sociable, calculating, and practical. They might be a bit impatient, so they can get frustrated easily. These individuals are culturally aware and curious enough to learn about everything.

Chapter 7: Virgo, the Perfectionist

Virgo symbol.
Phantom Open Emoji maintainers and contributors, CC BY 3.0
<*https://creativecommons.org/licenses/by/3.0*>, *via Wikimedia Commons:*
https://commons.wikimedia.org/wiki/File:Phantom_Open_Emoji_264d.svg

Date: August 23 - September 22

This constellation represents Virgo, the maiden. According to astrologists, the 'M' symbol stands for 'Maiden.' It's the only one representing a goddess, which makes it unique.

Now, you might be asking yourself, why does Virgo have a goddess as its symbol? In the Golden Age of Ancient Greece,

Astraea, the daughter of Zeus, lived among humans. She looked after them, provided them with grains and other gifts, and often shared her godly wisdom. However, it quickly changed with the beginning of the Silver Age. Mankind got angrier, more volatile, and rejected the gods. The gods punished them, and mankind repented and disobeyed, which created a vicious cycle.

One day, the goddess gathered the humans together and warned them that their lives would be destroyed if they did not work on their behavior. Unfortunately, they didn't heed the goddess' warning and continued with the same behavior.

Astraea could not bear to live among the humans any longer, so she flew to the sky and lived among the stars like Virgo. She is known as the maiden because she is wise, humble, and pure.

Key Phrase: "I Analyze"

Virgos are blessed with an active and sharp mind. Their brain scans and analyzes everything in its way. They are natural observers who don't miss anything, especially details.

Virgos observe everything; nothing escapes their gaze in their social or professional lives. After they are done with their observations, they begin to analyze them and critically judge them. They need to make sense of everything they see. They cannot let any questions go unanswered, so they will spend an infinite amount of time deciphering and analyzing until they have reached an answer.

Strengths

- Altruistic
- Analytical
- Helpful
- Logical
- Modest
- Organized

Weaknesses

- Controlling
- Critical

- Obsessive

- Perfectionism

- **Pet Peeves:** Crowded spaces

- Tardiness

Ruling Planet

Mercury rules this constellation. This planet is known to rule the logical side of the brain. It rules the analytical side, conversations, writing, reading, and other mental faculties. People with significant Virgo placements are affected by Mercury.

Mercury makes Virgo intelligent, analytical, logical, and quick on its feet. This planet is the reason behind Virgo's organizational skills and sharp mind. Astrologers advise people with prominent Virgo placements should check their Mercury aspects. These aspects will provide them with valuable insights.

For instance, people who suffer from concentration problems, depression, anxiety, and disorganized thinking, can find out which planet is causing this unfavorable aspect with Mercury and how they can overcome it.

Sun Sign

Virgo Sun signs are hardworking, modest individuals. They can dedicate themselves completely to anything they set their mind to. They are independent and perfectly capable of tending to their own needs.

Even though Virgo Suns do not need anyone to take care of them, they might need someone to take care of them. This might result in co-dependent relationships, so Virgo Suns need self-awareness when entering a relationship.

They love conversing with others, and they love to gossip. Not that they necessarily love to gossip, but nothing escapes Virgo's gaze, so they will have a thing or two to talk about when it is gossip time.

Virgos will not ask for support, but that does not mean they do not need it. They deal with various emotional hurdles and need to be reminded of how amazing they are by their friends.

Moon Sign

Virgo Moon signs love feeling needed. They feel their best when they know they are being useful to others because, deep down, they need to know that their existence is valuable and worthwhile.

These individuals' helpfulness knows no bounds, as long as it is not being abused. A little appreciation goes a long way with these folks. They do not need others to reciprocate their help; they need to know someone is also looking out for them.

This placement suggests a strong inner critic, judging everything they do. Virgo Moons need to learn to be more compassionate and kinder towards themselves. They need to know how to conquer and silence this voice and replace it with some self-care.

Unfortunately, these people quickly feel overwhelmed by stressful situations. They might overthink situations or feel like they are lost because of how much they are stressed. They are often shy and worry a lot; they get a sense of security by completing mundane errands daily. They are not the most ambitious people – but are dependable, realistic, and practical.

Rising Sign

Virgo rising people are well-put together, feminine, and have a classy look. They are always willing to help others and make their lives better. They are good planners and enjoy life more when they are organized or following a plan.

They are sweet, generous, and logical. They are willing to help you, so long as you listen to them. They do not like feeling like other people are not taking their advice, and this is where their controlling tendencies come to the surface.

Virgo rising is mentally agile, which is a great trait. However, they tend to overthink many details or develop anxiety. They are detail-oriented and meticulous, which makes them professionals in whatever they do. They always produce high-quality products.

They are known for being judgmental and critical. They do not have an ill intention when criticizing or judging someone; in reality, they are projecting. They have a strong inner-critic that judges everything they do, so Virgo risings project their inner-critic onto others, as well.

Virgo through the Houses

Second

People with this placement are difficult to satisfy. They are rarely happy with anything they have, and they feel like they always need to do more. Natives with this placement will work hard to earn their money, and even then, they will find something to criticize.

This is a difficult mindset to live with, which is why these natives need to work on feeling grateful. They need to recognize that it does not matter how much they have or how hard they have worked; what they already have is enough.

When these natives express gratitude, they will start to feel lighter and truly satisfied with what they have. People with this placement also struggle with self-worth. They feel like they are not enough or always find something to criticize about themselves. Expressing gratitude will also make them see their worth and value.

Third

Natives with this placement are blessed with intelligence, conversational skills, and mental agility. On the other hand, they are likely to develop an anxiety disorder. According to astrologists, individuals with this placement suffer from hypochondria prompted by their anxiety.

They need to restore their faith in themselves. At some point, they will see how much pain they have endured and seek healing. They are smart and disciplined enough to commit to their healing. However, their controlling tendencies might get in the way. They need to be strong enough to recognize that they are afraid to abandon their old ways and welcome new ones.

Fourth

Virgo in the fourth house indicates people who grew up with critical parents. As kids, they never felt as if they were enough, and they were made to feel as though they were always lacking or just not quite good enough – as if nothing they ever accomplished was sufficient.

These individuals had a cold relationship with one of their parents as kids. This took a toll on them, and as a result, they have developed a multitude of emotional hurdles that need healing.

Kids who grow up with Virgo in the fourth house either become high-achievers or underachievers. They either try their hardest to prove they are perfect, or they do not bother at all because they believe that whatever they accomplish will still not be enough.

Fifth

People with this placement find joy in fixing things or paying attention to details. They have a natural talent for pointing out problems and fixing them, and this makes them feel happy and useful.

The problem arises when these people start looking for companionship because they attract the wrong crowd. Either Virgo in the fifth house picks someone who needs healing or fixing, or damaged people flock towards them.

Unfortunately, these natives will learn the hard way that they do not need to fix anyone, nor does their worth come from fixing others or being useful to others.

Sixth

Virgo in the sixth house is in its home. This is a comfortable placement for the natives; they will lead healthy professional lives and care for themselves. Individuals with this placement have a natural talent for healing other people.

This placement indicates a career that the natives will absolutely love. They will feel joy and happiness when they are at work, and they will most likely help others through their job. Their career could entail anything from healing people to helping by offering some kind of service.

Individuals with Virgo in the sixth house are known for caring for their physical health. They will put themselves on a healthy diet, exercise, and hydrate regularly. They might take up yoga or any other activity that centers them.

Seventh

Natives with this placement have a caring side that is healing to other people. They are the kind of people who will lend a helping hand, whether they were asked for it or not.

They are likely to attract perfectionist partners. On the one hand, these partners may overwork themselves to achieve the unachievable; on the other hand, they might be too insecure to work for what they want.

Virgo in the seventh house will step in to help their partners, but they will also be critical of them. These natives need to accept people for who they are and provide help only when it is in their energy and time to do so.

Eighth

This placement is a bit difficult to manage. People with this placement can make their partners feel insufficient. They might focus on a lot of details that do not matter instead of staying present in reality and enjoying it.

These people do not know what it means to go with the flow, and everything needs to be mapped out and detailed. They are likely to have a mechanical sex life or one that follows a certain routine. Their lives are missing the spontaneous moments that make them enjoyable.

With Virgo in the house of death, these individuals might undergo a complete transformation in the areas associated with the eighth house. This transformation might be painful, but it will change them for the better.

Ninth

This is a comfortable placement for these natives. According to astrologers, these people will involve themselves in charity work. Virgos generally love helping others, but people with this placement are driven to help the collective as well.

They care about humanity and all living creatures. Their charity might take them abroad. They may be helping people from other countries or are involved with a foreign company that helps its people.

People with this placement will be challenged by their ego. They will need to go through a deep healing journey so that they understand who they are and who they are meant to be.

Tenth

Natives with Virgo in the tenth house are fixated on their professional goals. Astrologers describe them as "working bees," which is a very accurate description. These individuals have an early inkling of what they want to do in life.

They know what kind of career they want to have, and they are ready to do whatever it takes to achieve it. They are likely to be buried in assignments or paperwork; astrologists say this placement indicates careers in journalism or writing.

Eleventh

This is not an easy placement to manage. Usually, these people are sociable and love to make friends. However, the problem arises when they start getting close to people. They start to pick out flaws in their friends and become unhappy with them.

These natives find themselves in a cycle that has them building bridges and then burning them. These natives need to learn to accept people and, more importantly, accept themselves for who they are.

Twelfth

This karmic placement indicates that these natives need to learn to get in touch with their emotions so that they can help others as well. With Virgo in the twelfth house, these natives are here to raise other people's consciousness.

The more in tune they are with their emotions, the more compassionate they are. Their compassion will help them help others. Empathy and kindness are the tools that they will use to fulfill their karmic purpose.

These individuals are intelligent but will have trouble showing it. People will notice how smart they are when these natives are not showing just how bright they are.

Virgo and Lunar Houses

Uttara Phalguni Nakshatra

Second Pada

Individuals born in this Pada approach life with practicality and realistic expectations. They are neat and organized and have a structure for everything in their lives. They have walked into life with high standards and always try to live up to them. Their standards might look like a good thing on the surface, but in reality, it makes them judgmental and critical of others and themselves.

Third Pada

These natives are known for their sharp intelligence and intellectualism. They are successful in their professional lives and might reach managerial positions. However, they are known to take advantage of their positions and manipulate the system and people for their own gain.

Fourth Pada

These individuals are honorable and smart. They know how to take accountability for their actions and are not ashamed of them. They honor their health and bodies by taking care of their health. They are financially wealthy, and they are respected among their peers.

Hasta Nakshatra

First Pada

Natives who are born in this Pada are known for their intelligence and confidence. People describe them as fearless individuals who are not afraid of facing challenges. However, they might want to work on their communication skills because they come off as aggressive and hostile.

Second Pada

Vedic astrologers describe these natives as lovers of nature. They like to be next to the water, and they love animals. They are also musically gifted and fond of all types of art. They have problems with their parents and can be arrogant sometimes.

Third Pada

People who are born under this Pada make great debaters. They are naturally skilled when it comes to communication. They know how to access the information that they need just by conversing with others. Astrologers say that these natives will have careers related to trading or communicating with people.

Fourth Pada

According to Vedic astrologers, these people will receive an average education and possibly lead an average life. They might have to give up their career for their family. These individuals are inclined to become alcoholics, and they may become manipulative.

Chitra Nakshatra

First Pada

Astrologers describe these natives as physically attractive. During their lifetime, they will desire fame, power, and authority. They are said to be disloyal, cold, and cruel. They are likely to destroy people who stand in their way.

Second Pada

These people are perfectionists. They are likely to take on many projects in their lives and oversee other people's work. They have a great eye for detail and always strive to fix flaws and problems.

Chapter 8: Capricorn, the Disciplinarian

Capricorn symbol.
Phantom Open Emoji maintainers and contributors, CC BY 3.0
<https://creativecommons.org/licenses/by/3.0>, via Wikimedia Commons:
https://commons.wikimedia.org/wiki/File:Phantom_Open_Emoji_2651.svg

Date: December 22nd - January 19th

This constellation has one of the most interesting symbols. Many people think that Capricorn's symbol is the goat, but that is not entirely true. Capricorn is actually half goat and half fish.

Different civilizations drew the same interpretation of this constellation. For instance, the Ancient Egyptians noticed that this constellation had goat horns and a fish tale, but they did not give it a name.

On the other hand, Ancient Babylonia associated this constellation with Enki, the god of water, creation, and knowledge. Later the Ancient Greeks also assigned Pan, the satyr, to this constellation.

According to mythology, Zeus was escaping from Typhon, the monster with 100 dragon heads; Pan advised the god to turn into a goat with a fishtail to swim faster and escape to Egypt. When the god successfully escaped Typhon, he rewarded Pan by making him a half goat and half fish constellation.

Key Phrase: "I Use"

Capricorns are high-achievers and naturally logical - n they will find the necessary means to get to what they want. Nothing is too high or too impossible to reach, as long as they find the appropriate tool and use it.

As ambitious as Capricorns are, they are also morally ambiguous or take morally vague decisions. There is nothing wrong with having an active drive and an ambitious spirit. However, Capricorns will use anyone and anything to reach their goal.

Ideally, these people use their knowledge and similar means to achieve their goals, but since they are obsessed with status, they can use people or take advantage of certain situations just to have their dreams materialize in front of their eyes.

Strengths

- Ambitious
- Dedicated
- Disciplined
- Goal-oriented
- Leadership skills
- Practical
- Responsible
- Strong-willed

Weaknesses

- Condescending
- Greedy
- Irritable
- Materialistic
- Shallow
- Spiteful

Pet Peeves

- Cockiness
- Immaturity
- Irresponsible behavior

Ruling Planet

Saturn rules this constellation. This planet is like an authoritarian figure; in other words, it is like the father of the zodiac. It governs responsibilities, rules, laws, discipline, dedication, structure, life lessons, limitations, and hard work.

Capricorns are responsible and hardworking individuals. Their eye is always on the prize, and they never waver. They are not afraid of the amount of responsibility they need to take on to achieve their goals.

They are disciplined and dedicated to their daily routine. They don't feel bored as long as they know they are working towards their goal. Saturn is known for its limitations and restrictions, which is something that Capricorns learn during their lifetime. They need to understand their limitations and their place in this world.

More importantly, they need to know the value of the things they already have. Depending on their Saturn placements, they will experience a limitation in a certain area so that they learn their life lesson from the planet itself.

Sun Sign

Capricorn Sun signs are reliable and realistic. They have a serious outlook on life and know who they want to become and what their goals are. People may see Capricorn Suns as people who lead boring lives, but this is just a matter of perspective.

People with this placement do not think they have boring lives; on the contrary, their lives are full of purpose. They live their days achieving little goals, making baby steps towards fulfilling l their dreams.

This is why Capricorn Suns are responsible, dedicated, and detached from distractions. Their lifestyle can make them seem cold and distant, which would not be accurate. These individuals have a dry, sarcastic sense of humor, and their friends love that about them.

Moon Sign

Capricorn Moons are avid planners and taskmasters. This placement indicates that these individuals are at their best when they are being productive and working for something. It also suggests that they need healthy emotional boundaries so that they can function normally with others.

These individuals are innately financially literate. They do not need to be taught how to take care of themselves financially; they probably have been saving up and investing before anyone their age.

Their financial awareness gives them a sense of security and control. As long as Capricorn Moon feels that they are on top of things, they feel secure and comfortable. This placement also suggests that these individuals are harsh on themselves and expect unrealistic expectations of themselves.

This fuels their over-achiever side, but it also fuels their negative self-talk. Most Capricorn Moons hide behind their sarcasm and indifferent demeanor just to protect their vulnerable parts.

Rising Sign

Capricorn risings are focused and calculative. They may appear as cold and aloof at first, but their sharp demeanor fades away the more you know them. They have a unique sense of humor; they tend to be sarcastic most of the time.

They are not known for their friendliness, but they do not mean to be rude either. They just know better than to let anyone into their lives. They scan their surroundings and assess who is worth their time and who is not. In other words, they know their worth and do not let random people into their space.

They care a lot about finance and status. This can make them seem materialistic, but Capricorn risings do not agree. To them, status and money are power, and power is success, which is what they are after.

Capricorn risings like to be around similar-minded people, but they prefer to be around people who are powerful and successful. As standoffish as they seem, Capricorns attract and are attracted to people with Cancerian characteristics.

Capricorn through the Houses

Second

Natives with this placement measure their worth by how much they have built or the amount of wealth they have cultivated. These natives can be frugal with their money because they fear losing it.

They are unthinkingly careful with how much money they spend. One would think that they are being mindful of their money, but the truth is quite the opposite. These natives lack self-awareness. They do not see that their financial habits are robbing them of their happiness and joy. They do not see that they place a lot of emphasis on a pile of paper. They need to see that true value is within them, not in money.

Third

Capricorn in the third house indicates a tough individual. They are hard on themselves and others. Everything needs to meet their expectations; otherwise, it is not up to standards. Their way of communication may be sharp and curt, and people will be distancing themselves from these natives.

Eventually, people with this placement will grow tired of their mindset and their stubborn ways. They will recognize that they need to be more forgiving and compassionate with themselves and others. Once they have adopted this new mentality, they become approachable. These natives will enjoy a new side to themselves once they learn to be compassionate.

Fourth

Children who grew up with Capricorn in the fourth house struggled with their parents and in their house. Their home lacked affection and love. Their parents were probably cold, distant, and strict.

Kids with this placement are robbed of their childhood because they do not know what it means to be a child. They grew up with a lot of responsibilities, rules, and consequences. They did not feel much joy or happiness around their parents.

As a result, when these children grow up, they notice a coldness in their emotional world. They will need to begin their healing journey to regain warmth and love and experience it with other people.

Fifth

Natives with this placement have a difficult time relaxing. They do not know how to have fun or enjoy their lives. They take life too seriously and end up suffering from health conditions caused by stress.

They are deep thinkers and lead successful professional lives. However, their professional goals rob them of being carefree and enjoying their time with their partners.

If they do not learn how to balance these areas in their lives, they will have a distant relationship with their partners. They are also likely to become strict parents and will not know how to be active, present parents in their children's lives.

Sixth

One of the challenges that this placement brings about is balance. Capricorn in the sixth house suggests these individuals cannot sustain a healthy balance between work and personal life. Their health might be compromised by how stressed or overwhelmed they are.

This position might also indicate a lot of responsibility or a power struggle at work. These natives are known for their dedication and commitment to their goals, but they also need to prioritize themselves and know when to stop.

These individuals will enjoy a lot of blessings in their careers, but they need to remember not to overfill their plates and take a break now and again.

Seventh

People with Capricorn in the seventh house are loving partners. They might be closed off at first, but they open up the more you get to know them. They like to play the role of the provider in the family.

Individuals with this kind of placement can attract two types of people. They can either attract someone who will take care of them and play the authoritarian, or they will have a partner who they have to care for emotionally.

Capricorn in the seventh house means Cancer in the first house. This is an interesting placement because these natives will have to balance their emotional life with the cold realities of life. They need to be responsible for both sides of the coin; otherwise, they lose their balance.

Eighth

Natives with this placement might suffer from anxiety. Their fear of losing control brings this on. They feel as if they need to plan everything; otherwise, they might end up in a chaotic situation. On the other hand, they see how planning robs the joy from their lives. Once they have a handle on their anxiety, they will be able to enjoy life in a whole different way. These people are also likely to lead long lives and have a peaceful death.

Ninth

This placement indicates stubborn individuals who cannot let go of their control. They think they understand and know everything, even though it is impossible. These individuals have a hard time opening their minds to others.

Their beliefs are fixed, and no one can change them. These individuals will sometimes be held back because of their stubbornness and arrogance. They need to understand that they cannot know all there is to know and that life might surprise them if they open their minds to the possibility.

Tenth

People with this placement are ambitious and full of energy. Their careers mostly consume them, but they don't mind hard work. They are keen on following their plans and like to have a structure in their professional lives.

These individuals will have strict routines, leaving little room for being spontaneous. They might grow bored and tired with age, which is why they are advised to let go of their control and learn to go with the flow.

Eleventh

Capricorn in the eleventh house indicates karmic friendships. Karmic friendships can be either a reward or a debt to pay. In other words, people with this placement probably met certain people in a past life and are now meeting them again. They are bound in this life to pay their karmic debts or to enjoy a healthy friendship.

These natives might not have a large social circle, but they will meet a few people with whom they will be strongly bonded. They will need to build some structure to their social life to fully enjoy it; otherwise, they might lose all balance. They can either ignore their social life for work or personal responsibility or abandon their private life to sustain their social life.

Twelfth

This karmic placement will challenge its natives so that they can finally fix the error of their ways. They will deal with anxiety and burnout patterns until they learn that their career is not enough.

They will be put in situations where they need to trust the universe and have to take a leap of faith. They will be put under heavy pressure until they learn to draw boundaries and connect with their emotions.

The more these natives grow and learn, the sharper their intuition will become. Eventually, they will know how to be in tune with their feelings and will develop trust in their intuition.

Capricorn and Lunar Houses

Uttara Ashadha Nakshatra

Second Pada

These natives are known for their strength and focus. People sometimes mistake these qualities for being cold-hearted. However, that is not the case with these natives; they just do not allow themselves to get distracted. They fixate on earthly goals, which suffocates their spiritual side. They are exceptionally goal-oriented and use every ounce of energy to reach their hearts' desires.

Third Pada

People born in this Pada are strongly attached to their families. Tradition is important to them, and it is vital for them that their social circles respect their families and traditions as well. They are hardworking individuals who are smart, practical, and flexible.

Fourth Pada

These individuals spend their time thinking or conversing about philosophical topics. They value their spirituality and spend a lot of time in worship. They are attached to their spiritual beliefs and able to see God in everything and everyone.

Shravana Nakshatra

First Pada

Vedic astrologers describe these people as logical and ambitious. They will enjoy a successful career path during their lifetime. They are likely to take on a lot of projects brought on by their ambitious spirits.

Second Pada

These natives are known for their soft and diplomatic demeanor. They are fairly intelligent and are likely to have unconventional careers. Astrologists say that these natives are dedicated and committed to their craft.

Third Pada

People born in this Pada are often found working in the media. They might be journalists, podcasters, or talk-show hosts. They are good communicators and know how to talk to various people. This skill makes them successful in their field but also manipulates them when they want to be.

Fourth Pada

Vedic astrologers describe natives of this Pada as empathetic and sensitive. They are good listeners and give good advice. Their sympathy and kindness connect them to people and other living creatures. They are most likely to use their empathy in their line of work.

Dhanistha Nakshatra

First Pada

People born in this Pada will make great entrepreneurs. They know how and when to make strategic moves. In short, they have a sharp mind in business. During this lifetime, they will be making a significant amount of money. These individuals are generally blessed with good fortune, but this does not extend to their health.

Second Pada

These natives are flexible and know how to adapt to different situations. According to Vedic astrologists, these people will not have successful marriages during this lifetime. However, hope is not lost. If these individuals are ready to work with their partners on their relationships, they can achieve new heights.

Section Three: The Water Signs

The water element comprises Cancer, Scorpio, and Pisces. These three zodiacs are widely different from one another, but their element gives them a common foundation that adds to their mannerisms.

In Astrology and spirituality in general, water represents emotions. Water signs are deeply emotional and sensitive. This is not to say that they are emotional and all over the place. On the contrary, they often hide their emotions because they are aware that their feelings can overwhelm others.

With this high level of emotions and sensitivity, fear of rejection could accompany them, and each water sign has a different coping mechanism to deal with it. Cancer has its shell, so it completely hides its vulnerability. A Scorpio hides through secrecy, and Pisces escapes through art, imagination, and other means.

Water signs are known for their psychic abilities because they are in tune with their emotions and are highly sensitive. Highly sensitive folks are not just sensitive toward their own feelings, they are also receptive to their surroundings and messages from the universe, so it is easy for them to enhance their psychic gifts.

They are also observant, introspective, creative, protective, and intuitive. Water signs are also notorious for harboring anger, being vindictive, vengeful, and manipulative.

Remember that this does not mean that every water sign person embodies these qualities. The aim is not to generalize; instead, it fixates on the natural characteristics of water signs that may vary from person to person.

Chapter 9: Pisces, the Dreamer

Pisces symbol.
Source: Phantom Open Emoji maintainers and contributors, CC BY 3.0
<https://creativecommons.org/licenses/by/3.0>, via Wikimedia Commons:
https://commons.wikimedia.org/wiki/File:Phantom_Open_Emoji_2653.svg

Date: February 18th - March 20th

The Pisces constellation is symbolized by two fish swimming in opposite directions. Interesting, isn't it? Various factors went into assigning this symbol to this constellation. Let's start with the obvious one. The two fish swimming in opposite directions perfectly mirrors the Piscerian complex.

To understand this, you need to be familiar with this constellation's history and effect. Pisces is the last zodiac sign, making it the oldest of all the signs. The Pisces sign has ancient knowledge instilled within it. They are strongly connected to the spirit world; whether they like it or not, it is just the way they are.

That being said, Pisces struggles to keep up with their earthly lives. A part of them wants to live in their head, in their dream world. This part may want to engage in spiritual activities and not pay attention to the world.

The other part of them recognizes that they have a life, and they need to make the most of it. It knows that they have earthly responsibilities to tend to, and they cannot ignore them until it goes away.

Astrologists describe this as a dilemma of the ego and spirit. A Pieces' ego recognizes the urgency of tending to materialistic things, while the spirit is comfortable with not engaging with the world. Hence, the two fish swim in opposite directions.

Now you know the reason behind the opposite directions part, but why are they fish? Where did this come from? Well, this goes back to the constellation's rulership and mythology.

Neptune has rulership over Pisces. This planet also governs water, so it would only be fitting to give this constellation a fish or two as a symbol.

The mythology behind this symbol dates back to Ancient Egypt. Ancient Egyptians had acute observations of the sky, and they noticed that when the Nile reached its peak during its flooding season, the Pisces constellation would be in the sky. Historians found this symbol painted on the inside of an Ancient Egyptian tomb dating back to 2300 B.C

According to Greek mythology, the two fish represent Eros and Aphrodite, who latched onto the backs of two fish while escaping Typhon, the terrifying monster in mythology. After the gods successfully escaped this frightening creature, they honored the fish by making them into the Pisces constellation.

Key Phrase: "I Believe"

This constellation is mainly concerned with spiritual and intellectual transcendence. Pisces has an innate faith in humanity's divine essence. They don't need to prove to others that everyone is of a divine source; they just treat them as such.

This strong faith or belief system is why a Pisces does not bother with a lot of things. They do need to justify their spirituality to others; they just know or believe.

Strengths

- Compassionate
- Empathetic
- Grateful
- Intelligent
- Intuitive
- Kind
- Musically gifted
- Spiritual

Weaknesses

- Easily influenced
- Impulsive
- Lacks confidence
- Lacks discipline
- Manipulative
- Moody

Pet Peeves

- Inconsiderate people
- Over packed days
- Rudeness

Ruling Planet

Neptune rules this constellation as the ruler of the subconscious and spirit realm. The effect on this planet is very prominent. Pisces is a water sign, which means that they are intuitive, sensitive, and have emotional depth. They are blessed with psychic abilities, and their intuition is sharp.

They like to be by the water, which is caused by the planet. They feel like they are at home when they are near or in the water. They are very dreamy, just like this planet; however, this may manifest in various ways.

These individuals might receive prophetic dreams or spend their day daydreaming. The planet rules the subconscious, water, secrets, and what we cannot see. It also rules addiction, drugs, isolation, mental institutions, and prison. Pisces' placements are not going to mirror the planet completely, but Neptune's energy definitely shapes this constellation.

Sun Sign

Pisces Sun is highly empathetic, romantic, sensitive, dreamy, and spiritual. These natives are blessed with emotional depth. Of course, this can sometimes seem like a blessing and a curse, but this gift greatly aids them in their life mission.

People ruled by Pisces are very artistically talented. Their talents may be related to music or painting, but they are definitely not limited to these categories. Regardless of the nature of their talent, this Sun sign has a great amount of creativity. Their creative energy fuels anything they are genuinely interested in, which inevitably makes them shine.

They might suffer from a concentration problem, and their attention span may not be the best. They also feel too much and get affected by everything around them. This does more harm than good because Pisces Sun finds it challenging to find their own voice amidst all the emotions that they have absorbed from the outside.

Moon Sign

Pisces Moon signs are very intuitive. They sense the energy in the room as soon as they enter it; their feelings about people are accurate. They most likely have natural psychic abilities. This is not to say that every Pisces Moon has the same psychic ability; every chart should indicate what kind of gift they have. Some receive prophetic visions; others receive dreams, etc.

They are also very spiritual. They might not be religious, but they lead spiritually rich lives. They most likely partake in activities that leave their spirit feeling content and serene. Pisces Moon is advised to follow their spiritual paths because it is detrimental to their mental health.

These individuals have a heightened sensitivity. They can anticipate people's moods and provide care before anyone asks for it. They are also compassionate and caring. They care about everyone's emotional and mental well-being. These people make great friends and are often an integral part of their friends' support systems.

Their emotions may blind them from time to time. Their feelings are often exaggerated, and this creates a thick mental fog. They shouldn't always act on their strong feelings because things can end up unfavorably.

Rising Sign

People often find Pisces rising confusing. Their personality seems to be altered frequently. This may have to do with the fact that they are emotionally and energetically sensitive. Furthermore, they will often mirror a particular person's energy. This behavior will persist until they learn to put boundaries between themselves and others.

Another possible reason for this is that they want to be liked, which is understandable. However, finding their individuality will make them much happier individuals. In terms of physical attributes, Pisces risings have shiny eyes and small hands.

Overall, people view them as compassionate, caring, and loving. Pisces risings are also consummate daydreamers. They often seem out of reach, as if their minds are constantly elsewhere. They might be using escape as a coping mechanism, which is okay until it is out of balance. They often overdo it or use dangerous means to escape, so they need to be wary of this habit.

Pisces through the Houses

Second

Second house Pisces may find that they are always in search of their belongings. They seem to lose them or find them with great difficulty. Their concentration levels drop when it comes to their property. For instance, they always lose their keys, wallets, etc.

They are also prone to over or underestimate their capabilities. Their sense of worth seems to be unbalanced, not in the sense of extremities, but they never seem to have a fixed sense of self or worth; it is always changeable.

They are unclear on how to make money. They might find jobs, but they will not feel a sense of satisfaction until they search their hearts and find the kind of career that suits them. Usually, these careers involve changing people's lives for the better or making the world a better place.

Third

This is not the best placement for this individual. Pisces in the third house means that this person will have a serious problem with thinking clearly, communication, writing, and self-expression. They might have stage fright or seem to have difficulty speaking to a group of people.

However, since this constellation evokes musical and artistic talents, these individuals may find that they can self-express through music, painting, or any kind of artistic endeavor.

This placement predominantly indicates challenges with communication and mental faculties, but people can work on these areas and enhance their skills.

Fourth

This placement indicates that this person does not feel like they belong anywhere. They may have had emotionally unavailable parents, or they may have a family with a lot of secrets. This individual might have idealized one of the parents or both of them.

Pisces in the fourth house, people might feel like they have been abandoned or were literally abandoned by their parents. It also indicates emotional neglect, and it leaves the child feeling disconnected from their parents.

This placement also suggests that one of the parents, or a close family relative, has an addiction problem, and it affects the house in some way. All in all, this is a challenging placement, and this individual will have to deal with emotional challenges like feeling isolated and depressed.

Fifth

People with this placement are incredibly gifted. They have a talent or two that makes them shine. Often, they will find their muse in the person they love. Sadly, they will face a lot of disappointment in their lives, especially from people they associate with.

They might deal with deception, and it might cause serious trust issues. However, this person needs to find it in themselves to not give up on people. They need to realize that not everyone they form a connection with will end up lying or betraying them.

Sixth

Pisces in the sixth house; these people have a rocky relationship with their health. They might not tend to it or take care of themselves as much as they should. They may be slapdash with their work if they feel like it is not making a difference in the world.

The best approach for these individuals is to find a job or an activity that leaves a positive impression on the world. They need to recognize that no matter how much work they pour into this job, the world will not change, but they might have helped a few people or creatures have a better life, and that should be enough.

These people are natural caregivers and generous with their time and emotions. They might be the coworker who listens to you about your problems or the kind of friend who empathizes with you so much that it impacts their mental health. This is why they need to learn about emotional boundaries and lead healthier lifestyles while still being the helpful individuals that they are.

Seventh

People with Pisces on the cusp of the seventh house are complete sweethearts. They are caring, loving, and romantic. They might have an idealized idea of love that may hurt them the more they expose themselves to it. These individuals that love and partnerships might not look like what they have imagined it to look like, but it is still magical in their way.

These individuals might be disappointed in what love and relationships look like in the real world, but they need to understand that magic exists in reality too. Now, in the way they might have expected, it is still there.

They may develop a co-dependent relationship when they are in a comfortable partnership. They need to realize that in doing so, they are harming themselves and the relationship. They need to understand that no one can or will save them other than themselves.

Eighth

Pisces in the eighth house is the furthest away from their Piscerian nature. They have a very tight grip on reality, probably too tight, to the extent that they have a grim outlook on reality. They are goal-oriented, which is great for them, but on the other hand, they have a paralyzing fear of failure and betrayal.

These fears might hold them back a bit in life, but the more they know how to regulate and manage their emotions and fears, the faster they accomplish their goals. Another thing that needs their attention is boundaries.

They need to be careful of how much they give themselves to others because, more often than not, this ends up being the thing that hurts them the most. Once they have mastered their boundaries, their relationships will become much healthier.

Ninth

Individuals with this placement need to understand that they need to be free to discover themselves. They generally want their space but often fear it because they think it might send the wrong message.

That is not true at all. They need to let go of attaching to people too strongly. Only then can they understand the value of their freedom. This placement indicates educating or receiving education in psychology, chemistry, hypnosis, or pharmacy.

This placement also indicates that these natives have rich spiritual lives. They might meditate or meditate on religious texts. They are not necessarily religious, but their faith is strong.

Tenth

Pisces- in-the-tenth-house people have a reputation for being compassionate, wise, kind, and artistically gifted. They are most likely empaths, so they might enjoy spiritual or psychological work.

However, most people with this placement face a lot of difficulty in choosing a career path. More often than not, they feel clouded and are not sure what they want for a job. The kind of careers that would match their Piscerian energy is anything related to the arts, spiritual gurus, or therapists.

They might also be talented in metaphysical art. They can put their intuition to use and help people through astrological readings, palmistry, tarot readings, etc.

Eleventh

People with this placement may not be the luckiest in their friendships. They may have long-distance friendships. Usually, their friends will live by the sea or are across the continent. This placement also might manifest in deception and betrayals in friendships. They could also find themselves in a cycle of friendships that do not amount to anything.

Pisces in the eleventh house might find that their connection to others is disconnected, or their friends seem to be distant. A Pisces in the eleventh house might wonder about their friends' feelings towards them, and they are not sure if their friends genuinely love them or not.

However, once this individual finds their kind of people, they become emotionally available to them. They show a lot of love, care, and understanding towards their friends.

Twelfth

Pisces is the natural ruler of this house; naturally, all of its energies are exaggerated in this house. Picture the typical Pisces in this house, so these individuals are beyond compassionate, sensitive, and intuitive.

These individuals will be dealing with unforeseen forces in their lives, and it will be one of the most prominent features in their lives. They might be a medium, and they might be in contact with spirits or be able to see into the other realm.

Their journey and life mission could also be purely spiritual, which would make them perfect at being spiritual gurus, tarot readers, astrologists, light workers, etc. People with this placement can find true meaning and happiness in causes that help others.

Pisces and Lunar Houses

Purva Bhadrapada

Fourth Pada

Vedic astrologists describe these natives as dangerous. They are either dangerous themselves or are attracted to danger. They are capable of being both the victim and perpetrator. These individuals are compatible with the first, second, and third Pada in Purva Bhadrapada.

Uttara Bhadrapada

First Pada

People connected to this Pada are productive and lead active lives. They are a bit proud, but on a more positive note, they are a joy to be around. They make everyone around them feel better and know how to cheer people up.

Second Pada

According to Vedic astrologists, people who are connected to this Pada are fans of classical literature. They are introverts and are more comfortable being comfortable and vulnerable to the opposite gender. They are good planners and like to weigh everything carefully before reaching a decision.

Third Pada

Individuals associated with this Pada care a lot about balance as a concept. Balance is incorporated into every facet of their lives. They consider it a vital factor in all of their relationships, and they tend to fall off the passive side in partnerships.

Fourth Pada

These natives express their feelings aggressively. They are secretive and tend to go to extremes. Life is black and white for them, and this is reflected in their mindset and how they express themselves. People find them mysterious, and these individuals tend to have unusual interests.

Revati

First Pada

Revati first Pada natives are smart, wise, and wealthy. They are generally popular and liked by everyone who meets them. They may be a bit arrogant, but deep down, they are selfless and kind. They tend to go out of their way to help others, which sometimes does more harm than good. They need to learn how to establish healthy boundaries with others. These individuals also need to work on their concentration levels. They are physically attractive people, and they know it.

Second Pada

Unlike the typical Pisces, these individuals are very clear on their desires and know what they want from life. They are realistic and goal-oriented, which helps them achieve whatever they seek. They might be a bit too independent on their own; they need to work on getting along with others in group projects. They could also be a bit more modest and need to be careful because people may treat them rudely.

Third Pada

These natives are very attracted to spirituality and seek to live a spiritual life. They are very keen on helping others. People feel like they can trust these individuals. Third, Pada people need to be careful because others may abuse their characteristic kindness and willingness to listen.

Fourth Pada

Similar to the third Pada people, these natives are also interested in the spiritual path and willing to experience different spiritual experiences. Vedic astrologists say that, physically, they are slightly short and a bit overweight. They may also lead somewhat of a chaotic lifestyle and get into fights with others. They are interested in high education and are embedded within their own culture.

Chapter 10: The Mysterious Scorpio

Scorpio symbol.
Phantom Open Emoji maintainers and contributors, CC BY 3.0
<https://creativecommons.org/licenses/by/3.0>, via Wikimedia Commons:
https://commons.wikimedia.org/wiki/File:Phantom_Open_Emoji_264f.svg

Date: October 23rd - November 21st

Scorpio is one of the most misunderstood constellations, even in ancient times. Firstly, the constellation's symbol is the scorpion's tail, not the arachnid itself. This is significantly interesting because this constellation's symbol is part of a creature. You might be asking yourself, "Why?"

Well, the answer can be found in Greek mythology. One day, Orion and Artemis were out hunting, as they were known for their professional skills. As they were capturing beasts, Orion pompously bragged that he could hunt down all the beasts that roamed the earth if he wanted to.

Gaia, the goddess of the Earth, heard him and was not pleased with his disrespectful manner towards her creatures. In return, Gaia sent down Scorpius, a giant, venomous scorpion, to kill Orion and avenge the beasts. After a long battle between the two, Scorpius stung Orion and threw his corpse into the water.

The battle sent tears trickling from Athena's eyes as she prayed to Zeus to help her. At her request, Zeus honored both Orion and Scorpius by turning them into constellations in the heavens.

Scorpios are known for their determination and vengeful spirits. Both of these qualities can be found in Scorpius, the creature that fought until the end and avenged earth's beasts. The more you read about this constellation, the more you will understand its attributes and characteristics.

Key Phrase: "I Desire"

Fun fact about this constellation, it rules the genitalia. No wonder its key phrase is "I desire" However, it is much deeper than this. Pluto rules Scorpio. This planet mainly rules over transformation, but it also rules power dynamics, sex, death, and rebirth. A lot of intensity surrounds this sign, and Scorpios carry this intensity within them.

This intensity precludes logic in a Scorpio's mind and makes them have a black-and-white mentality. In other words, they have a binary mindset; if they are not the most powerful, then they are weak. For instance, a lot of Scorpios are power hungry or have a problem with authority, so they will work to reach high levels in society just to feel powerful. Other Scorpios will work to have ownership over necessary and unnecessary items.

This can translate in different ways with Scorpios; there is not necessarily one single narrative they follow. It also depends on the kind of placements that exist with this sign. One Scorpio may outgrow this mentality and adopt a new one; after all, Scorpio is about transformation. Other Scorpios may stagnate and feel stuck in their mindset.

Scorpios can also be quite materialistic. They might fixate on worldly things, whether status, property, or anything that strokes their ego. Materialism can make them feel confident and secure, but it also makes them arrogant and worldly.

Strengths

- Brave
- Determinate
- Emotional
- Insightful
- Passionate
- Perceptive
- Psychic
- Sensitive
- Sex appeal
- Transformative

Weaknesses

- Clingy
- Insecure
- Jealous
- Paranoid
- Possessive
- Unforgiving
- Vindictive

Pet Peeves

- Being challenged
- Disrespectful attitude
- Prying eyes

Ruling Planet

As referenced earlier, Pluto rules this constellation. This is one of the heaviest planets energetically. Astrologers always associate this planet with transformation. This association elevates some heaviness of this planet and sends the wrong message.

Pluto is about transformation, but it is not as peaceful as a worm going into its cocoon. Pluto wreaks havoc before you are transformed. These phases are painful, and it feels as if your world is falling apart. After this phase is over, you welcome your new self to life, knowing it did not come into this world easily.

As you welcome your new self, you grieve your old self in the process. This is why this planet rules death and rebirth. Pluto's death is more of an ego death than literal physical death. But, still, its death is painful and intense, so brace yourself.

Pluto rules sex, sexuality, and primal urges. Certain Plutonian placements can indicate many things in regard to these topics. Some people may have sexual problems or active sexual lives. They may be addicted to sex or like sexual promiscuity. They may have challenges with power dynamics in sex or unorthodox sexual activities.

People with certain Pluto placements may have a sexual awakening in regard to their own sexuality or gender. They might go into a transformative phase to find who they are in terms of their sexuality, gender, and who they are in their sexual lives.

This planet also rules the occult and anything that is unknown or hidden in nature. This is why Scorpios are secretive and mysterious. They are like an onion that you need to peel until the end until you reach the core.

Sun Sign

People often think that Scorpios are dark and dangerous, but that would be an oversimplification. Scorpios are not either, but they will let you believe that they are. Scorpios are sensitive and emotional; they are one of the water signs, after all. They are capable of feeling a lot of emotions at once, and it gets the best of them.

They are prone to feeling overwhelmed by their emotions and may partake in impulsive behaviors. The nature of their emotions is behind their vindictive mindset. When someone hurts a Scorpio, Scorpios take it personally and plan to strike back.

They are calculating and strategic and do not mind waiting a long time to get their revenge. "Revenge is a dish better served cold" is a proverb that definitely applies to them. People often do not see it coming, and after they have been stung by a Scorpio, they are often left in disbelief.

This quality made Scorpios prone to living in the past and fixated on their wounded ego. It also makes them unforgiving and prone to having a cold, dark heart that is weighed by burdens only they can remember. They often live with their pain alone; this is why most Scorpios are lonely at heart; the rest is purely for show.

On a more positive note, they can make loyal and protective friends. They are also determined to reach their goal, no matter what stands in the way. They are hard-working individuals and are not easily scared by life's challenges.

They can easily enter a meditative mindset thanks to their psychic abilities. Water signs are in touch with the universe's magic and emotions, so it makes sense that Scorpios are psychic. Their intuition is at its sharpest when they feed their spirit and partake in spiritual activities.

Moon Sign

Scorpio Moon signs have an intense emotional life. They have great emotional and psychological depth. This placement is a difficult one to live with, for the most part, because people who have their Moon in Scorpio are prone to dark moods. Their emotional life is not particularly balanced; they go to the extreme sides of the spectrum.

They are also very private and do not reveal all their cards at once. They need to really trust someone to reveal who they are, and even when they do, they don't reveal everything all at once.

According to astrologists, people with this placement have a mother wound that needs work. They might have a problem with their vulnerability, confidence, and self-esteem. These people can make great psychologists because they understand their psychological depths and can, therefore, understand others.

People with this placement are emotional and particularly sensitive. If they have an artistic placement, they can put their feelings and sensitivity into use. This way, they can express themselves in a way that does not threaten them.

These individuals are also very intuitive and psychically gifted. Their sixth sense will depend on the kind of placement that they have, but whatever it is, it is powerful. The more Scorpio Moons work on their psychic gift, the sharper it will become.

Rising Sign

People view Scorpio rising as mysterious and attractive. They feel like they cannot figure them out, which is part of their charm and sex appeal. This might offend some people, but those who are not afraid to approach Scorpio risings find it absolutely mesmerizing.

Individuals with this placement are fearless but also a bit impulsive. They might make snap decisions without thinking them through or acting based on their feelings. This does not always end well for them. More often than not, they create their own challenges and blame them on life.

These individuals struggle with financial security. They either spend a lot of time and energy worrying about it or put in a lot of time working to make a significant amount of money. They always want to make sure that they are financially secure.

They are also a bit suspicious of people, making up narratives and believing them. This stems from trust issues they need to overcome, but unaware Scorpio rising people do not see that. They might think that people are out to get them or that anyone they come into contact with will try to hurt them.

Scorpio through the Houses

Second

People with this placement are secretive about their money. Their financial situation is a very private matter to them; they will not share this kind of information even with their partners. They are the kind of people who will have to work hard to earn their money.

This does not mean they will have financial difficulties; it is actually easy for them to make money. However, they will need to earn, for the most part, even if they come from money.

This placement also indicates that their ancestors may have left money for them. If these people did not come from money, they might experience a transformation in this arena. In other words, they will go through a financial transformation and build their way up.

These people are also most likely to become bosses, whether in a company or in their own business. They might create their own business and become entrepreneurs, but this depends on their planetary placement, especially in the 2nd house.

Third

Individuals with Scorpio in the third house often view life as dark and full of hardships. They will eventually find that the best way to deal with life is to just laugh at it. Laugh through their hardships and laugh at the absurdity of it all.

They also might have a dark sense of humor, which is obvious in how they communicate with others. They like to be in the company of those who see the darker shades of life and laugh at them. They also enjoy shows and movies with a dark sense of humor because they feel seen and represented by them.

They admire people who are not afraid to talk about the dark side of life or the dark side of themselves. They like honesty and love people who are not afraid to speak freely.

These individuals need to work on seeing the softer sides of life so that they can get rid of their pessimistic mindset. This practice will be challenging at first; however, the more they try, the easier it will become. They will gradually notice a change in how they feel about life and feel lighter and a bit happier than their gloomy past self.

Fourth

Unfortunately, this is one of the difficult placements in the natal chart. This person did not have an easy time growing up. They were not close to their family and were most likely neglected or unaccepted in their home.

Their childhood home might have been cold and distant. This child did not feel cared for or even loved. This is why adults find they are stuck in the past and cannot let go.

They find it incredibly difficult to let go and forgive their parents. However, since both Pluto and the Moon rule this placement, this person will go through an emotional transformation that relates to their family, mothers, and inner child. It will be a deep healing journey, but only if they allow themselves to do it.

They might deal with dark moods, vulnerability, trust, low self-esteem, and attachment issues. As this individual matures, they will find that it is best to resolve their issues by receiving professional help from therapists.

Fifth

These individuals are fascinating. They like going through emotional challenges and facing their pain and fears. They might seek out experiences that kill their ego or their sense of self, like certain meditations or psychedelics.

These people can make fantastic psychologists, energy healers, or researchers. Not only do they understand how dark life can be, but they have a positive way of approaching it. They see the value and good that come from these challenges, which helps them help others with their challenges and work with them until they, too, see the brighter sides of their hardships.

These people might have problems with their relationships because they can be a bit possessive. They will learn the lesson once they notice their pattern and listen to the people in their lives. Only then will they work on themselves and heal.

Sixth

People with this placement struggle with change. They are not the most flexible and prefer things to stay the same. Stability gives them a sense of safety, while change threatens the structure they have become comfortable with.

They also have self-destructive tendencies, be dismissive of their health issues, and do not pay attention to or downplay the seriousness of their condition.

More often than not, these individuals need psychological help. They need a guiding hand to point to a different perspective for them. Mental health professionals will teach them how to accept their deepest truths because their denial is the root of all their psychological problems.

Once they learn to accept themselves, they will find that they have an endless amount of energy and that their lives have become much easier than before. They will have enough mental energy to deal with their repression, suppression, and self-destructive mentality.

Seventh

Individuals with this placement have to deal with self-love issues. They might not know what it means to love themselves and have problems with learning to love themselves. They will seek extreme intimacy from their partners or relationships until this is resolved.

They will face disappointment after another because no one can give them the kind of love and affection they are looking for. It is not that their partners are not sufficient; it is the person with this placement who is confusing self-love with intimacy in relationships with others.

They really need to love themselves, but instead, they seek this kind of affection from others. This placement teaches them that loving themselves is vital if they are to enjoy relationships with others.

Eighth

This placement gives people a different way of looking at life and death. They accept these concepts with ease and are not generally afraid of death; to them, it is as natural as anything else in life.

These individuals tend to go to the extreme sides of the spectrum when dealing with their fears. At times, they are absolutely fearless, no matter how scary their situation is. Other times, they panic and often get stuck in their fear-induced state.

They also may be attracted to the occult. They have an innate knowledge of how the universe works and are aware of the magic that surrounds them. They are skilled at making money from unconventional businesses.

Ninth

Scorpio, in the Ninth house, people live unconventional lives. People often comment on how weird their life choices are. People with this placement do not pay attention to what people have to say about them.

They have a deep thirst for understanding how the universe works. They will most likely become their own teachers during this lifetime because the things that they seek knowledge in are not typically taught in schools or by family.

They are also connected to their ancestors and will communicate with them once they learn how to. They enjoy learning about the occult and adopt its teachings in their daily lives.

Tenth

People with this placement have a role to play in life. They need to understand their own emotional depth to understand others. Once they know this about themselves and accept it, they will start cleansing their social circle of people who are not of the same caliber.

These people will make amazing psychologists and healers. They are drawn to helping others reach their emotional depth and open their eyes to their truths. Once they have achieved their desired profession, they will help great numbers of people.

Through their life's journey, they will learn that true satisfaction comes from answering their calling. Their task is to find out what their calling is and seek it with determination and patience.

Eleventh

This placement suggests difficulty bonding with others. These individuals have the skills and depth to build powerful bonds; however, their emotional blockages stand in their way.

They need to understand that the emotional depth they seek in others exists within themselves. Once they feel tired of looking for something they will not find in others, life will teach them to look within themselves first.

Their true friendships will be rooted in deep honesty, complete vulnerability, and trust. The kind of people they are looking for is out there, but they will not find them before they work on themselves.

Twelfth

Individuals with this placement know how to hide their feelings even from themselves. They know how to shove things under the rug, and they would rather bury their emotions and problems than deal with them.

The more time passes, their suppressive nature causes them to become more vulnerable to the point where they are likely to implode and get themselves into dangerous or weird situations. They need to be careful with this because it may lead them to unwanted destinations.

They need to learn how to face and accept themselves. This will not be the easiest thing for them, but it is their karma in this life. They will face a lot of situations that will teach them to face their emotions with compassion.

Scorpio and Lunar Houses

Anuradha Nakshatra

First Pada

Individuals born in this Pada approach life with practicality and a logical mindset. They seek knowledge to reach their professional goals. They always work on themselves to sharpen their skills. They are not necessarily family oriented, but their life revolves around their profession and career path.

Second Pada

These people are calculating and are more logical than sentimental. They are committed and disciplined enough to seek knowledge. They often wonder about the universe, so they spend time learning about it. Their communication style is direct, and they love having conversations about the universe and its power.

Third Pada

Vedic astrologists describe these natives as tall and hairy. They can make skilled numerologists and astrologers. They have a large, diverse social circle and enjoy the friendships they will make during this lifetime.

Fourth Pada

These natives will seek knowledge that is hidden from others. They might specialize in unique professions or have a lot of knowledge about unknown topics. They will likely succeed in their profession because of their powerful energy and research skills.

Jyeshtha Nakshatra

First Pada

These natives are interested in abstract topics. They like spending time thinking about different philosophies and various thinking methods when approaching common life situations. They are likely to become a teacher to others or themselves. They are seen as knowledgeable, intrinsic, and intelligent.

Second Pada

People born in this Pada will most likely become authority figures. They are very strict and disciplined when it comes to their routine and goals. Vedic astrologers describe them as materialistic, self-serving, vengeful, and stingy.

Third Pada

These people feel a calling to help those in need, especially old people. They often fixate on their professional knowledge and skills. They are generally hard-working and decent human beings.

Fourth Pada

These natives have difficulty connecting with their emotions. They are exposed to sexual encounters early in their lives and spend their time in their minds rather than in real life. They daydream a lot and have unearthly fantasies, which makes them unique individuals with unprecedented ideas.

Chapter 11: The Emotional Cancer

Cancer symbol.
Source: Phantom Open Emoji maintainers and contributors, CC BY 3.0
<https://creativecommons.org/licenses/by/3.0>, via Wikimedia Commons:
https://commons.wikimedia.org/wiki/File:Phantom_Open_Emoji_264b.svg

Date: June 21st - July 22nd

The crab represents cancers. This might seem strange at first, but the crab is a very fitting symbol for Cancerians. Crabs live in water, have hard shells that protect their soft bodies, and they like burying themselves in the warm sand.

Cancers are a water sign, which is evident in their rich emotional life and sharp intuition. They develop thick skin or a tough exterior to protect themselves from getting hurt by others. They are aware of just how sensitive they are, so they need to mask their vulnerability with a hard shell. They also often seek solitude and hide from the world because life can be very overwhelming for them.

A fun fact about the constellation is that it was not always associated with the crab. Ancient Egyptians perceived this constellation as a scarab, which was considered divine at the time, and Ancient Babylonia assigned the tortoise to this constellation. However, this changed when the Ancient Greeks came along.

The Ancient Greeks associated this constellation with the crab as a tribute to the great crab that fought Hercules. This mythology involves Hercules completing the 12 tasks set by Hera. In the second labor, the crab tries to defend Hera by pinching the hero. In response to the crab's attack, Hercules kills it. The goddess appreciated the crab's heroic act and honored it by placing it in the heavens.

Key Phrase: "I Feel"

The Moon rules Cancer placements. One of the many things that the Moon rules are his feelings. This is why most Cancerian placements begin their sentences with "I feel." These individuals have a deep emotional life.

They are emotionally intuitive; they walk through life feeling everything that crosses their path. Of course, this exhausts them, which is what promotes their introversion. The real world is too overwhelming for these sensitive individuals. This is why they tend to retreat from activities and social stimulation. They need to have some alone time to relax and check in with themselves.

Strengths

- Compassionate
- Empaths
- Humorous
- Intelligent
- Intuitive
- Nurturing

- Protective
- Psychic
- Sensitive
- Witty

Weaknesses

- Brooding
- Manipulative
- Moody
- Sharp-tongued
- Vindictive

Pet Peeves

- Criticism
- Forgetfulness
- Insensitivity
- Selfishness
- Superficiality

Ruling Planet

The Moon rules this constellation. This luminary planet is associated with maternal instincts, home, family life, mothers, and roots. This is why individuals with remarkable Cancerian placements are often nurturing, caring, and loving.

They care about familial connections. Not only do they care about their blood-related family members, but they can also find family in friends and other relationships. They are nurturing towards everyone, not just children.

The Moon also rules intuition, spiritual knowledge, psychic abilities, emotions, and sensitivity. Natives ruled by the Moon are intuitive and emotionally intelligent. They are able to sense the energies of animals, plants, objects, and people. They can walk into a room and immediately sense the vibrations in it.

They are emotionally in tune with themselves and others. Their psychic abilities will be determined by the kind of placements they have, but usually, people ruled by the Moon exhibit different psychic gifts.

Sun Sign

Cancer Sun signs have caring personalities. They are nurturing, intelligent, funny, and emotional. They can easily get swept away in their emotional life, which usually drags them down and leaves them with low energy levels.

They are loving and giving, and while these are nice qualities, they often end up feeling hurt because other people don't reciprocate the same feelings or with the same intensity.

This is why Cancers develop their hard shells so that they can avoid getting used to or hurt by others. They do not want others to see them as sweet and loving; they want people to think they are tough and indifferent.

Cancers are naturally strong people, but their strength lies in their ability to love and give, not in appearing indifferent to other people's feelings. Unfortunately, when Cancerians are hurt or betrayed, they use their sharp claws to hurt those who have caused them pain.

Moon Sign

Cancer Moon signs are sweet and loving individuals. They love tending to themselves and others. They have a deep understanding of other people's emotions. Individuals with this placement are most likely empaths. They feel for every living creature and sympathize with them.

They do not care for superficial conversations and interactions. They often get stuck in the past and can't let go of it, especially if they are hurt. They are often overwhelmed by their sadness, which can get tiring.

They are emotionally reactive and often impulsive. Once they develop emotional awareness, they will notice that they have obtained a better grip on their emotions. These individuals can anticipate people's wants and needs. They notice when people's energies drop and often feel like they want to tend to them.

These individuals need to understand that they do not have to fix people or make them feel better all the time. They need to tend to themselves and not overextend themselves for the sake of others.

Rising Sign

Cancer risings have distinctly feminine appearances. People view them as welcoming individuals and enjoy being in their presence. Cancer rising makes people feel at home when they are in their company.

If you are a Cancer rising, then your chart ruler is the Moon. This means that your mood is susceptible to change and changes frequently. This might emotionally exhaust you, so you need to learn ways to unwind and find practices that relax you.

You also need to understand that the Moon makes you intuitive and sensitive to people and creatures. You go about your day absorbing other people's emotions; this is why it is vital to spend some alone time and learn how to create healthy emotional boundaries. The lack of these emotional boundaries could exhaust you emotionally, and you will feel burnt out eventually.

Cancer through the Houses

Second

People with Cancer in the second house are financially blessed. They might have their own company, where they are making a significant amount of money. Another interpretation is that they have inherited money from their family.

This individual is most likely to work from home. They could be a freelancer, or they could be managing their company from the comfort of their own home. This person also likes to provide for their family.

They are nurturing and most likely enjoy cooking for themselves and their loved ones. Their sense of security comes from owning their house, and they might get into real estate businesses or rent one of their houses. This person enjoys passive income and likes to have more than one source of income.

Third

These natives are caring and thoughtful but often experience challenges when trying to express themselves. They can seem a bit cold and distant to others at first, but when people get to know them, they find that they are caring and warm individuals.

People born with this placement feel the need to shield themselves with a hard shell when they first meet people. It takes some time for them to come out of their own shell to show who they truly are.

These individuals are shy, sensitive, and nurturing. They have a lot of love for their friends; they just need to trust them or feel safe enough to be fully themselves around people.

They can be a bit aggressive and sharp-tongued when they are being aggressive or provoked. They can also show their aggressive side when they are being protective of a loved one.

Fourth

Cancer in the fourth house can indicate a caring and nurturing family. This person's mother might have been emotionally attentive and available. Their parents cared about them, and they grew up in a loving environment.

They enjoy a healthy, loving relationship with their mothers. This individual also cares about creating a home and a family. They might enjoy activities like decorating a house, cooking, or taking care of little ones.

One of this person's life missions is to find love within themselves. They must fully accept their identity and not compare themselves to their parents. They often romanticize the idea of building a family, but they will not find what they are looking for until they truly love themselves.

Fifth

Individuals with this placement are highly empathetic and artistic. Their creativity shines through in everything they do. There are a lot of musicians, singers, and comedians with this placement.

Cancers are naturally funny, and they feel on such a deep level. This is why people with this placement turn their sadness and disappointments into funny anecdotes. They can use their sensitivity and active emotional life to their advantage by inducing their creativity into the mix.

These people are prone to idolize their partners or put them on a pedestal. This idealization causes a rift in their perception of reality. It may cause problems in the relationship because of their high expectations of their significant other.

Sixth

Cancer in the sixth house indicates a person whose emotional state affects their health, house, and job. They may appear to others as disorganized and lacking structure, which would be an unfair assumption.

People with this placement do not complete any tasks out of obligation; they usually feel that they want to finish their tasks. They do not feel like they have to do anything per se. Problems start to arise in this area when they are not feeling well.

This is when their work suddenly begins to lack quality, and often they are not taking care of themselves, and their house becomes dusty and chaotic. Unfortunately, this makes them feel worse, and it is a downward spiral from there until they pick themselves up or receive help from others.

Seventh

These individuals are introverted with low social energy. They love everyone they have a relationship with, but they feel like they run out of energy quickly when they are around others.

This is why they prefer to spend time around certain people, especially since their close friends know them and will not feel offended. This person is mostly home oriented and prefers to spend time when they are most comfortable.

Their romantic relationships are successful, but they can have trouble finding the right person. They have a lot of love and care to give, provided that the other person reciprocates the same energy.

Eighth

This placement suggests fears that were inherited from parents or ancestors. This individual is also likely scared of pregnancy or of bringing children into the world. They have a lot of emotional hurdles that they need to work through, but they need to stop running away from them before they can fix anything.

Unfortunately, when these people feel overwhelmed by their problems, they shut down and run away. They need to understand that ignoring problems will not make them go away. They also need to see that they have the proper tools to deal with their challenges.

They are generally strong-willed, meaning they can overcome any emotional hurdles if they put their mind to it. The more compassion and self-love they cultivate for themselves, the better they will feel.

Ninth

This placement indicates a long life journey of finding peace. This suggests that this individual will be put in circumstances and situations in life that will drive them to want peace.

They need to figure out what peace means and what it looks like for them. Is it inner peace? Is it peace from certain people or places? This is where the journey takes on a unique form.

On this journey, they will also find out that they are their best teachers. They will understand that they do not have to find answers from other people, books, or gurus. They are the only ones holding the keys to their questions, and they will not find these keys unless they search inwards instead of outwards.

Tenth

Cancer in the tenth house natives might enjoy a career that has to do with healing, nurturing, teaching, cooking, or taking care of others. These natives may find themselves in the spotlight regarding their careers, especially if they have relevant placements in this house.

They tend to be career oriented and fixated on their professional goals. This placement suggests that these individuals will learn how to be forgiving, empathetic, compassionate, and loving during this lifetime.

Eleventh

Natives with this placement are sensitive and full of love for everyone they meet. They often run into people who soon turn into family. They are likely to get emotionally attached to people quickly, which can result in a lot of emotional pain.

Their mission in this life is to obtain emotional awareness and draw healthy boundaries with others. They will eventually know how to cultivate healthier friendships and relationships and enjoy a more peaceful environment.

Twelfth

This karmic placement indicates that this individual does not have a healthy sense of self. They have a lack of emotional boundaries and awareness. They are sensitive and empathic, meaning they unconsciously absorb other people's emotions and internalize them.

During this lifetime, they will find out family secrets or secrets kept from them in relationships. These experiences might prove to be painful, but Cancer in the 12th house natives are meant to find out for their own good.

Cancer and Lunar Houses

Punarvasu Nakshatra

Fourth Pada

Natives born in this Pada are known for their altruism and strength. Jupiter blesses these people with good fortune for their altruistic mindset and selflessness. These people are nurturing and caring for their loved ones.

Pushya Nakshatra

First Pada

These natives are blessed with pride, wealth, and success. They are most likely to have nurturing parents, but if they don't, they will become nurturing figures to others later in life.

Second Pada

Vedic astrologers claim that these natives have slim, lank bodies with a fair complexion. They might suffer from a physical illness and are more likely to be secretaries or work as servers in various fields.

Third Pada

People born in this Pada will fixate on the materialistic side of life. They will work to achieve the home of their dreams and will fill it with luxurious items so that they can be fully comfortable.

Fourth Pada

According to Vedic astrologers, this Pada is not favorable. They say that individuals who are born in this Pada will struggle with their education and career because of their irresponsible mentality and love affairs. They will become successful later in life or after their 36th birthday.

Ashlesha Nakshatra

First Pada

These natives are hard workers and eventually become wealthy individuals. They are sensitive, emotional, and caring. It is important for them to be accessible to others and help them. These natives might open a charity service or donate money to the needy. The more these individuals help others, the more they balance their karma.

Second Pada

People born in this Pada are highly ambitious but often use their negative traits to achieve what they seek. Vedic astrologists say that these natives cannot be trusted because they are cunning, manipulative, intelligent, and dishonest. These people will backstab anyone who stands between them and their goals. They are also attached to their possessions and tend to speak harshly to others when it suits them.

Third Pada

These natives will most likely be found working in a hospital. They might be nurses, doctors, or work in the general medical field. They are clever and can anticipate their own illnesses and others. They will become financially blessed after their 26th birthday. These people are secretive and private and are no strangers to plotting, strategizing, and scheming.

Fourth Pada

People born in this Pada come from wealth. They enjoy a life of luxury and joy. They were also born in a nurturing home. These individuals will have to work on the quality of their relationships later in life. They need to understand that real relationships need commitment and hard work.

Section Four: The Air Signs

The air element is associated with the following zodiacs - Gemini, Libra, and Aquarius. These signs carry different energies and, of course, manifest differently. However, their common air element makes them share air sign qualities. The more you learn about each sign, the more you will understand how their elements make them a bit similar.

Air signs are known for their knowledge. They are curious learners who like to know everything. Of course, this differs from one air sign to another.

For instance, Geminis are the type of people whose interests change frequently, so they will read a bit of everything. This is noticeable when talking to a Gemini; they usually display only surface-level knowledge.

Aquarius and Libras are not avid readers like Gemini, but they are most likely to go in-depth about a subject that intrigues them. Usually, these subjects will relate to humanity, equality, innovation, and justice.

These air signs are also intelligent. They may have different types of intelligence, but Gemini and Libra are exceptionally socially smart. Aquarius is more of an analytically smart kind of person.

They are a bit hard to read; not everyone can tell what they are thinking most of the time. This tends to confuse people a bit. They are also a bit unconventional and emotionally flighty. For instance, the three signs may not reply to texts or emails for days. Gemini and Libra are likely to forget about commitments that they have made. Aquarius and Gemini have commitment issues and distance emotionally once things feel serious.

Chapter 12: Aquarius, the Pioneer

Aquarius symbol.
Phantom Open Emoji maintainers and contributors, CC BY 3.0
<https://creativecommons.org/licenses/by/3.0>, via Wikimedia Commons:
https://commons.wikimedia.org/wiki/File:Phantom_Open_Emoji_2652.svg

Date: January 20 - February 18

This constellation, known as Aquarius, is represented by the cupbearer. Now, you might think this is a weird symbol to give to a constellation. However, three ancient civilizations would disagree with you.

The actual constellation looks like a figure that is pouring water out over the earth. In Ancient Egypt, people saw this constellation in the sky and noticed that every time it was there, they experienced a flood. They believed that Aquarius dipped its jar into the river and flooded their soil, which meant that spring was on its way.

In ancient Babylonia, Aquarius was associated with the god Ea, who was depicted as a man holding an overflowing cup of water. Every time Aquarius was in the sky, they would experience destructive flooding that ruined their land.

In Ancient Greece, Aquarius was Zeus' cupbearer. This man was taken, as a boy, by Zeus because Zeus was struck by his beauty. He wanted to be close to him, so he made him immortal and assigned him as the official cupbearer for the gods.

Key Phrase: "I Know"

Aquarians are visionaries and futuristic by nature. They have this deep sense of knowing how their ideas will unfold and how they could change their surroundings and, ultimately, the world. They are firm believers in the ripple effect and know that their unconventional ideas are what society and the world need right now.

They are also highly attuned to the universe and know things that would take other people forever to learn. It is as though they receive spiritual downloads that make them understand themselves and others more.

They are also active learners; they seek knowledge and like to stay on top of things. There is not much that an Aquarius does not already know. They can only access this part of themselves by attuning to their subconscious and investigating their emotional and internal life. Once they do so, they will be awakened to many truths they were previously blinded to.

Strengths

- Free-thinkers
- Individualistic
- Life-long learners
- Observers
- Peaceful

- Unique
- Visionaries

Weaknesses

- Emotionally cold
- Self-righteous
- Stubborn
- Uncompromising

Pet Peeves

- Feeling confined
- Judgmental people

Ruling Planet

Uranus rules this constellation. This planet rules innovation, sudden changes, the unusual and eccentric, scientific discoveries, rebelliousness, freedom, and awakenings. You can see all of these themes with Aquarius, or rather these themes manifest in significant Aquarius placements.

People who are associated with this sign are eccentric in one way or another. They seek to break free from anything that confines them. Their views or how they look might seem unconventional because they are trying to break the mold.

On a subconscious level, Aquarius shows that they are different and bravely walk into the world so that they can free everyone else. They believe that if people saw a true expression of freedom, they would also free themselves from their confined selves.

They bring innovation and positive change into the world, whether it is through their views, creations, or simply how they look. Aquarius cares about the collective wellness of humanity, and they are mostly concerned with the lack of awareness in humanity, so they aim to open people's eyes to the bigger picture.

Sun Sign

To put it simply, Aquarius sun signs are individualistic and independent. They might not look physically eccentric, but their behavior, or rather their personality, definitely raises some eyebrows.

They might be misunderstood because people don't understand who they truly are and why they behave in the way they do. However, once people are accustomed to their Aquarius friends, they become fond of them.

Aquarius Sun is someone who is a joy to be around. They are joyful social butterflies who like to spend time with people. They like to make a lot of friends because they do not like getting too attached to people. They have commitment issues, and close emotional relationships suffocate them.

Moon Sign

Aquarius moon signs are emotionally distant and cold. People feel they are unpredictable and unreadable. These people make wonderful friends, so long as their attachment issues are not threatened by their friendships or relationships.

There are plenty of Aquarius moon signs who have unconventional or unorthodox types of relationships. However, these connections work because they keep the flighty Aquarius at ease. These individuals value their independence and freedom above all else, so it is important to them that they do not lose their identity in any relationship they get into.

It is also important that these individuals express their needs to their friends and partners. They require some alone time and do not appreciate it when people are clingy. This is why they need to communicate their needs so their relationships can thrive.

Rising Sign

This is a person who is eccentric and flamboyant. They do not look or behave in any conventional way. They are the out-of-the-box kind of people. They don't accept or respect social norms.

They have unusual ideas about how the world should work. They tend to be emotionally flighty. They might have commitment issues and are not fully emotionally comfortable with themselves or others.

These individuals need to find their center and accept how beautifully unique they are. In return, they also need to accept that everyone is different, and that is okay. They need to respect that other people have different views and that they should be heard.

Aquarius through the Houses

Second

This is an uncomfortable placement. This position signifies irresponsibility in financial matters. These people will go through financial fluctuations quite often. They might also have strange jobs or more than one job at a time.

They also might have self-esteem issues. They will question their sense of worth and value, leaving them feeling negative about themselves. However, they will find comfort with their friends. These individuals will discover that true value is not in money or possessions but in the meaningful bonds they share with their loved ones.

Third

These individuals are rebels at heart. They have unusual, brilliant ideas and convictions. In other words, they march to the beat of their own drum. They have a rich social life and like meeting people from different backgrounds.

They are prone to giving in to their ego, which will get them into all kinds of trouble. They are also known to give unsolicited advice, which is ironic because they do not appreciate it when others give them advice.

These people need to honor their bodies because they might get so lost in their plans and goals that they forget to tend to them. They need to understand that if they have poor health, they will not be able to accomplish everything they have set their mind to do.

Fourth

This is an uncomfortable placement. People who were born in this position lacked stability, especially during their childhood years. They might have been moving around a lot, or their home life was insecure.

They might have watched their parents separate and compromised their sense of safety in the house. These individuals have a deep need for emotional independence. This could prove difficult to find in real life because they are not good at managing relationships or dealing with authority figures. They will achieve a sense of inner peace through the most unexpected situations.

Fifth

These individuals are dreamers. They have big goals and even bigger dreams to achieve. Their creative outlet is always strange and weird, but it is where they shine. Their creativity is unique and brings new things to the table.

They have this deep desire to create something new and remarkable. Once they know how to channel their inner personality into their creations, this will be achieved. They will experience a lot of change in their lives, and their priorities might get blurry, but their friends and loved ones will keep them grounded. These individuals have a deep sense that everything will be okay in the end.

Sixth

Individuals with this placement have unhealthy routines and habits. They could be involved in an unhealthy family dynamic or be coping through unhealthy coping mechanisms. They are prone to eating fast food and distancing themselves as a way to cope with their stress.

Physical activity is necessary for these natives. They need a bit of structure when it comes to their daily routine. They also need to set some alone time to soak in their feelings and rest instead of hurting themselves with their coping mechanisms.

These natives are likely to meet their close friends through their work. Their friends will ground them and give them an outlet where they can be at ease.

Seventh

People with Aquarius in the seventh house have unusual relationships with people. There is a lack of balance with their partners. They could be either distant or emotionally out of sync with their significant others.

These individuals will find themselves in relationships that end suddenly or haphazardly. They might not know the reason, but they can spot the problem once they notice the pattern.

Everyone with this placement will have a unique case, but they will likely have problems with commitment, attachment issues, or have cold, emotional natures. Once these people have attained equilibrium and figured out a way to balance themselves in relationships, they will notice a significant change in their romantic encounters.

Eighth

Aquarius is a fascinating constellation. However, in the eighth house, it is dimmed and parched of its merits. This house only brings out the negatives of this sign, which is a difficult position for the native.

This manifests in their inability to cope with changes, life stressors, and fast-paced encounters with people. They feel lost in the world and cannot hear their voice, wants, and needs.

As sociable as these people are, they need to understand the value of solitude and learn to sit alone. They need to ground themselves and listen to their inner selves. They need to have the time and energy to connect with their emotions. They will most likely cultivate grounding rituals before stepping foot out into the world, which will be helpful to them.

Ninth

In this placement, natives are on a journey to find out how to live out their dreams and desires. These individuals have extraordinary minds; their interests can make them true pioneers in their fields. However, their lack of determination stands in the way.

These people have a hard time accepting responsibility for their lives. They find something or someone else to blame for their unrealized dreams. These natives find themselves in a loop of dreaming dreams and watching them fade slowly.

To avoid this pain, the ninth house tells these natives that they are capable of taking this journey, but they need to be serious about their dreams so that they can experience the self-actualization they have been craving.

Tenth

People with Aquarius in the tenth house are individualistic. They are completely unconventional inside and out. Their minds are open to the magic of the universe, but they cannot fully understand it. They understand that everyone and everything is connected, but they do not know what to do with this information.

They feel as if they can reach enlightenment, but they do not know how to do so. Their life will be a journey to find meaning. Their minds work in fascinating ways, and this shows in their appearance. They are the kinds of people who wear flamboyant fashion with unconventional colors and look comfortable in their skin.

Eleventh

This placement is about ultimate freedom. These individuals recognize how they are confined in the world. Internally, they see how they are held captive by their thoughts, habits, and subconscious behavior. Externally, they see how they are confined to social rules.

They want to break free from societal standards and expectations. They do not relate to social class, jobs, and other rules. They believe that everyone is a unique expression of the universe, and that people should not be groomed to blindly follow society.

The world can be depressing for them, but on the other hand, these individuals are blessed with friends who balance them and give them more realistic expectations.

Twelfth

This karmic placement speaks of a mysterious, stressful, and sudden death in a past life. As a result, these individuals feel a bit out of place in their current life. It is almost as if they are disconnected from themselves and others.

According to astrologists, these people need to connect with humanity so that they can reconnect with humanity. They suggest charity work or an activity where they are helping others and feeling good about their activities. Their relationships are good for them as well. Their true friends and life partners ground them and give them a sense of safety. These individuals feel like they belong with their loved ones, which is why they should always remain close to them.

Aquarius and Lunar Houses

Dhanistha Nakshatra

Third Pada

These individuals are blessed with good personalities and strong moral compasses. They are artistic, so they have various creative outlets. They can be self-righteous at times, which is why they should ground themselves in reality and remember that everyone is different.

Fourth Pada

People born in this Pada are athletic. They have a lot of energy and channel it into different physical activities. They tend to be aggressive sometimes, so they need to learn a healthy way to channel and release their anger.

Shatabhisha Nakshatra

First Pada

Natives born in this Pada are a bit impulsive. These people often act before they think, and they are known to make decisions based on their emotional state. They are sweet, loving, and make good friends. They are also known for their bravery and confidence.

Second Pada

These people make amazing parents. They are career-oriented but do not let their work take over their lives. They try to balance their career with family life and try their best to be present and loving parents.

Third Pada

These people are visionaries and futuristic. They have eccentric views, and they bring something new to the table. They are unapologetically themselves, which is inspiring to everyone around them.

Fourth Pada

These natives are very good-looking. They could become spiritual healers or doctors. They will have a successful family life, but they need to keep their unhealthy coping mechanism at bay.

According to Vedic astrologers, these natives can easily become addicted to alcohol.

Purva Bhadrapada Nakshatra

First Pada

These natives have great determination to reach their goals. Once they have set their minds to do something, they become disciplined and consistent. They are also short-tempered and might hurt others with their words.

Second Pada

These individuals have good looks and noticeably large eyes. They do not grasp reality well and might lose themselves in the occult. Astrologers say that they can make great astrologers and magic workers.

Third Pada

People born in this Pada are amazing communicators. They might be a bit talkative, but it is how they show others that they are interested in getting to know them. These individuals like to spend time-consuming knowledge, so they are fairly intellectual.

Chapter 13: The Well-Balanced Libra

Libra symbol.
Phantom Open Emoji maintainers and contributors, CC BY 3.0
<https://creativecommons.org/licenses/by/3.0>, via Wikimedia Commons:
https://commons.wikimedia.org/wiki/File:Phantom_Open_Emoji_264e.svg

Date: September 23d - October 22nd

This constellation has scales as its symbol, which says a lot about this sign. Ruled by Venus, Libra is mainly concerned with balance and harmony above all else.

Libras are concerned with fairness and balance. They uphold these values in everything they do, big or small. For instance, if someone is left out of the conversation, a Libra would make sure to include them. A typical Libra is most likely an activist who stands up for people's rights.

Other factors contribute to this sign's symbol. When the Romans were studying this constellation, they noticed a point that the sun crossed while it was traveling from the Northern Hemisphere to the South. This is the exact time when the days and nights were equal.

Based on their discovery, the Romans found it appropriate to give this constellation the symbol of the scales. One scale contained the night, the other the day, and they were in perfect balance.

However, long before the Romans, Babylonian astrologists also associated the constellation with balance. They called it "Zibbaanna," which translates to "the balance of Heaven."

Before the Romans' time, this constellation was actually part of Scorpio. The Greeks thought of them as the claws of Scorpio. At that time, the Scorpio constellation was much bigger than it is today. The Romans changed this; they dislocated the claws from Scorpio and separated them into the two constellations that we are familiar with today.

Key Phrase: "I Balance"

As mentioned before, Libras are concerned with balance. Naturally, their key phrase is going to be about balancing things. Libras are known as skilled negotiators and are usually the person in the group who takes on the role of mediator. They bring back the group's balance. They dislike conflict and would not let it proceed if they can do something about it.

Strengths

- Artistic
- Charming
- Diplomatic
- Easy going
- Fairness
- Harmony
- Refined taste
- Strategic

- Social butterfly
- Socially Intelligent

Weaknesses

- Avoids conflicts
- Avoids confrontation
- Easily distracted
- Indecisive
- Passive-aggressive
- Repress feelings
- Self-sacrificing attitude

Pet Peeves

- Bossy attitude
- Interruption
- Injustice

Ruling Planet

Similar to Taurus, Venus also rules Libra. This means that the two signs share similar qualities because the same energy influences them. However, they still retain their unique qualities because of how the two signs' different energies manipulate this Venusian energy.

For instance, Libra has a strong theme relating to the idea of two's: partnerships, relationships, the scales, etc. Venus is the planet of love; naturally, Venus highlights the idea of partnerships with Libra. After all, they are the rulers of the seventh house, the house of relationships. Venus blesses Libra with extensive social life and sharp social skills.

Venus influences Libra to appreciate art and create it themselves. They adore beauty and have the talent to see it everywhere they look. Libras might be a bit lazy and messy, but they would still make sure that their space looks neat. However, chances are that they hid all the mess in the closet room.

Sun Sign

Libra Sun signs are about the friendliest individuals you could meet; in fact, some people mistake their friendliness with being flirty. The beautiful thing about Libras is that they treat everyone they care about with the same love and kindness. They are very sociable, and it is generally nice to be around them.

They make excellent negotiators and mediators. They often handle disagreements with compromise, yet a lot of Libras would rather sacrifice their needs to keep their person happy. Evolved Libras know better than to do that, so they suggest a middle ground that they can meet.

Libra is an air sign, so any Libra Sun sign is bound to be flighty, hesitant, and occasionally unconventional. Their intention is always good; they do not mean to hurt others with their flakiness.

Their indecisiveness stems from having full knowledge of any situation. They can see different sides and perspectives of the same situation. This makes them feel like they can make a fair judgment, yet at the same time, it often leaves them in a mental space where they want to be on the fence.

Libras are very self-aware individuals. They need to know that they are being fair in their platonic and non-platonic relationships. They would rather create a harmonious environment than a negatively charged one.

Libras dislike confrontations and will play mind games before facing and addressing a situation. However, when someone pushes them to fight, they fight back. They make excellent debaters and are usually strategic about what they say.

Moon Sign

Libra Moon signs are attuned to their friends' and partners' needs and feelings. They can anticipate what their loved ones might need or want at the moment. They make amazing friends; they are the type of people you know who will understand and empathize with you.

These individuals have excellent communication skills and know exactly how to express their feelings. Typically, Libras are not upfront about their emotions. However, once a Libra Moon is comfortable enough, they communicate about how they feel emotionally. So, you will never be in the dark with a Libra Moon because they will be communicative enough with you.

They are also charming and optimistic people. They know how to bring out the best in others just by being friendly and kind. Their strong need for fairness and well-balanced relationships is inspiring. However, sometimes this causes strain on a Libra Moon because they often feel like they are the ones who need to restore the balance in every situation.

They are also sensitive and might be a bit passive in relationships. More often than not, they put the other person's feelings and priorities first. They do it out of love, but they also have a tendency to sacrifice themselves for others. People can abuse this quality about them, but it takes an evolved Libra Moon to draw strong boundaries out of love for themselves and their partner.

Rising Sign

Libra risings signs are attractive and charming. They are social butterflies and like talking to everyone. The dark side of this is that they are also people pleasers and need to be liked. They are notorious for giving too much too quickly. This stems out of their people-pleasing mindset. Somewhere in their minds, if they give you everything, you will love them and stay, but life does not work this way.

They can anticipate conflict and are attuned to their loved ones' moods. This sensitivity, occasionally, sends them down an anxiety spiral because they do not want you to be upset or part of a conflict. However, they will try to resolve conflict and cheer you up even when you are not in the mood to be cheered up.

A Libra rising feels like it is their role to fix what is broken. It is a burden that they wholeheartedly want to carry because anything off-balance makes them uncomfortable. However, there is a dark side to this; if there is nothing to fix, a Libra rising might create conflict or a situation that needs fixing.

Libra risings are artistic and appreciate art. They are fairly messy and can be lazy at times, but they perform and feel much better when they are in a neat environment. They like to be in aesthetically pleasing spaces, probably too much.

They adore beauty, but sometimes this makes them a bit vain, and they can dismiss alarming behaviors just because someone looks pretty. They care about their physical beauty but can spiral if they do not have a balanced approach to it.

Libra through the Houses

Second

Ruled by Venus, Libra in the second house will fixate on money, probably as much as a Taurus would. This placement will give this individual a gifted approach to business, especially with business partnerships.

These individuals might be anxious about their financial security, which will inevitably drive them to make their own money. However, Libras are spenders, so their money will most likely be spent on clothes, art, or whatever they feel like buying at any given moment.

Third

Libras in the third house are charming communicators and a bit flirty. They are diplomatic and love absorbing knowledge. They are not the type to spew facts or seem like a know-it-all, but they will be able to provide stimulating conversations with anyone.

Their communication style is graceful and serene, and they are also less likely to cuss. They may be a bit poetic in their communication and enjoy wordplay. They are excellent debaters, and their words can be a bit sharp when provoked.

Fourth

Fourth house Libras were probably raised in a house that valued harmony and balance. This placement could play out in two ways. One, it is a benefic placement, in which case this individual was brought up in a peaceful household. In the other scenario, if this house is malefic or badly aspected, then their home was withholding and passive-aggressive.

Fourth house Libras should have a close relationship with their parents, especially the mother. These individuals will uphold balance, fairness, and harmony when they have a family of their own. They are also most likely to decorate their house with different art pieces.

Fifth

Fifth-house Libras know how to have fun and are a blast to be around. They have artistic self-expression, and they often express themselves creatively. They might be artists and talk a lot about their creations.

They make amazing romantic partners and parents. They might be a bit pushy, but raising their kids to be intellectuals and culturally aware is really important. So, they will be making sure that their kids are well-read and exposed to different cultures.

Sixth

People who have Libra in their sixth house are very health conscious. They like to balance out their day between their responsibilities and tending to their bodies via eating healthy, working out, relaxing, etc.

They work hard in their marriage or serious relationships, but there seems to be a part of them that is not fully satisfied in the relationship. More often than not, a Libra in the sixth house needs to realize that the love they seek comes from within, not from another partner.

Their balanced nature allows them to escape the perfectionist energies in this house. They are also responsible for their professional tasks and try to be helpful and available to everyone as much as possible.

Seventh

Libra in the seventh house is the perfect placement since it is its natural ruler. Individuals with this placement enjoy relationships. They do not strive for it; they are like a magnet for relationships. Even though relationships come to them with ease, they have challenges to overcome.

One, they need to learn to stop losing themselves within the other person. Seventh house-Libras tend to mold their identity with their partner to reach perfect harmony. But these individuals do not see that they are creating a rift between themselves and their partners. They need to have a more yin-and-yang approach within their partnerships. They need to learn that peacefully co-existing is also an example of harmony.

Second, these individuals need to learn how to communicate effectively because they are most likely to bottle things or forget about them to keep the peace. Again, this is counter-productive because the more they don't communicate t honestly, the more their connection fades away.

Eighth

These natives might have had a rocky history with love, relationships, and control. They might have first witnessed it with their parents and internalized the idea that love is often more hurtful than rewarding.

They feel the need to self-isolate out of fear of getting hurt. They may have control issues in relationships or attract someone who is controlling. This individual will need to self-heal and rearrange their idea of love and intimacy.

They are likely to have active sex lives once they are comfortable with their sexual nature. They are also likely to be financially stable through business or romantic partnerships.

Ninth

Natives with this placement often deal with a harsh inner critic. They are almost never fully satisfied with anything that they do. They are confused about their beliefs and views of the world. They seem to be spiritually lost and unsure which path they should take.

They might find love with a person from another land. This person could be from a different country or have a drastically different background from them. The kind of conversions that stimulate them are usually about philosophy, faith, and other abstract concepts.

They might find that they need to work hard to sustain their friendships and relationships. They need to overcome the urge to have superficial relationships because it does not save them from getting hurt.

Tenth

People with this placement have an amazing reputation. They are known for being friendly, fair, charming, and elegant. They always make sure that they look good; they have an overall neat look. These individuals are most likely to succeed in careers that are related to architecture, design, fashion, and counseling.

Career-wise, they might be working with a partner or within a group. Their scope of work can also revolve around one-on-one meetings, as with counseling. These people are most likely to become friends with their work acquaintances. They also might be a bit flighty when it comes to their career, especially when they are looking for their professional interests.

Eleventh

Eleventh house Libras have a wide circle of friends. This is where their social skills and natural charming attitude shine. They attract a lot of people to them, and they absolutely love it.

Most people with this placement are concerned with justice in the world. They are likely to be activists and educate themselves about the injustices of the world. They try to help as much as possible because they truly believe justice can be achieved.

They hold these morals tightly - in their inner and outer circle. The microcosm mirrors the macrocosm for Libras in the eleventh house. They also educate their friends about the world's injustices because they believe there is power in unity. They are very vocal about it the things they believe in, whether in their home or online.

Twelfth

With the twelfth house representing Karma, Libra on the cusp of this house means that this person needs to pay their karmic debts in relationships. This placement could be indicative of many things.

This person might not know how to cope without a partner, so they will need to be independent in their lifetime before they find themselves in a healthy relationship. Another reason might be that they were selfish in their previous relationship or lost their identity. So, they are being given another chance to rebalance the scales.

People with this placement tend to lie to themselves to keep things going. The sooner they understand that they can control their fears, the sooner they will see who they truly are and the amazing talents they possess.

Libra and Lunar Houses

Chitra

Third Pada

Vedic astrologists say that natives associated with this Pada are wealthy and make a great impression in their field. They are socially adept and experts in various things outside their fields. They are artistically gifted and are interested in exotic science. They make a great deal of money through traveling, and they are passionate and caring partners.

Fourth Pada

Individuals connected to this Pada are highly ambitious and plan to follow their goals but do not always do it. They have a lot of potential within them, but they need to make a conscious effort to channel it.

Swati

First Pada

These natives are highly cultured and intellectual. They are intelligent and spend their time learning about well everything. They like having conversations with others, especially the ones that stimulate their mind. Vedic astrologers describe them as charming individuals who are quite attractive. However, they tend to be a bit arrogant and flaunt their knowledge.

Second Pada

These individuals are grounded in reality and have calming energy. They have a great mind for business and can give helpful professional advice. They might be a bit selfish because they over-prioritize their wants and needs. They are also described as materialistic and a bit vain.

Third Pada

Natives associated with this Pada spend time thinking about abstract concepts, like philosophy; they connect best with people who share the same mindset and have similar views. They are blessed in their career paths and function better in business partnerships. They spend a lot of money and are not very disciplined.

Fourth Pada

Swati fourth Pada people are sensitive, intelligent, and flexible. They innately know how to adapt to any new situation, so they do not fear change, and it does not cause much disturbance to their lives. Their friends are their support system, which would help this individual reach out to them.

Vishakha

First Pada

These natives tend to be a bit short-tempered and expect unrealistically quick results. They are passionate and make amazing partners. They might seem to be rude and stubborn, but on a more positive note, they are intelligent and intellectual.

Second Pada

These individuals are skilled in their professions and lead successful lives. They are very strategic and know how to defeat their opponents. They will gain a lot of wealth easily and make great researchers. They might suffer from an ear disease, and they might indulge themselves a bit too much.

Third Pada

According to Vedic astrologists, these natives will achieve success during their 32nd year. They love reading about different topics and are interested in religions and different faiths. These natives have great social and communication skills.

Chapter 14: The Extroverted Gemini

Gemini symbol.
Phantom Open Emoji maintainers and contributors, CC BY 3.0
<https://creativecommons.org/licenses/by/3.0>, via Wikimedia Commons:
https://commons.wikimedia.org/wiki/File:Phantom_Open_Emoji_264a.svg

Date: May 21st - June 21st

The twins represent this constellation. Looking at the night sky's constellation, you will see two figures holding hands. No wonder the ancients associated the constellation with twins.

In ancient Babylonia, this constellation was called "the twins," and it referred to two underworld gods. One of the gods is

Meshlamtaea, and the other is Lugalirra. Both of these gods were manifestations of Nergal, who brought pestilence and plagues. Nergal also ruled the underworld.

In Ancient Greece, this constellation is said to be named after Castor and Pollux. Now, these two boys were not twins, but they had the same mother and looked identical. Castor was mortal and was King Tyndareus's son, while Pollux was the immortal son of Zeus.

The two brothers were attached to one another, so Pollux prayed to Zeus that he would bring his brother back when Castor died. Zeus agreed and united them in the heavens as the Gemini constellation so they would never be separated again.

Key Phrase: "I Think"

Geminis are ruled by Mercury, which rules the brain. This makes them active thinkers and avid learners. Geminis are eternal students at heart; they might not learn everything to its full extent, but they will try to get a taste of everything that interests them.

You might have noticed that you can discuss any topic with a Gemini, and they will have something to say about it. However, their knowledge tends to stop at the surface level. This does not apply to the topics that interest them. Once they get fixated on a topic, they will know everything there is to know about it.

Strengths

- Conversationalists
- Curious
- Fast learners
- Flexible
- Intelligent
- Outgoing
- Socially intelligent

Weaknesses

- Flighty
- Eccentric
- Unpredictable

- Moody
- Talkative
- Impulsive
- Indecisive

Pet Peeves

- Being ignored
- Being misunderstood
- Interruption

Ruling Planet

Mercury rules this constellation. This planet rules the logical side of the brain, left-brain functions, reading, writing, communication, speech, technology, transportation, and short travels.

Communication is important to Geminis. They might be a bit talkative, but this is how they express themselves and connect with other people. They are also avid learners who are keen on soaking up knowledge.

They like to read about anything that catches their eye. Their brains are filled with a lot of information, which makes them fun to talk to. Speaking of which, Geminis are social butterflies. They can converse with everyone, and they make a lot of friends wherever they go.

They are smart with technology and might use it to express themselves and make a profit from it. People with significant Gemini placements find themselves in careers that have to do with technology, writing, or the media. They might also take up jobs that are either far away from where they live or call for them to travel a lot.

Sun Sign

Gemini Sun signs are energetic beings who love to learn and meet different people. Their curiosity knows no bounds. Geminis who operate on a lower octave might find themselves interested in gossiping, thinking, and talking about things that are none of their business.

Awakened Geminis, recognize that gossip is a waste of mental energy and time. They channel their curiosity into learning about themselves and the world. They always want to expand their knowledge into uncharted territories. The more they know about the world, the better they feel. Geminis have a deep desire to know everything if they can.

These individuals are fun to be around. They are funny, smart, and just a joy to be around. They are also usually flexible and like to go with the flow. However, they can be moody and snappy at times, making them a little inflexible - it all depends on how they feel.

Moon Sign

Gemini Moon signs are hilarious. They have a humorous outlook on life and often use their humor to defuse tension or negative feelings. They are intelligent and intellectual. Communication is very important for them. They like to spend quality time with their loved ones.

Their emotional environment fluctuates frequently, and it can confuse them. They feel lost at times, and they are not sure which path they should be following. This is why their friends can be the people who ground them and help them find their center.

These individuals can be too logical for their own good and, at times, see things in a very literal sense. This ends up perplexing them, but they eventually learn not to take things so literally.

Rising Sign

Gemini ascendants are full of energy. They cannot stay in the same place for too long; they always need to be moving. They are intelligent, and they let people know it. They have a strong thirst for knowledge.

They are talkative, sociable, and funny people. They like to have a rich social life and enjoy meeting people from different walks of life. They are the type of people who strike up a conversation with a stranger just because they feel like it.

These individuals are moody and shift perspectives a lot. One day, they will approach life with rationality and logic. Then the next, they are ready to throw logic out of the window. They can be unpredictable, but that is what makes them unique.

Gemini through the Houses

Second

People who have this placement are most likely freelancers. They despise the idea of conventional jobs that bring in stable money. These individuals need to have stability when it comes to their finances, which is why they make sure that they have different freelance jobs that bring in earnings.

The reality is that their financial situation will fluctuate, but they always know how to turn the situation around. They are talented individuals who can make a profit from different sources. They utilize their talents so that they can be financially prosperous. They are likely to be writers, journalists, or authors.

Third

These people are skilled with their words. They do not speak mindlessly and know what and when to say it. They are talented communicators and blessed with clear, logical minds. These individuals are attached to their siblings and love communicating with them.

Communication, in general, is something that they value above all else. They make this clear to people when they are not getting the hint to be more communicative. These people have a problem with being in sync with themselves. They need to learn how to listen to their bodies and honor them. They need to build a healthy routine that grounds them and gives them a sense of stability.

Fourth

This placement signifies a childhood that was filled with inconsistencies. Their parents might have sent mixed signals. One day they are approachable; the next, they are not. As children, they might have felt unsafe around their parents.

Also, their parents might not have allowed the child to express themselves; they might have interrupted them or not have given any weight to what the child had to say. They did not have clear communication in the house they grew up in. There might have been lies and a lot of murky communication growing up.

Fifth

Gemini in the fifth house indicates a person with a deep desire to express themselves. There is a multitude of ways they could do so, but since the fifth house is connected to creative expression, these individuals might find an artistic outlet. These individuals need to get in touch with their inner children to tap into their creativity.

This could be done through writing of any kind. They could be poets, use words in their art, or portray themselves in a book or a script. They could also do this through the art of speech, so they might be podcasters or use their words artistically through media.

Sixth

These individuals are multitaskers. They are more focused when they are juggling a few things simultaneously. Ideally, their place of work should allow them the space to do a few things at the same time.

For example, while they need to finish their tasks, they do this at the same time as managing a project and keeping up with their work colleagues. These individuals function better when they are in a friendly working environment. They do not need to be friends with everyone at work, but they will need to have their own circle at work.

Seventh

People with this placement connect with people through communication. Their love language is probably quality time. They love to be seen and heard by others to feel loved, but they also love to get to know people through conversations.

As close as conversation brings them to others, it could also be the downfall of the true emotional bond they can have. These individuals need to understand the difference between a good conversation and a conversation that allows for closeness and bonding.

They might confuse conversations that make them feel good with tough conversations that make room for closeness. When these lines are blurred, these people emotionally distance themselves from each other, and their conversations do not come to fruition. Their relationships will become deeper once they have emotionally opened themselves to others and allowed others to do the same.

Eighth

This is a fascinating placement for these individuals. They have this ease when dealing with big life changes that astound them and everyone watching. They are not necessarily the most flexible people, but they are practical and optimistic enough to deal with these changes in a stress-free mode.

These individuals cannot stand small talk with others. They would rather have meaningful conversations. However, not everyone feels the same or has the same mindset, so they really need to pick their people to avoid disappointment.

Individuals with Gemini in the eighth house will find their happiness in unconventional places or situations. Life will show them that it can offer them joy beyond their expectations; they only need to be open enough to receive it.

Ninth

People in this house have a passion for learning. They learn fast and seek knowledge on a daily basis. They are ambitious and feel they have a lot of goals to accomplish.

The problem arises when they compromise their single-mindedness by focusing on too many goals at the same time. Their powerful ambition upsets the balance between expectations and reality.

It gives them a sense that they can accomplish everything at the same time, which is impossible. These natives feel disappointed and exhausted when their plans do not materialize. They need to have realistic expectations so that they can accomplish their goals, one at a time.

Tenth

Natives born with this placement want to make a splash in the world. They want to be seen and heard by all. They are talkative and have a lot to share and say. They are the kind of people who share their opinions, whether they are asked or not.

Their social media could be a big outlet for them, but this is not what they are after. They will probably seek a career where their opinions and beliefs are in the spotlight. They speak in a carefree manner, which can get them into trouble. If they are to approach this line of work, they need to be mindful of their words.

Eleventh

People born with Gemini in the eleventh house develop exciting and adventurous friendships. They have a busy social life, and they love that they have a lot of friends they can reach out to.

These natives feel the need to share their thoughts constantly. Most of their conversions involve a rich brainstorming session, which is one of their favorite activities. People here have a constant desire to have enlightening conversations, but they do not yet understand that true enlightenment comes when one is vulnerable and honest with themselves and others.

Twelfth

This karmic placement suggests that these individuals died before speaking their truth. They had so much to say and more to show, but their lives ended before they could. During this lifetime, they will be challenged by speech difficulties of some kind.

It could be a result of low self-esteem, a physically challenging speech problem, or any kind of manifestation of a blocked throat chakra. Whatever the case is, these people need to find a way to express themselves.

Acceptance and confidence are key here. Once they feel comfortable with who they are, they will begin to shine and show who they truly are. They will share their thoughts and opinions with honesty, and it will fill them with absolute glee.

Gemini and Lunar Houses

Mrigashira Nakshatra

Third Pada

People born in this Pada are intelligent, intellectual, and curious. They like to spend their time exploring places they have never been to. They tend to be impulsive, which is why Vedic astrologers suggest checking in with a counselor when they feel like they are out of sync with themselves.

Fourth Pada

These natives have a suspicious nature, and it often threatens their relationships with others. They are good observers, but they sometimes create different realities in their heads based on their observations. Needless to say, these observations tend to be inaccurate, and it weakens their relationships.

Ardra Nakshatra

First Pada

These individuals are bright and quick. However, they can have an overall active mind, which brings about difficult feelings and anxieties. Astrologists recommend that these people meditate to relax and keep their composure.

Second Pada

People born in this Pada are reliable and dedicated to their work. However, this is a difficult Pada to work with because it brings misfortune into one's life. These people might deal with a lot of difficulties that stem from their fixation on materialism.

Third Pada

This Pada speaks of people who have short bursts of energy throughout their day. Their energy level is not consistent, so they need to figure out a routine that matches their energy level. It is also recommended that they find activities that increase their energy and help them maintain their productivity.

Fourth Pada

These natives are humanitarians at heart. They are empathetic beings who have a lot of love and kindness in their hearts. They involve themselves in charity work because they have this deep drive to help those who are in need.

Punarvasu Nakshatra

First Pada

These natives are creative and sociable. They like to surround themselves with friends and loved ones. They like to be on the move constantly and are ready for any adventure that comes their way. They also like juggling different tasks simultaneously, keeping them productive and focused.

Second Pada

People here are financially blessed. They find their joy in materialistic luxuries, so they always look forward to spending their money on earthly items. They like to travel to different countries and explore different cultures and cuisines.

Third Pada

These people have an active imagination. They are mentally active and like to spend time studying science. They are more scientifically inclined, so it is natural for these individuals to become astronomers, doctors, or involved in any career that allows them to study science at a more advanced level.

Section Five: The Fire Signs

Welcome to the final astrological element, fire. Aries, Leo, and Sagittarius are the final three fiery signs you will learn about. These signs are known for their energy, eagerness, and so much more.

There are a lot of qualities these signs share. For instance, they make loyal friends. This is a little-known quality about this element, but it is absolutely true. This is how it manifests. All of these signs are full of love and generosity.

If you are friends with anyone who belongs to one of these fire signs and you are in trouble or not feeling good, Aries and Sagittarius will listen to you and will volunteer head-on solutions to help you. A Leo will understand what you are going through and will try to comfort you.

These signs are enthusiastic and eager to tackle things; however, these qualities manifest differently. Sagittarius is almost always optimistic about things and is so full of enthusiasm that it is contagious. Aries likes to tackle life obstacles or tasks head-on. They might not give it much thought, either, as they hurtle headfirst to the solution. Leos are eager to work on their creative expression and are usually very excited about their creations.

Fire elements often feel frustrated when they cannot find their motivation or when nothing is stimulating them. It is as if their energy has been contained in a tiny space and is about to erupt. They will do just about anything to get rid of this feeling, which is usually easy since all of these signs will always create or find something to do.

Chapter 15: The Confident Leo

Leo symbol.
Source: Phantom Open Emoji maintainers and contributors, CC BY 3.0 <https://creativecommons.org/licenses/by/3.0>, via Wikimedia Commons: https://commons.wikimedia.org/wiki/File:Phantom_Open_Emoji_264c.svg

Date: July 23rd - August 22nd

The lion represents this constellation. It is one of the most recognized constellations by ancient civilizations. Ancient Sumerians linked the constellation to a terrifying monster known as "Humbaba the Terrible." This creature was the guardian of the Cedar Forest, where the gods lived. It had the head of a lion, sharp scales on its back, bull's thorns on top of its mane, vulture's claws, and two snakes attached to its body.

In Ancient Greece, the constellation was actually a lion sent by Hera to kill Hercules. However, the hero tricks the lion and kills it. The goddess appreciated the lion's bravery and effort and placed it in the stars as Leo, the constellation.

Key Phrase: "I Will"

Leos are the kinds of people who are sure of themselves and sometimes too confident. They do not doubt their abilities, so they know they can put them into existence when they want to achieve something. Of course, this does not always work because this is real life. However, their confidence and optimism are admirable.

These individuals are also creative. They love to brainstorm and create all the time. So, no wonder their key phrase is "I will." They will bring things into existence all the time just by being their creative selves. Leos can also be determined when they want to be. This key phrase speaks volumes about their willpower.

Strengths

- Confident
- Creative
- Generous
- Kind
- Loving
- Natural leaders
- Passionate

Weaknesses

- Arrogant
- Egotistic
- Immature
- Rigid
- Selfish

Pet Peeves

- Feeling used
- Feeling unheard and unseen

Ruling Planet

This constellation is ruled by the sun and rules the ego, identity, personality, life force, creativity, authority figures, and fathers. The sun has rulership over this constellation. This makes Leos creative and full of life.

Think of Leos as sunflowers; they always want to be facing the sun and in the spotlight. Leos love expressing themselves, but to do so, they need an audience who will see them. Leos are also generous, caring, artistic, and loving, which are not well-known facts about them. They have ego battles and often get into trouble with authority figures. Their ego makes them seem immature, putting them in uncomfortable situations with others.

Sun Sign

Leo Sun signs are full of life. They like to entertain, lead, and inspire others. They are sociable and surround themselves with like-minded people. Leos are creators, so they will most likely spend time with creatives.

They are, of course, charming and loving creatures. They enjoy helping others and are usually generous with their time and energy. They also relish being the center of attention, so they are guilty of leading conversations, talking most of the time, or talking over others.

They can be a bit manipulative when they want to get their own way, not to mention a bit passive-aggressive. They are also childish and stubborn at times, but some Leo suns grow out of it.

Speaking of age, young Leos tend to be egotistical, arrogant, and self-centered. However, when they are awakened to their truths, they work on themselves to change these qualities.

Moon Sign

Leo Moons are unapologetically themselves. They are passionate beings who love to create and work on their skills. They are very loving and can make incredibly supportive friends. They have this bold personality that attracts others to them like a magnet.

They have a lot of inner light to share with the world, but only when they are ready. They do like to be the center of attention, but with their selected people. They are also very creative; they always have a unique perspective that makes their creativity and whatever they create stand out.

They are also hopelessly romantic. They love being in relationships, both platonic and non-platonic ones. They love showering their loved ones with attention and gifts. Truly, these human beings have a lot of love to share with the world.

Rising Sign

Leo risings are fun, loving, and caring. Of course, this is Leo, so you know this individual loves to be in the spotlight. Not only do they like to be the center of attention, but they also somehow find themselves in situations where the spotlight is on them. Maybe the spotlight likes them too.

They are artistic and creative, and they look it. They are also generous and do not mind giving other people their time and energy. These people might struggle with their self-image and vanity and might create a persona just so they never look bad in front of anyone. They need to accept themselves as they are so that they can get rid of this unnecessary ego battle.

Leo through the Houses

Second

People with Leo in their second house are most likely models, actors, or artists who make a profit off their looks. These individuals have careers that put them in the spotlight. Needless to say, they enjoy it at first.

These types of careers are lucrative, but they have a lot of downsides. Depending on their planetary placements, these people can have a difficult time at work. This placement also indicates a sensitivity towards people's criticisms.

These people are always in the spotlight and get affected by people's thoughts and opinions about how they look. If these natives do not protect their feelings and place strong boundaries, they will be negatively affected by people's negative attention.

Third

These individuals can be a bit self-centered. This is a difficult placement because it is challenging to be friends with someone who only fixates on themselves and their feelings.

These natives have a habit of taking people's comments to heart. They take everything too personally, and the slightest things can upset them. They think that a change of tone or a facial expression is targeted at them.

This comes from their insecurities and low self-esteem. Once they have nurtured their inner child and given themselves some love, they will notice that everything that used to hurt their feelings no longer has power over them.

Fourth

This placement is a bit tricky because it depends heavily on the planetary placements and the location of the sun in the chart. If the sun is in a powerful place, then this individual had a loving, generous home – a home that allowed them to live their childhoods and shine in life.

However, if the sun is in an unfavorable placement or has challenging aspects, then this individual is outshone by their parents or siblings. When they were kids, instead of receiving attention and love, their parents received it instead. The child might have had a challenging relationship with one of the parents, most likely the father.

Fifth

This is such a favorable position because this is the natural place for Leo. These individuals are full of life and creativity. They are definitely artistic and are most likely talented in various things.

They might spend time perfecting their skills and performing for others. They could show their talents through social media or in real life in front of people. They will most likely express themselves through their art. It is their way of saying, "Hello, world; this is who I am." Leo in the fifth house is at its happiest when they are publicly showing who they are to the world.

Sixth

These individuals can be a bit childish and irresponsible at work. They have a lot of creativity and would rather work with it than complete the task as their superiors instructed them.

These people make their workspace fun and lively. Their colleagues love being around them because they are a joy to be around. They might have ego battles with their bosses, which is unfavorable. However, they have to learn to be more flexible, especially with authority figures.

These people might become entrepreneurs because they would rather be independent than work for someone else. Besides, they have a lot of creativity that they would love to incorporate into their professional lives.

Seventh

These natives are loving and caring in their relationships. They are generous and passionate about their partners. However, they often experience difficulty in maintaining a healthy balance between their own wants and needs and their partner's.

They do not have a sense of "we" in the relationship and can often become engulfed in their own world, so they forget their partner has their own world. They can get so fixated on their feelings that they do not ask their partners how they feel.

Their relationships will, unfortunately, be rocky until they learn how to be flexible enough with their lovers. They need to maintain the balance so that their relationships work.

Eighth

This placement indicates a big problem with authority. They need to change their attitude before they get into trouble. They tend to be too childish and inflexible, which attracts strict authoritative figures towards them.

However, with Leo in the watery eighth house, they are bound to experience a powerful transformation that will completely alter their behavior. If these individuals do change, life will feel much lighter and easier. They will no longer need to engage in fruitless ego battles or have unnecessary fights with others.

Ninth

This individual wants to set themselves apart from their relatives and family. They want to prove that they are truly individualistic and independent. They are firm believers in their adopted philosophies. However, they often fall into the trap of thinking that the truth is not relative.

Sometimes, their pride makes them think that they are the only ones with valid opinions, thoughts, and beliefs. Eventually, people will feel like they are being preachy and pushy with their beliefs. Once they are ready to let go of their pride, they will be able to see the beauty that comes from various beliefs.

Tenth

This placement speaks of powerful leaders. This is where the leader or manager archetype really shines. Now, these natives are not necessarily bosses; however, they have the same personality. They will be constructive and gentle leaders if the Sun is in a favorable position. They will know what it truly takes to be an effective leader who is part of the team and helps others.

However, they might have low self-esteem if the sun is badly aspected. This will result in a person trying to get everyone's attention by showing off or displaying grandiose behavior. This person might think other people are inferior to them, but this belief comes from the ego that shields them from facing their insecurities.

Eleventh

These natives have a complicated situation when it comes to friendships. They like the idea of having friends more than creating genuine bonds with others. They often fall into the trap of associating with people who will make them look good. However, when it is put into this perspective, one starts to see that this is not the basis of a healthy friendship.

They can also sometimes get too attached to their friends and idealize them. They turn them into something that they are not. Once these individuals can see every friend of theirs as their own person, they will start having healthier friendships. They will finally attract people who are loving and genuine.

Twelfth

This karmic placement speaks of people who do not know who they are. Their ego and sense of identity are blurry and unclear. This is the story of someone who finally realizes who they are through different life situations.

During this lifetime, they will meet themselves after everyone else has already met them. They will experience themselves and hopefully fall in love with who they are. These natives are truly loving, generous, and caring, but they do not know it. They are talented and creative, but they need someone to tell them. In due time, the universe will show these people who they are and what they are made of, and hopefully, it will be a nice experience for them.

Leo and Lunar Houses

Magha Nakshatra

First Pada

These people are natural-born leaders. They can be a bit idealistic at times, which is why they need to regain perspective whenever they idealize concepts, etc. They might reach powerful positions during this life. Their ego and pride can make them attract enemies, so they should be careful and try to keep the peace with others.

Second Pada

These natives are late bloomers. They will feel lost in life, especially if they do not know who they are. They will get a sense of their personality after their 28th birthday. They will achieve success and reach their potential later in life.

Third Pada

These individuals are intelligent and sociable. They know how to be part of a team and, more importantly, they enjoy working with others. According to astrologers, they will begin to shine after their 35th birthday. One of the best qualities of this person is that they know how to relax and enjoy themselves.

Fourth Pada

This placement indicates a person who is involved in education or politics. This placement is not fit for people in managerial positions, mainly because they make decisions based on their emotional state instead of thinking rationally. These people love spending time with their family and derive pride from their ancestors.

Purva Phalguni Nakshatra

First Pada

These natives are fiery, passionate, and intense beings. They will gain popularity among their peers, and they will be able to influence others easily. These individuals have strong personalities and are respected in their community. However, this can go to their heads and make them pompous and arrogant.

Second Pada

Individuals born in this Pada are neat, organized, and hardworking. They are intelligent and skilled communicators who know how to use their words. They can be very charming when they want to be. They usually speak their mind and are honest about how they feel.

Third Pada

These natives are a bit vain. They care about their appearance and people's approval of them. They spend a lot of time taking care of their physical appearance just so that other people will idealize them. Deep down, they just want to be loved, but this kind of love will only come from within.

Fourth Pada

People who are connected to this Pada are fierce competitors. They are often associated with the warrior archetype because this is the kind of energy they channel into the universe. They love their family and are willing to do anything to protect them.

Uttara Phalguni Nakshatra

First Pada

These people are fond of education. They will most likely become teachers, professors, or private tutors. They are intellectuals who read a lot and spend time researching different topics. They love philosophy and often wonder about abstract concepts in life. They also give great advice because they have this unique inner wisdom.

Second Pada

These natives are highly organized and neat. They have a practical outlook on life, which helps them achieve their goals. They like to have a structured routine to follow, especially in their professional lives. They are often critical of the quality of their work and others.

Chapter 16: The Passionate Sagittarius

Sagittarius symbol.

Phantom Open Emoji maintainers and contributors, CC BY 3.0
<https://creativecommons.org/licenses/by/3.0>, via Wikimedia Commons:
https://commons.wikimedia.org/wiki/File:Phantom_Open_Emoji_2650.svg

Date: November 22nd - December 21st

This sign is the only constellation given a weapon as a symbol, which has given rise to many queries regarding the chosen image. The story behind this symbol dates back to the Sumerians, who named the constellation after the god Pabilsag. Scholars decoded this name and found that it translates to "the archer."

Babylonians also assigned this constellation to their god Nergal, who was described as a Centaur with wings and a fiery bow. This explains why this constellation depicts a Centaur that is hunting something, but what is it hunting?

According to Greek mythology, the centaur was a warrior who was sent after Scorpios to avenge Orion, who was murdered by Scorpios' sting. The archer is aiming for Antares, which is said to be Scorpios' red heart.

This begs the question, does this mean that Sagittarians are inherently revengeful? No, they are more defenders of moral codes than vengeful beings. However, it is not this simple; this chapter will analyze Sagittarian qualities and persona in-depth.

Key Phrase: "I Understand"

Sagittarians are knowledge seekers. They are thinkers and debaters and are unafraid to wander into the unknown. They spend time thinking of abstract concepts or learning about them. More importantly, they do not reject any new idea that comes their way, no matter how unconventional it is, and as long as it does not violate their moral code, they will accept it. They like to think about the spiritual realm and wonder about the things that exist beyond our knowledge. They might meditate, travel, or experience spiritual experiences so that they understand and be connected to the spirit world.

Strengths

- Adventurous
- Fun
- Humorous
- Optimistic
- Philosophical
- Spiritual
- Spontaneous

Weaknesses

- Lack structure
- Overindulgent

- Preachy
- Prone to boredom
- Undiplomatic

Pet Peeves

- Clinginess
- Stinginess

Ruling Planet

The planet of good fortune, Jupiter, rules this sign. Astrologists describe Jupiter as the king of kings. It is known for its generosity and infinite wisdom and blesses humans with good luck, knowledge, and travel opportunities. Astrologists also describe this planet as an advanced version of Mercury because it rules the abstract mind. This sign is capable of breaking down and understanding complicated concepts.

Sun Sign

These folks look for things that can make their lives meaningful and worthwhile. This is why they are avid travelers, adrenaline junkies, and love taking up any new opportunities. They are cultured and concerned with abstract topics.

To them, learning is a valuable experience like any other and is necessary to expose oneself to new knowledge whenever it is possible.

These individuals are social creatures, so they might have friends everywhere they go. They might be a bit self-centered and self-serving. However, mature Sagittarians know better than to fall into these pit holes.

The more the Sagittarius sun understands the workings of the universe and spirit, the more they will open themselves up for service. They will be helping people in any way they can, and they will express gratitude for the blessings and good opportunities they have been given.

Moon Sign

The moon sign Sagittarian is an optimistic ray of sunshine. They often find the good side in everything. When they are feeling down, their brain automatically thinks about the good that can come out of the situation.

They can be a bit insensitive because they are truth speakers, and their words are often sharp and blunt. These natives do not mean to hurt others or have ill intentions, but they think that the truth should be prioritized over everything else.

They are also social butterflies and can accept people who come from different backgrounds or are vastly different from themselves. They have the same approach to different faiths and spiritual beliefs.

Romantic relationships can pose a threat to them. They fear commitment and dislike being stifled by a person or a relationship. Whoever is dating needs to understand that this person needs their space and freedom.

These people are goal-oriented, although their approach can be a bit unconventional. They sometimes lack the structure and dedication to actually get to their goal. Yet, their optimistic hearts do not look at these details and believe they will reach their goal by using their own methods.

New experiences and traveling can cheer up these natives when they are feeling down. However, they need to find the balance between running away from problems and traveling to catch a break. Otherwise, their coping mechanism will prove ineffective after a while.

Rising Sign

Sagittarius risings are some of the most outgoing and adventurous people you can meet. They are fun and spontaneous, and it is rarely boring to be with them. In terms of physical attributes, they have pointy noses and look smart.

They are optimistic and goofy and have a smile on their faces most of the time. These individuals have a lot of opinions and insight about various topics. A conversation with them can last for a very long time because you will never run out of things to talk about.

People view them as intelligent, highly educated, and intellectual people. Others admire them, and Lady Luck seems to be taking care of them in life. When Sagittarius's risings are feeling low, they cheer themselves up by finding something funny in the situation or by looking at things with a more positive eye.

Sagittarius through the Houses

Second

Second-house Sagittarians may find it difficult to earn money and save it. They might find it easy to find a job that matches their interests, but this job is less likely to satisfy their financial needs. These people feel that the moment they receive money, they immediately spend it. They are generally lucky, but they also need to cultivate a more realistic approach to their finances.

These natives also strongly display the energies of the second house. So, if they have money, they will spend it quickly and then spend the rest of the month worrying about their financial security. They might over-eat, earn a significant amount of money, spend money on a lot of purchases, and have an unrealistic perspective on their worth and value.

Third

Individuals with this placement are sociable and a bit talkative. They can't help it, though; they are usually enthusiastic about sharing their knowledge and having philosophical conversations.

They have a broad perspective but do not hold onto them too tightly. They like hearing about different views as well. They are generally optimistic. They might be the kinds of people who give unsolicited solutions to problems.

They are more of a cup half-full kind of people until they feel lost in life. When they go through this phase, their views and opinions are scattered, and they cannot seem to make up their minds on anything.

Fourth

People with this placement frequently travel in search of a place that feels like home, but their endeavors always end disappointingly. They do not feel like they have roots, and they cannot find a good enough place where they can establish roots.

They often feel like their country of birth is not a hospitable place for them. They feel like they cannot live as per their beliefs and values because it may not be appropriate or match their country.

They find momentary relief or satisfaction through travel and knowledge. Eventually, they will find their kind of home, but before they do, they need to soul-search before jumping to conclusions. This placement also suggests that they come from wealth or are blessed financially.

Fifth

This placement usually means that this individual is very creative. They have a lot of creative energy rushing through them and always incorporate it into their work. Their love for education, traveling, philosophy, and exploring different faiths is exaggerated in this placement.

These people might teach children at some point, which fits them perfectly because they have a lot of positive energy within them. It is also possible for them to teach unprivileged kids abroad.

People with this placement instinctively know what they want to do with their lives. They know which path to follow, and they are usually so excited to follow it that they make a lot of plans and follow through with them.

Sixth

In the sixth house, Sagittarius feels like they are destined for something great, but they are often confused, especially in their early years. They are not sure which path to take or what they should be doing to find their path.

They care a lot about other people and are always ready to sacrifice for the well-being of others. They have a lot of energy and enthusiasm that cheers up their colleagues at work. They are generally okay with their jobs, even if they are not exactly what they want.

They do not show extra love or attention to their own health, but they care about their loved one's health and are ready to preach about the importance of taking care of oneself when they should be taking their own advice and living by it. All in all, these people are humanitarians with a lot of love to share and give. They are generally optimistic about life and are a joy to be around.

Seventh

People who have Sagittarius in the seventh house are often inconsistent in their relationships. This placement suggests that this individual might feel stifled by their partner and relationship norms.

They might feel like they want to have a relationship tailored to their needs; they are not interested in participating in a relationship based on society's norms and expectations of what it should be or look like.

Other times, they might feel like their partner will betray them. This sense of doom looms over their relationship because the native is waiting for the other shoe to drop. They might prefer long-distance relationships or a relationship that provides enough space and freedom for both of them.

Eighth

This placement indicates frustration for its natives. They feel they have a lot of potential or so much to offer, but they cannot seem to find it. They are spiritual in nature and seek to be in harmony with the universe, but their views continue to change the more they grow.

Their spiritual paths will take them in multiple directions, leaving them confused and disoriented. However, once they trust the journey, they will feel content. Everything they have gone through, good and bad, will make sense when they have gained wisdom from their journey.

They are inherently lucky people, given that Jupiter is their ruler. However, if they abuse their luck or take it for granted, it will slowly be taken away from them. A good way to avoid this is to be humbled by the universe's gifts and feel and show gratitude.

Ninth

This is the natural placement for this sign, which means that its energies will be exaggerated in this placement. This native will find contentment when they embrace their Sagittarius nature.

This means that this person will find contentment when they explore the world by traveling and learning about it. The more they delve deeper into philosophical topics and investigate spirituality from various points of view, the happier they will become.

They do need to watch out for being self-centered, self-serving, and preachy. They need to understand that knowledge is to be shared, not used as a tool to stroke one's ego. The more they help out others and open themselves to serving people, the more Jupiter will bless them with its gifts.

Tenth

People born in this place are most likely to become educators, specifical professors in universities. They might teach philosophy or a class that is philosophical in nature. So, they could be discussing theories with students and teaching them how to look at things from different perspectives.

They could also be highly religious, especially since this placement conjuncts the MC. They might be spiritual gurus, preaching and helping others in their place of worship. The MC here in the tenth house indicates that this individual will somehow be in the public eye. However, their career of choice will heavily depend on planetary placements, especially ones in this house.

Eleventh

This is a person who surrounds themselves with a lot of people who come from different backgrounds. Their social circle will consist of people who give back to the world. They will enjoy a lot of conversations that are very Sagittarius in nature. In other words, they will be discussing theories, philosophical views, spirituality, etc.

This person is likely to have friends from different countries, which makes sense since Sagittarians are sociable and friendly. They will also enjoy spontaneous activities with their friends, like buying plane or train tickets without prior planning.

Natives with this placement are fun to be around, but they are not exactly the most sensitive people. So, they can hurt their friends' feelings by being too curt or too blunt with their words.

Twelfth

Given that this is a karmic placement, these natives have a long, deep spiritual journey ahead of them. They need to find out who they truly are and how to connect with their spirit. Life will be their greatest teacher, and all they need to do is trust the process.

They will feel lost from time to time; they might feel confused as to what they believe in and what aligns with them. This individual needs to remember that the longer their faith prevails, the clearer the picture will become.

This placement also suggests that just as these natives need to listen to their spirits, they must also listen to their bodies. They need to know when it is time to rest and when it is time to work or have fun. They need to take care of their body and keep it healthy and clean. They will also be receiving blessings from unexpected people and situations. The universe will aid them when the time is right.

Sagittarius and Lunar Houses

Mula Nakshatra

First Pada

According to Vedic astrologists, these natives have a noticeable nose, shining teeth, small testes, and a piercing gaze. They take pleasure in philosophical and spiritual discussions, as well as traveling. They are also described as arrogant, self-centered, and prone to developing an unhealthy ego.

Second Pada

People born in this quarter have enough potential to be good astrologists and have a gift that can make them work with unseen forces and practice different types of divination. During their early years, they will work hard to earn material possessions. However, they will enjoy mental peace and a good relationship with their mother in their later years.

Third Pada

These natives have good communication skills, and they enjoy delving into philosophical conversations. They have a lot of ideas about how people can be more spiritual, and they are driven to awaken people to their spiritual selves. They are described as mature and professional. When the planets are on their good side, they can enjoy an equilibrium between the material and spiritual worlds.

Fourth Pada

Individuals born in this quarter are intelligent, nurturing, and have an urge to take care of everyone. They believe that to truly take care of someone, you need to stimulate their minds with spiritual and philosophical concepts. They might suffer from emotional disturbances because they are extremely sensitive and are challenged to balance the spiritual and emotional plane and the material world.

Purva Ashadha Nakshatra

First Pada

These natives have a strong moral code. They care about ethics and philosophy and take great pride in their spiritual life. In terms of physical appearance, they are said to have noticeable eyebrows, big eyes, ears, and nose, and a large overall face. People are impressed by their charisma and personality.

Second Pada

People born in this Pada are intellectual, logical, and realistic. They are not necessarily spiritual or religious. They are generally successful and hardworking. This Pada suggests that they will achieve success in the material world. They like to be of service to others, which makes sense, given that they are kind and honest.

Third Pada

These people are described as kind and respectful. The material world consumes them, and they are often too impatient for their work to pay off. They may expect unrealistic results and be disappointed by reality. They fall in love too easily because they like the idea behind the person, not the individual themselves. They are also sensual and creative and love to express themselves creatively.

Fourth Pada

People connected to this Pada are intellectual, self-centered, secretive, and passionate. They are a bit impatient and impulsive. People view them as charming and sensual, which is true because these natives have a strong sexual allure. They are said to be an average height and have a somewhat flat nose.

Uttara Ashadha Nakshatra

First Pada

These people are said to be helpful and kind. They have powerful willpower, and they are ambitious. So, needless to say, it will be easy for them to achieve their goals and go after them what they want in life. They might be a bit vain and care a lot about their place within the high-class society.

Chapter 17: Aries, the Leader

Aries symbol.
Phantom Open Emoji maintainers and contributors, CC BY 3.0
<https://creativecommons.org/licenses/by/3.0>, via Wikimedia Commons:
https://commons.wikimedia.org/wiki/File:Phantom_Open_Emoji_2648.svg

Date: March 21st - April 19th

The ram symbolizes this constellation, which is a fair connection given how feisty and stubborn rams can be. Ancient civilizations, however, associated this constellation with various symbols and gods.

For instance, Ancient Babylonia recognized the constellation and named it the "hired man." They noticed that their rams and sheep would multiply in number whenever the constellation was visible in the sky.

Ancient Egyptians also recognized the constellation and linked it to Amun, the god of the sun, who was depicted as a human figure with a ram's head. They believed the sun would be at its peak power whenever Aries was in the sky.

In Ancient Greece, Nephele, the goddess of clouds, wanted to save her children from being slaughtered. So, she sent a flying ram to save them. The ram managed to save one of her children, and as a token of appreciation, the goddess sent it to the heavens, where it became the constellation that we now know as Aries.

Key Phrase: "I Am"

Aries is the first sign of the zodiac. They are in a constant state of finding out who they are and then feeling sure of themselves. From an astrological point of view, Aries is a child just gaining consciousness. They are concerned with everything to do with themselves.

This is why they can be a bit selfish and childish at times. They are just like how a child would act when they are still gaining their sense of self. However, because Aries are children at heart, they are also lovers of all that is new. They get easily excited and always look forward to going on adventures and exploring uncharted territories.

Strengths

- Bold
- Brave
- Energetic
- Fierce
- Independent
- Initiators
- Leaders

Weaknesses

- Childish
- Impatient
- Impulsive

- Selfish
- Stubborn

Pet Peeves

- Being controlled
- Being told what to do

Ruling Planet

This constellation is ruled by Mars, which rules energy levels, vitality, sex drive, sex, desire, libido, aggression, dominance, war, and violence. This fiery planet gives Aries its passionate and intense nature. Aries has a reputation for being hot-tempered, stubborn, and impatient.

These individuals are self-assured, confident, and sensual. Mars gives them this kind of confidence that makes them sure of themselves and feel comfortable in their own skin. Of course, this is if Mars is in a favorable position in the natal chart.

Aries is bold and fierce. They are not afraid to speak their minds or fight back when needed. They might hurt people with their sharp words when they are defending themselves. Sometimes, their words are subtle, but they still hurt. However, that is just fiery Aries when they are snappy, moody, or defensive.

Sun Sign

Aries are freedom-loving, adventurous beings. They are direct and honest when they want to be. They have a childish side that wants to roam around and explore, but this comes with the burden of having to carry responsibilities, which they are not fond of.

They have bold personalities, and they love beginning or starting new projects in their lives. They might not complete them, but they get so excited about their new endeavor that they convince themselves that they will complete it this time. Aries are determined beings, though, so if they really set their minds to it, they could finish the project.

They are fun to be around and love taking their friends on new adventures. They can be a bit impulsive and impatient at times, but this gets better with age. They also like to engage in healthy competition.

They are full of energy, so they spend their time exerting their energy on physical or mental activity. They also like to fill their days with activities and tasks because they despise feeling bored.

Moon Sign

Aries Moon signs are adventurous, spontaneous beings. They are passionate about the people and the things they love. They have all the determination in the world to chase and achieve the things they want in life.

They are a bit hot-tempered and easily irritated by inconveniences. One of their best qualities is their clarity about their wants and needs. This kind of clarity makes them feel accomplished and well-rounded human beings.

These people are infamous for acting on their emotions. This sometimes results in complicated situations because of their impulsiveness. They also fight back a bit too hard when they are confronted. They are capable of hurting someone in the heat of the moment and then regretting it later if they are not too proud to admit it to themselves.

Rising Sign

Aries ascendants are children at heart. They are full of energy, enthusiasm, and life. They like to stay physically active because, otherwise, they will be fidgety and irritable. They can be a bit immature, but they mean well. They are adventurous and love all things new.

They are confident and comfortable in their skin. They have a good sense of themselves and are sure of who they are. They can be impulsive and a bit selfish sometimes, but you have to remember that Aries risings can sometimes be like little kids. One of the things they might want to work on is their compassion. Sometimes they are so rooted in their reality that they forget that there are other people around them.

Aries through the Houses

Second

These individuals do not know how to enjoy the slow-paced moments in life. They do not know how to embrace the comfort of a home or quiet times. They like to live a consistently fast-paced life, but that is no way to live, relax, or enjoy the little things in life.

When it comes to money, they follow their instincts. Their gut guides them, and they usually reap good results. However, they can be impatient with their profit and expect unrealistically fast results. If they do not change their perspective, they frequently feel disappointed with themselves.

Third

People with Aries in the third house are known to speak in a fast-paced manner and sometimes aggressively too. They might not mean it, but their words can be sharp and unfriendly.

They are bright and intelligent, but they often have a difficult time keeping up with their minds. They have fast-paced thoughts that are sometimes illogical and do not make any sense.

These individuals are not good communicators, and this results in pent-up feelings that make them angry, impatient, and irritable. They can be stubborn at times as well, and they do not listen to people as much as they should.

Fourth

Aries in the fourth house indicates a house that is charged with energy. This individual might have grown up in a loud, noisy home. They might have witnessed a lot of aggressive fights that took place in their house. This person might have had parents who did not listen to them or were too stubborn to accommodate the child. They might have been the kind of parents whose motto was "My way or the highway."

Their parents were not good communicators. They talked over their children and did not listen to them or channeled their anger through physical activities. If Mars is badly aspected or in an unfavorable position, this child might have endured physical abuse from one of the parents.

Fifth

This is a really nice placement. These individuals are naturally joyful and happy and feel happiest when they are physically active. They love feeling like winners and often chase this feeling during their lifetime.

These individuals will probably pursue some kind of sport where they can exert physical energy and be a part of healthy competition with others. These are the kinds of activities that make them feel alive and happy.

They might also be personal trainers for children or train kids in any kind of support. If this individual is to have children of their own, they will most likely spend time with them by playing games or exercising.

Sixth

These individuals like to stick to a routine. Their routine will most likely include meal prepping and exercising. They also like to follow a work routine, which makes them hardworking individuals.

They can be a bit competitive with their work colleagues, but there is nothing wrong with a bit of healthy competition as long as it does not go off the rails. They are also likely to follow their instincts at work. They might not listen to their bosses and can be stubborn with them. These individuals have a difficult time being a team-player, but there is nothing that these people cannot achieve once they have set their minds on something.

Seventh

This is a challenging placement, but these natives can learn to work with it. See, Aries, the active, aggressive child, is the house of balance and relationships. This means that this individual has a hard time addressing conflict. They do not know how to communicate their feelings, especially when they are negative. They might repress their emotions to avoid any kind of clash with their partners.

Eventually, these natives will learn how unhealthy this is and learn to communicate their feelings constructively instead of blowing up in a fit of anger. Once they have mastered this position, they will feel alive in their relationships, and they will have more exciting sexual encounters than they were used to before.

Eighth

This placement is a bit rocky. These individuals have a lot of pent-up anger. They suppress their feelings, especially when they are angry. What makes matters worse is that they do not know how to channel their anger into a healthy activity. Their anger comes out in a volatile manner, and it is often uncontrollable.

These natives are also prone to overthinking and suppressing their gut feelings and instincts. On a brighter note, these natives enjoy active sex life. The nature of their sexual activity can be seen more through their Mars placement and other planetary positions.

Ninth

These natives find their purpose in things and subjects that truly inspire and speak to their passions. When they find something they truly believe in, they fight for it vigorously.

They are not the most open-minded or flexible people because they do not allow others to express their beliefs as much as they allow themselves to speak of them. They can be a bit stubborn, and no one can change their minds or show them other perspectives simply because they will not listen.

Tenth

These are the kinds of individuals who channel all of their energy into their careers and professional goals. They are likely to become entrepreneurs because they love working independently. This placement indicates innovators who create new and different things in their field of choice.

They will likely become pioneers in their field because Aries in the tenth house is a powerful placement. However, this placement also indicates low self-esteem and a low sense of worth because these natives measure their worth by how much they have accomplished and achieved.

They need to understand that their sense of worth and value has nothing to do with how much they have accomplished professionally. Their values and accomplishments are two separate things. Once they have figured this out, they will be more energetic, lively, and just happier.

Eleventh

These natives make a lot of friends during their lives. However, they are never around them long enough for the bonds to become stronger and deeper. They will likely experience superficial friendships because they always move on to new people.

They are sociable beings who easily make friends but are also likely to lose them due to a lack of consistent communication. These individuals have low self-esteem; they might compete with their friends and lose their friendships due to a competition that only existed in their minds.

Twelfth

This karmic placement indicates a poor set of boundaries. These individuals do not know how to build healthy boundaries for themselves. Unfortunately, they will be put into situations where people do not respect their personal space, time, or energy. Once this person has had enough, they will work on their boundaries and start communicating with others.

They need to understand that they fear boundaries because they do not want to be rejected by others. They need to speak their minds and fiercely fight for their rights, as an Aries would. Placing healthy boundaries is the first step to having happier, healthier relationships with other people.

Aries and Lunar Houses

Ashwini Nakshatra

First Pada

These natives are fiery beings. They are competitive, smart, and aggressive. They can get into fights with their colleagues at work due to unhealthy dynamics. According to Vedic astrologers, these individuals have slim and tall bodies. They have a low voice and small eyes.

Second Pada

People who are connected to this Pada have realistic expectations in life. They are driven, ambitious, and practical people. They know how and where they should place their energy, which is a rare skill to have.

Third Pada

These people have great communication skills. They speak their minds and expect others to do the same. They are also intelligent and know how to charm others. They have a lot of passion and drive within themselves.

Fourth Pada

According to Vedic astrologers, these people might become doctors or trainers because they are fascinated by the human body's inner workings. They will be interested in human anatomy early in their lives and easily soak in this knowledge. They also help individuals, so they will want to help others through their profession.

Bahrani Nakshatra

First Pada

These natives are selfless and altruistic. They are likely to have a successful marriage that is built on love and trust. Astrologers say they will have many friends of the opposite sex. They will also likely become teachers, dancers, dance teachers, or sportsmen.

Second Pada

These individuals are attractive, and they will enjoy an active sexual life. They will most likely become entrepreneurs because they do not want to be bound by other people's rules and restrictions. They will also inherit wealth from their grandfather.

Third Pada

These natives might find successful careers in modeling, acting, or dancing. They are comfortable in their skin and know how to use their body. They are also likely to have their own business later in life. According to astrologers, these natives can make great sex counselors.

Fourth Pada

People born under this Pada will try to find shortcuts in life instead of working for what they want. They are a bit manipulative and know how to get what they want by using their words. They can be successful as photographers, researchers, explorers, or detectives.

Krittika Nakshatra

First Pada

These natives are a bit short-tempered, but other than that, they have strong spiritual lives. They are generous beings who follow their moral compass. They are also intellectual and like to share their knowledge with others.

Conclusion

Perhaps while reading the introduction, you wondered whether you really needed to understand every astrological sign to be able to understand your natal chart. It's a common trap that most of us fall into when starting out. After all, understanding twelve signs - each with its own twelve houses - isn't really easy to do.

Take a moment to look back at what you've learned throughout the chapters of this book. Has it deepened your understanding of each sign? Do you find yourself able to work out how a particular sign would manifest in a house using your critical thinking skills rather than memory?

Anyone can memorize planets, houses, and signs, but that doesn't make an astrologer. What makes a remarkable astrologer is that they understand the delicate natures and influences of the elements of astrology and the connections between them.

This deep understanding of all aspects of the craft is how you, too, can end up with accurate and whole readings that tie together a whole natal chart. Instead of haphazard guesses based on which sign lies in which house.

On the topic of accurate readings and deeper understandings, as you develop your chart-reading skills, it's important to remember that astrological knowledge doesn't substitute other forms of knowledge.

In other words, getting stuck can easily reduce people to their signs, ruling planets, and natal charts. The fact of the matter is that while astrology provides a great deal of unparalleled knowledge, it shouldn't be your only source when it comes to human beings.

You'll go a long way when doing your readings by just listening to the person in front of you. How they talk, how they handle themselves, and how they respond to what they tell you. This will not only help you fine-tune your readings, but it will also help you with personal relationships.

Astrology can provide a more sheltered alternative to putting yourself out there in a friendship or a relationship. You may think getting hurt is impossible if you've already counted the red flags and carefully vetted the person in front of you. The truth is people are constantly changing.

A natal chart will show you what the individual is born with, including their aspects, challenges, and properties. This, however, doesn't mean they haven't done the work to heal, change, and overcome their challenges. If you don't take the time to supplement your astrological data with real-life interactions, you may end up losing out on a few good people and opportunities.

Last but not least, one thing that will give you a great head start as an astrologer is psychological knowledge. For example, understanding how one's relationship with their mother could affect them later on in life could give a sense of direction to your readings. It could also help you when it comes to delivering sensitive information to an individual.

Remember, astrological knowledge is a great gift, but it also comes with great responsibility. People display trust in you by revealing their time and date of birth. Take this into account whenever you're doing your readings. May you have a beautiful and blessed journey.

Here's another book by Silvia Hill that you might like

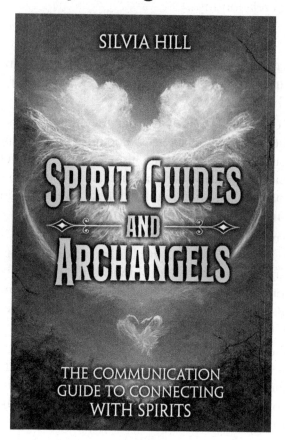

Free Bonus from Silvia Hill available for limited time

Hi Spirituality Lovers!

My name is Silvia Hill, and first off, I want to THANK YOU for reading my book.

Now you have a chance to join my exclusive spirituality email list so you can get the ebooks below for free as well as the potential to get more spirituality ebooks for free! Simply click the link below to join.

P.S. Remember that it's 100% free to join the list.

~~$27~~ FREE BONUSES

- 9 Types of Spirit Guides and How to Connect to Them
- How to Develop Your Intuition: 7 Secrets for Psychic Development and Tarot Reading
- Tarot Reading Secrets for Love, Career, and General Messages

Access your free bonuses here
https://livetolearn.lpages.co/astrology-and-the-zodiac-signs-paperback/

References

Campbell, C. (2014, August 16). A brief introduction to astrology. Retrieved from Com.au website: https://www.introinto.com.au/a-brief-introduction-to-astrology/

Groom, C. J. (n.d.). An introduction to astrology and zodiac signs. Retrieved from Westwoodhorizon.com website: https://westwoodhorizon.com/2018/10/an-introduction-to-astrology-and-zodiac-signs/

Hammonds, O. (2014, August 5). 3 benefits of astrology. Retrieved from 3Benefitsof.com website: https://www.3benefitsof.com/3-benefits-of-astrology/

Introductions to Astrology. (2020). In *Prognostication in the Medieval World* (pp. 814–817). De Gruyter.

Logan, J. (2017). *Astrology basics: A quick reference guide.* Jayne Logan.

As above, so below - astrology for Aquarius. (n.d.). Retrieved from Astrologyforaquarius.com website: https://astrologyforaquarius.com/articles/363/as-above-so-below/

Astrology planets and their meanings, planet symbols and cheat sheet. (2018, January 27). Retrieved from Labyrinthos.co website: https://labyrinthos.co/blogs/astrology-horoscope-zodiac-signs/astrology-planets-and-their-meanings-planet-symbols-and-cheat-sheet

AstroTwins. (2013, October 19). The 12 houses of the horoscope wheel. Retrieved from Astrostyle.com website: https://astrostyle.com/learn-astrology/the-12-zodiac-houses/

Kahn, N. (2020, July 29). The ruling planet for your zodiac sign & how it affects you. Retrieved from Bustle.com website:

https://www.bustle.com/life/ruling-planet-zodiac-sign-meaning-astrology

Planets Signs & Houses - astrology information. (2013, January 4). Retrieved from Thejewelledsky.com website: https://thejewelledsky.com/articles/planets/

Team Jothishi. (2019, November 29). Classification of astrological knowledge - history, significance and more - jothishi. Retrieved from Jothishi.com website: https://jothishi.com/classification-of-astrological-knowledge-history-significance-and-more/

(N.d.). Retrieved from Costarastrology.com website: https://www.costarastrology.com/natal-chart/

12 astrology zodiac signs dates, meanings and compatibility. (n.d.). Retrieved from Astrology-zodiac-signs.com website: https://www.astrology-zodiac-signs.com/

FrancosWriter, E., & 04/02/, Z. (2021, April 2). Sun sign meaning: What the sun means for your zodiac sign. Retrieved from Yourtango.com website: https://www.yourtango.com/2019328837/what-your-sun-sign-means-astrology

Goodman, L. (2006). *Sun Signs*. Edinburgh, Scotland: George G. Harrap.

Hall, M. (n.d.). The Sun Sign. Retrieved from Liveabout.com website: https://www.liveabout.com/the-sun-sign-206735

Naylor, R. H. (2014). *Home astrology: A non-technical outline of popular astrology tradition*. Literary Licensing.

Rocks, D. (2019, September 25). What is A Sun Sign? Discover your purpose. Retrieved from Com.au website: https://www.starslikeyou.com.au/what-is-a-sun-sign/

Fenton, S. (1992). *Rising Signs*. London, England: Thorsons.

Maria. (2020, October 8). What is your Ascendant Sign & What does it Mean. Retrieved from Trusted-astrology.com website: https://trusted-astrology.com/how-does-your-ascendant-sign-affect-you/

Marie, A. (n.d.). Rising Sign - Ascendant. Retrieved from Astrosofa.com website: https://www.astrosofa.com/astrology/ascendant

Pemberton, B. (2021, May 6). What is my rising sign and what does it mean? *The Sun*. Retrieved from https://www.thesun.co.uk/fabulous/horoscopes/5621885/rising-sign-horoscope-calculate-meaning-star-sign-personality/

Sargent, C. (1990). *The astrology of rising signs*. London, England: Rider.

Secrets, M. A. (2019, October 4). Zodiac Text Symbols - not emoji - my astro secrets. Retrieved from Myastrosecrets.com website: https://myastrosecrets.com/zodiac-text-symbols-not-emoji/

Angel, J. (2015, April 6). *What's Your Emotional Mode of Operation?* Harper's BAZAAR. https://www.harpersbazaar.com/horoscopes/a10491/whats-your-emotional-mode-of-operation/

Balancing the Light and Dark: Understanding Your Sun and Moon in Astrology. (n.d.). Byrdie. https://www.byrdie.com/astrology-sun-and-moon-5086414

Cafe Astrology .com. (2021, March 14). *The Moon in Astrology/Zodiac.* https://cafeastrology.com/moon.html

Kahn, N. (2020, July 23). *How Each Planet's Astrology Directly Affects Every Zodiac Sign.* Bustle. https://www.bustle.com/life/how-each-planets-astrology-directly-affects-every-zodiac-sign-13098560

Moon Sign Calculator, Astrology Moon Phase Lunar Horoscope Online. (n.d.). Astro-Seek.Com. https://horoscopes.astro-seek.com/which-moon-phase-was-i-born-under-calculator

Contributor, G. (2020, November 23). *What is Numerology? How it can change your life?* The Times of India. https://timesofindia.indiatimes.com/astrology/numerology-tarot/what-is-numerology-how-it-can-change-your-life/articleshow/79314743.cms?from=mdr

Hurst, K. (2017, December 18). *Numerology: What is Numerology? And How Does it Work?* The Law Of Attraction. https://www.thelawofattraction.com/what-is-numerology/

J, S. (2021, March 30). *How Does Numerology Work with Astrology?* MIND IS THE MASTER. https://mindisthemaster.com/astrology-and-numerology/

Numerology: History, Origins, & More - Astrology.com. (n.d.). Astrology. https://www.astrology.com/numerology

Numerology number characteristics. Learn what your numbers mean. (n.d.). See You. Be You. https://seeyoubeyou.com/pages/numbers

Destiny Numbers. (n.d.). Retrieved from Prokerala.com website: https://www.prokerala.com/numerology/destiny-numbers.htm

Felicia. (2017, March 23). What your Destiny number reveals about your life purpose. Retrieved from Feliciabender.com website: https://feliciabender.com/the-destiny-or-expression-number/

GOSTICA. (2017, March 23). THIS is what your Destiny Number is saying about your life. Retrieved from Gostica.com website: https://gostica.com/spiritual-lifestyle/destiny-number-saying-life/

McClain, M. (n.d.). Numerology - the birth name. Retrieved from Astrology-numerology.com

Coughlin, S. (2021, January 19). Your life path number is more than A personality type. Retrieved from Refinery29.com website: https://www.refinery29.com/en-us/life-path-number-numerology-meaning

Faragher, A. K. (2020, April 10). Numerology 101: How to calculate life path & Destiny numbers. Retrieved from Allure website: https://www.allure.com/story/numerology-how-to-calculate-life-path-destiny-number

Hurst, K. (2015, December 15). Numerology calculator: Your life path number and meaning. Retrieved from Thelawofattraction.com website: https://www.thelawofattraction.com/life-path-number-challenges/

the Cut. (2020, May 14). What is your life-path number? Retrieved from Thecut.com website: https://www.thecut.com/article/life-path-number.html

Adams, A. (n.d.). *Personality Number – what others see when they first meet you.* Retrieved from https://thesagedivine.com/personality-number/

Decoz, H., & World Numerology. (2001, September 1). Do Your Own Numerology Reading - Personality. Retrieved from Worldnumerology.com website: https://www.worldnumerology.com/Do-reading-numerology-02-Personality.html

Discover your personality number | numerology calculator. (n.d.). Retrieved from https://mattbeech.com/numerology/personality-number/

Adams, A. (n.d.). *Heart's Desire / Soul Urge number | meanings, calculations, and more.* Retrieved from https://thesagedivine.com/hearts-desire-number/

Heart's Desire number - numerology center. (n.d.). Retrieved from Numerology.center website: http://numerology.center/heart_desire.php

The Heart's Desire Number. (2009, July 30). Retrieved from Tsemrinpoche.com website: https://www.tsemrinpoche.com/tsem-tulku-rinpoche/numerology/the-hearts-desire-number.html

A brief history of tarot cards – articles. (n.d.). Retrieved from Bicyclecards.com

Brigit. (2018, May 9). What are Tarot cards + how do they work? Retrieved from Biddytarot.com website: https://www.biddytarot.com/what-is-tarot-how-does-it-work/

Tarot card meanings. (2011a, December 15). Retrieved from Biddytarot.com website: https://www.biddytarot.com/tarot-card-meanings/major-arcana/

Tarot card meanings. (2011b, December 18). Retrieved from Biddytarot.com website: https://www.biddytarot.com/tarot-card-meanings/minor-arcana/

Tarot.com Staff. (2019, February 25). The Major Arcana Tarot card meanings. Retrieved from Tarot.com website: https://www.tarot.com/tarot/cards/major-arcana

(N.d.). Retrieved from Squarespace.com website: https://static1.squarespace.com/static/5a07aca112abd96680bdc6fa/t/5b1d983d8a922ddcbe3a0ac4/1528666185262/MAJOR+%26+MINOR+ARCANA+QUICK+REFERENCE+SHEET.pdf

Coryna, O. (2020, November 22). Sagittarius energy & the Temperance card. Retrieved from Lilithastrology.com

Faragher, A. K. (2021, April 28). The personality of an Aries, explained. Retrieved from Allure website: https://www.allure.com/story/aries-zodiac-sign-personality-traits

King of wands tarot card meanings - aquarian insight. (2013, December 1). Retrieved from Aquarianinsight.com website: https://www.aquarianinsight.com/tarot-card-meanings/minor-arcana/suit-of-wands/king-of-wands/

Philips, S. (2019, April 28). Tarot cards for each zodiac sign. Retrieved from Tarot.com website: https://www.tarot.com/astrology/tarot-cards

SawyerAuthor, A., & 12/28/, Z. (2018, December 28). What tarot cards represent each of the zodiac signs in astrology. Retrieved from Yourtango.com website: https://www.yourtango.com/2018317524/how-tarot-cards-and-astrology-zodiac-signs-are-connected

Steve. (2019, December 4). What tarot card represents Leo? Retrieved from Vekkesind.com website: https://vekkesind.com/what-tarot-card-represents-leo/

Steve. (2020, January 28). What Tarot card is associated with Aries? Retrieved from Vekkesind.com website: https://vekkesind.com/what-tarot-card-is-associated-with-aries/

Tarot card meanings. (2011, December 15). Retrieved from Biddytarot.com website: https://www.biddytarot.com/tarot-card-meanings/minor-arcana/suit-of-wands/

Tarot.com Staff. (2016, July 14). A taste of tarot: Strength & Leo. Retrieved from Tarot.com website: https://www.tarot.com/tarot/strength-tarot-card-leo-zodiac-sign

Earth signs will inspire you with their groundedness. (2020, August 12). Retrieved from Cosmopolitan.com website: https://www.cosmopolitan.com/lifestyle/a33588028/earth-signs-astrology/

Knight of Pentacles: Upright and reversed love meanings & more. (n.d.). Retrieved from Kasamba.com website: https://www.kasamba.com/tarot-reading/decks/minor-arcana/knight-of-pentacles-card/

Page of Pentacles: Upright and reversed love meanings & more. (n.d.). Retrieved from Kasamba.com website: https://www.kasamba.com/tarot-reading/decks/minor-arcana/page-of-pentacles-card/

PSA: Your zodiac sign has its own tarot card. (2020, March 25). Retrieved from Cosmopolitan.com website: https://www.cosmopolitan.com/lifestyle/a31913908/tarot-cards-zodiac-signs-astrology/

Slozberg, M. (2020, April 4). 10 tarot cards that represent earth signs. Retrieved from Thetalko.com website: https://www.thetalko.com/tarot-cards-that-represent-earth-signs/

Virgo through the eyes of tarot. (2016, October 15). Retrieved from Tarotelements.com website: https://tarotelements.com/virgo-through-the-eyes-of-tarot/

Air signs can talk, think, and network faster than the wind. (2020, July 14). Retrieved from Cosmopolitan.com website: https://www.cosmopolitan.com/lifestyle/a33314375/air-signs-astrology/

Cabral, C. (n.d.). The 10 fundamental Libra traits and the best advice for Libras. Retrieved from Prepscholar.com website: https://blog.prepscholar.com/libra-traits-personality

Mukomolova, G. (2018, September 28). What tarot cards correspond to your zodiac signs. Retrieved from Nylon.com website: https://www.nylon.com/articles/what-tarot-cards-zodiac-signs

Steve. (2019, December 17). What tarot card represents Gemini? Retrieved from Vekkesind.com website: https://vekkesind.com/what-tarot-card-represents-gemini/

Tarot.com Staff. (2018a, January 15). A taste of tarot: Aquarius and The Star. Retrieved from Tarot.com website: https://www.tarot.com/tarot/star-tarot-card-aquarius-zodiac-sign

Tarot.com Staff. (2018b, September 25). A taste of tarot: Justice & Libra. Retrieved from Tarot.com website: https://www.tarot.com/tarot/justice-tarot-card-libra-zodiac-sign

The tarot suit of Swords meanings & interpretation. (2014, April 3). Retrieved from Sunsigns.org website: https://www.sunsigns.org/tarot-suit-of-swords-minor-arcana/

(N.d.). Retrieved from Gyanswers.com

Cabral, C. (n.d.). The 10 Scorpio personality traits to know. Retrieved from Prepscholar.com website: https://blog.prepscholar.com/scorpio-personality-traits

Carrillo, G. J. R. (2017). A King of Cups. In A. M. G. López & A. Farnsworth-Alvear (Trans.), *The Colombia Reader* (pp. 113–117). Duke University Press.

DLC Tarot Notebooks. (2019). *Page of cups: Tarot diary log book, record and interpret readings, lined notebook journal for tarot lovers.* Independently Published.

Douglas, M. (n.d.). The fundamental 6 Pisces traits, explained. Retrieved from Prepscholar.com website: https://blog.prepscholar.com/pisces-traits

Knight of Wands Tarot card meanings. (2011, December 22). Retrieved from Biddytarot.com website: https://www.biddytarot.com/tarot-card-meanings/minor-arcana/suit-of-wands/knight-of-wands/

Mantis Tarot. (2020, September 4). The chariot & cancer: The power of moving waters. Retrieved from Mantistarot.com website: https://mantistarot.com/2020/09/03/the-chariot-cancer-the-power-of-moving-waters/

Tarot card meanings. (2011, December 15). Retrieved from Biddytarot.com website: https://www.biddytarot.com/tarot-card-meanings/minor-arcana/suit-of-cups/

Tarot.com Staff. (2016, February 17). A taste of tarot: Pisces and The Moon. Retrieved from Tarot.com website: https://www.tarot.com/tarot/moon-tarot-card-pisces-zodiac-sign

Wen, B. (2019, October 29). Tarot's death card & the season of Scorpio - north Atlantic books. Retrieved from Northatlanticbooks.com website: https://www.northatlanticbooks.com/blog/tarots-death-card-the-season-of-scorpio/

(N.d.). Retrieved from Costarastrology.com website: https://www.costarastrology.com/zodiac-signs/cancer-sign

Brigit. (2016, January 13). Tarot by numbers: A fast and simple way to learn the cards with numerology. Retrieved from Biddytarot.com website: https://www.biddytarot.com/tarot-by-numbers/

Numerology of Tarot. (n.d.). Retrieved from Thethreadsoffate.com website: https://www.thethreadsoffate.com/blogs/news/numerology-of-tarot

Tarot & numerology - minor Arcana ace to ten - tarot study. (2015, July 1). Retrieved from Tarot-study.info website: https://tarot-study.info/articles/tarot-numerology-minor-arcana-ace-to-ten/

Tarot and Numerology: What do numbers in Tarot Mean for the Minor Arcana? (Infographic). (2016, November 14). Retrieved from Labyrinthos.co website: https://labyrinthos.co/blogs/learn-tarot-with-labyrinthos-academy/tarot-and-numerology-what-do-numbers-in-tarot-mean-for-the-minor-arcana-infographic

Tarot.com Staff. (2019, May 2). The Minor Arcana: Meanings behind the number cards. Retrieved from Tarot.com website: https://www.tarot.com/tarot/meaning-of-numbers-in-minor-arcana

The minor Arcana: How numbers and elements give tarot meaning. (n.d.). Retrieved from Gaia.com website: https://www.gaia.com/article/the-minor-arcana-how-numbers-and-elements-give-tarot-meaning

The Numerologist Team. (2010, February 13). Numerology and the minor Arcana cards in Tarot - numerologist.Com. Retrieved from Numerologist.com website: https://numerologist.com/numerology/numerology-and-the-tarot/

Chris, & Styles, S. (2020, June 12). Numerology meanings of Tarot Major Arcana. Retrieved from 365Pincode.com website: https://365pincode.com/numerology-meanings-of-tarot-major-arcana/

Major Arcana Correspondences. (2018, August 17). Retrieved from Tarotelements.com website: https://tarotelements.com/major-arcana-correspondences/

Meg. (2010, March 25). Numerological & astrological attributes of the Major Arcana. Retrieved from Padmes.com website: https://padmes.com/2010/03/numerological-astrolgical-attributes-of-the-major-arcana/

This story behind the Tarot major Arcana mirrors human experience. (n.d.). Retrieved from Gaia.com website: https://www.gaia.com/article/journey-of-the-tarot-how-major-arcana-meanings-mirror-the-soul

Boswell, L. (2017, August 28). Planet correspondences in astrology and Tarot — Lisa Boswell. Retrieved from Divinationandfortunetelling.com website: https://divinationandfortunetelling.com/articles/2017/8/28/planet-correspondences-in-astrology-tarot-and-divination

Mantis Tarot. (2020, April 20). The astrology of the Major Arcana: The planets. Retrieved from Mantistarot.com website: https://mantistarot.com/2020/04/20/the-astrology-of-the-major-arcana-the-planets/

Media, H. (n.d.). The tarot & planetary correspondences. Retrieved from Voxxthepsychic.com website: https://voxxthepsychic.com/tarotplanets.html

12 Houses Zodiac Tarot spread. (2015, December 21). Retrieved from Angelorum.co website: https://angelorum.co/topics/divination/12-houses-zodiac-tarot-spread/

learntarot. (2018, November 27). Learning & using the Zodiac Tarot Spread. Retrieved from Thesimpletarot.com website: https://thesimpletarot.com/learning-using-zodiac-tarot-spread/

Waits, P. (2020, July 23). Tarot spreads: The 3 most effective card spreads. Retrieved from themagichoroscope.com website: https://themagichoroscope.com/zodiac/tarot-spreads

Wigington, P. (n.d.). How to use the Celtic Cross spread in Tarot. Retrieved from Learnreligions.com website: https://www.learnreligions.com/the-celtic-cross-spread-2562796

Regan, S. (2021, January 21). The simplest tarot "spread" for quick insight anytime you need it. Retrieved from Mindbodygreen.com website: https://www.mindbodygreen.com/articles/one-card-tarot

Crawford, C. (2019, December 21). How to use a 3 card tarot spread for self care — the self-care emporium. Retrieved from Theselfcareemporium.com website: https://theselfcareemporium.com/blog/tarot-card-spread-self-care

Astrology symbols and glyphs. (2015, April 16). Retrieved from Cafeastrology.com website: https://cafeastrology.com/astrology-symbols-glyphs.html

https://link.springer.com/content/pdf/10.1007%2F978-1-4614-6141-8_148.pdf

https://www.constellation-guide.com/constellation-names/

https://astronomy.swin.edu.au/sao/guest/bacon/#:~:text=One%20such%20new%20idea%20was,relied%20on%20astrologers%20for%20counsel

https://depts.washington.edu/triolive/quest/2007/TTQ07030/history.html#:~:text=Chinese%20Zodiac%20%7C%20History&text=The%20Chinese%20zodiac%20consists%20of,was%20over%202000%20years%20ago.

https://www.purewow.com/wellness/chinese-zodiac-elements

https://kaleela.com/en/the-arabic-horoscope-what-does-it-say-about-your-future-holds#:~:text=Despite%20the%20fact%20that%20it's,and%20your%20parent's%20social%20standing.

https://www.mindbodygreen.com/articles/aspects-in-astrology#:~:text=The%20five%20major%20aspects%20in,i.e.%2C%20Sun%20conjunct%20Venus

https://www.bustle.com/p/being-born-during-mercury-retrograde-can-actually-be-a-good-thing-according-to-astrologers-18189808#:~:text=So%2C%20what%20does%20it%20mean,t%20know%20about%2C%20of%20course.

https://astrologyking.com

https://www.elephantjournal.com/2013/10/nakshatras-their-meaning-purpose-in-vedic-astrology/

https://vedicastrology.net.au/blog/vedic-articles/the-lunar-mansions-of-vedic-astrology/#:~:text=The%20ancient%20Indians%20looked%20up,called%20Lunar%20Mansions%20or%20Nakshatras.

https://www.mypandit.com/astrology/nakshatras-constellations/#:~:text=Each%20Nakshatra%20has%20four%20'Padas,Artha%2C%20Kaam%2C%20and%20Moksha.

https://www.ganeshaspeaks.com/astrology/nakshatras-constellations/#:~:text=Nakshatra%20Meaning,Pisces%20covered%20by%20Revati%20Nakshatra

https://greekerthanthegreeks.com/2021/03/pisces-the-ancient-greek-myth-behind-the-zodiac-sign.html

All the Padas: https://www.rahasyavedicastrology.com/

https://www.theoi.com/Ther/Skorpios.html#:~:text=SKORPIOS%20(Scorpius)%20was%20a%20giant,the%20beasts%20of%20the%20world.

https://www.rahasyavedicastrology.com/jyeshtha-nakshatra-4th-pada-characteristics/

https://divyavivaham.com/services/nakshatra-rashi-list

https://www.space.com/26088-libra-constellation-scales-origins.html

https://www.constellation-guide.com/constellation-list/libra-constellation/

https://birthdate.co/blogs/news/the-libra-symbol-weakness-personality-strength

https://divyavivaham.com/services/nakshatra-rashi-list

https://www.ganeshaspeaks.com/astrology/nakshatras-constellations/chitra/

https://www.rahasyavedicastrology.com/chitra-nakshatra-3rd-pada-characteristics/#:~:text=Chitra%20Nakshatra%203rd%20Pada%3A%20It,plenty%20of%20wealth%20through%20traveling.

All the Padas: https://www.rahasyavedicastrology.com/

The Mula Pada: https://www.rahasyavedicastrology.com/mula-nakshatra-1st-pada-characteristics

Made in the USA
Middletown, DE
13 October 2023

40762882R00215